THE ADAMS FAMILY

Gilbert Stuart 1825   *By permission of Charles Francis Adams*

John Adams in His Eighty-ninth Year

THE ADAMS FAMILY

BY

JAMES TRUSLOW ADAMS

With Illustrations

New York
THE LITERARY GUILD
1930

THE ATLANTIC MONTHLY PRESS BOOKS
ARE PUBLISHED BY
LITTLE, BROWN, AND COMPANY
IN ASSOCIATION WITH
THE ATLANTIC MONTHLY COMPANY

PRINTED IN THE U. S. A. BY
QUINN & BODEN COMPANY, INC.
RAHWAY, N. J.

PREFACE

THE family whose story is told in this volume (and with which I am in no way connected) is the most distinguished in the United States. Suddenly passing from village obscurity into international fame in the latter part of the eighteenth century, it has ever since maintained a preëminent position, due neither to great wealth nor to a hereditary title, but to character and sheer intellectual ability. It is this, in part, which gives it a unique interest, although the life of each of its members here chronicled has an interest also of its own. The volume, however, is not intended to be merely a series of biographies. It is essentially a *biography of a family*, thrown against the changing background of its times for a hundred and fifty years. Indeed, the family is in part used as a sort of measuring rod to measure the extent of the change in its environment. The chief purpose of the book is thus not at all genealogical, and only in a minor degree individually biographical.

The writings of the various members of the family from 1750 onward are extremely voluminous, and have been heavily drawn upon. I am particularly indebted to Messrs. Houghton Mifflin and Company for permission to quote at considerable length from works of which they hold the copyright. As always, Mr. Worthington C. Ford has proved among the kindest of friends and most helpful of scholars. Mr. William Adams Slade, of the Library of Congress, Mr. Henry Osborn Taylor, Mr. M. A. DeWolfe Howe, and others, have also helped me with material and counsel. Owing to my temporary absence in England, Professor Allan Nevins, of Columbia University, kindly took upon himself the task of reading the proof. I am greatly indebted to the Massachusetts Historical Society, the American Antiquarian Society, and the British Museum for much trouble taken on my behalf, as I am also to Mr. Edward Weeks, of the Atlantic Monthly Press, for suggestions made when reading the manuscript, and to members of the Adams family for their kind help in procuring the illustrations. One makes one's own mistakes, but one succeeds only with the help of one's fellows, and to those named above, and many more, I offer most cordial thanks.

JAMES TRUSLOW ADAMS

NEW YORK CITY
March 23, 1930

CONTENTS

ILLUSTRATIONS

THE ADAMS FAMILY

PROLOGUE

TITLES in an aristocracy, colossal inherited wealth in a modern democracy, may keep a family in the public eye for many generations, but in any country in the world it is so rare as almost to be unique that one family should remain leaders of their time, and play great parts upon the stage of their day, merely because of a sequence of individuals, generation after generation, who combine character and intellect far above those of the common run of their contemporaries. The line of a Cromwell or a Napoleon, a Kant or a Descartes, a Burke or a Pitt, a Shakespeare or a Scott, a Marlborough or a Grant, a Jefferson or a Lincoln, soon disappears in the multitude of society, like a stream lost in the sands of a desert.

In America there is one family, and only one, that generation after generation has consistently and without interruption made contributions of the highest order to our history and civilization. After four generations of simple but public-spirited yeomen, following the primal immigration from England, a something, we know not what, occurred in the blood or brain of the line and lifted it to a higher plane, from which it has never descended. The family story is an inspiring tale and a fascinating problem. That a farmer's son should become a President is, happily, no strange phenomenon in the great democracy, but it is strange indeed, that *his* descendants, for five generations, by public service in the highest of offices or by intellectual contributions, should remain leaders of the nation which their ancestor so conspicuously helped to found. This is the tale we have to tell.

About the year 1608, in the little village of Charlton Mackrell, on the River Cary, among the Polden Hills in the heart of

English Somersetshire, a young girl was being courted by a lad from the neighboring village of Barton St. David. We know little enough about them at that time, and their love-making is safe from the intrusion of even an historian's guess. The girl's name was Edith, and she was the daughter of a certain Henry Squire. Beyond that flicker of light all else is darkness. The lad, who made her his wife in the year 1609 or thereabouts, was Henry Adams, a young farmer who held some land, by the old English system of copyhold, from the Lord of the Manor of Barton St. David. How rapidly children came to fill the farmhouse we do not know, but, in all, eight sons and one daughter lived to grow up, and in those days of high infant mortality there may well have been more births of which history is silent. The youngest of the eight sons of whom we have knowledge was apparently born in 1626, and it is not until he was about ten years old that we can begin clearly to trace the family story.

By that year, 1636, times had become hard in England and all ranks in the population had grown restive. There were, of course, the religious disputes which had brought trouble to many and caused some to seek asylum in other lands. But, in addition to this, life had become suddenly difficult in other ways. There had been a great increase in the cost of living, which had completely upset the domestic economy and habits of a large part of the population. Farm lands had risen enormously in value and in rent, largely as a result of the vast expansion of the cloth trade, which now suffered a severe decline. Taxes and other exactions of the government had been steadily mounting. There were new rich and new poor, a general dislocation of old-established standards and modes of living and of comparative social and economic positions. Between 1620 and about 1640, sixty-five thousand persons emigrated from England for America and the West Indies, without counting the numbers who sought new fortune in Ireland. For some reason, Henry Adams decided to abandon the home where his family had probably lived for generations, and to try his luck in the New World. The moving cause may have been religious or it may have been economic, or, as was so often the case, a combination of the two.

We know no more as to why he chose Massachusetts as his destination. The New England colonies were not nearly so popular among emigrants as the other continental and West Indian ones, about as many persons having gone to the one island of Barbados alone as had settled in all the Puritan colonies together. It is possible, although unlikely, that Adams was a relative of the Thomas Adams who was one of the grantees of the Massachusetts charter, and that his attention was thus drawn to that colony. It may have been his form of religious belief or the lure of holding land in fee simple. At any rate, for whatever reason, about 1636 he arrived at Boston with his wife and nine children to start life over in a new and strange world. He was granted land at Mount Wollaston, afterward called Braintree, and managed to establish a foothold. After his burial on the eighth of October, 1646, the inventory of his estate reveals that he had a house and barn, a cow and a calf, some pigs, furniture and utensils, and three beds — one in *the* parlor and two in *the* chamber. More noteworthy, and probably relics of the old days in England, were a silver spoon and some old books. The estate was worth about £75, equally divided between real and personal property. He had done his work well. If he had not become a figure in his new small world, he had made the great resolve, taken the great responsibility, and had lived long enough to establish his transplanted family firmly in their new surroundings. He had given them opportunity, whether in his mind that lay in freedom to worship according to the Puritan mode or to become great in a new country.

His youngest son, Joseph, who was about twenty when his father died, married, four years later, November 26, 1650, Abigail Baxter, and lived till the sixth of December, 1694. He begat twelve children, established a brewery as an adjunct to his farm, became a selectman of the town of Braintree, and once served as a surveyor of highways. His second child, Joseph II, with whom we are concerned, was born December 24,

1654, but we may note in passing that it was from his next son, John, that Samuel Adams of Revolutionary fame was descended as grandson.

Joseph II had three wives and eleven children, but we need consider only one of each. Although the family was not as yet showing any ability to act on a wider stage than that of village life, Joseph got ahead a bit on that. He did, indeed, rise no higher in office than selectman and constable, but for his second wife he married, February 8, 1692, Hannah Bass, a granddaughter on one side of Deacon Samuel Bass, and on the other of John and Priscilla Alden. It was a step up, although John and Priscilla did not weigh quite so heavily as ancestors then as they do now, and the distinction of marrying a granddaughter of the Deacon may have been lowered a trifle by the fact that he had a hundred and sixty-two descendants born to him before his own death. However, a deacon was a highly important figure in the tiny village life of that day, and a budding ambition in the family for better things is shown by the fact that Joseph educated his oldest son at Harvard in order that he might become, as he did, a clergyman, which then spelled, locally, both political power and social prestige. The family, in a modest way, was evidently prospering, for, as against the £75 left by Henry, Joseph I had left an estate of nearly £350, and in 1690 Joseph II, although one of twelve children, was assessed nearly as heavily in taxes as his father. He lived on until February 12, 1737, nearly the beginning of our real story. With the birth, January 28, 1691, of Joseph II's second son, John, we reach a life that overlaps it.

John lived on a farm through which ran the main street of the town of Braintree, and besides being a farmer, as were over 90 per cent of the population of the colonies at that time, practised the trade of shoemaker. He was a constable, a selectman year after year, and a lieutenant in the militia, refusing a captaincy out of loyalty to his commanding officer in a squabble that gentleman, Colonel John Quincy, had with Joseph Gooch. Yet more important, by 1747 he had been made a deacon, and on October 31, 1734, had married Susanna Boylston, daughter of Peter Boylston of Brookline, of a family prominent in the medical history of the colony. Of their three children, the eldest, born October 19, 1735, was named John, for his father, and, fortunately for him, being the eldest, was given a college education at Harvard. The father died May 25, 1760, and the steady growth of the modest family fortunes is indicated by the value of his estate, £1330.

Thus far, the family had not displayed the slightest element of greatness or distinction of either mind or achievement. They had been hard-working, pious, reliable, public-spirited village folk. A few miles away in Boston countingrooms or State House, fortunes were being built up, reputations gained, and history made. In fact, in view of the amount of history spun in Boston, the smallness of the stage on which the actors played their parts is noteworthy. When the first Henry arrived in 1636 or so, the town had a population of about 3000, which had increased to only about 15,000 by the time Deacon John died. Yet in a hundred and twenty-five years not an Adams had played any speaking part in the crisis after crisis which had marked the history of the little community in its internal development or its relations with England. In spite of strong aristocratic tendencies in the social life of the day, there were self-made men in plenty, and the names of the leaders shift in every generation. There was no lack of opportunity for able men — opportunity in trade and land speculation, in military affairs from the war with the Pequots to that with the French; above all, there was political opportunity in the more than a century of incessant wrangling with England by the town deputies in the colonial legislature, known as the "Great and General Court." But of the four generations of Adamses, all doing their private and public duty well in the narrow sphere of their village, none had shown either the ability or the ambition to take part in the larger life of the colony. Thus far the most important man they had produced was, in the third generation, a village pastor in New Hampshire. With the fifth generation, in the person of John Adams, historian, publicist, diplomat, President of the United States, the family not only suddenly achieves national and international position, but maintains it in successive generations for two centuries. Was it due to some mysterious result from the combination of Adams and Boylston blood far beyond the ken of science even to-day; or to some unfathomable synchronism between the peculiar qualities of the Adamses and the whole social atmosphere of the next few generations, a subtle interplay of unknown forces; or to mere chance in a universe in which atoms rush and collide chaotically? Fascinating as the problem is, it is insoluble. All we shall see is that without warning, like a "fault" in the geologic record, there is a sudden and immense rise recorded in the psychical energy of the family. For a couple of generations this new energy finds itself in harmony with the greater lines of force acting upon human society; then, with little diminution in itself, its line of direction fails to continue to coincide with those of the greater forces driving human society along its path. It is the purpose of this book to describe the phenomenon, without attempting to explain it.

THE FIRST GENERATION

JOHN ADAMS

JOHN ADAMS

I

YOUTH

THE house in which John Adams was born was of the type still familiar among the older farmhouses throughout the northeastern United States — two stories in front, with a short pitched roof rising to the ridge, and sweeping downward thence in a long line to within six or eight feet of the ground at the back. Although we think of it as "colonial," it was merely the sort of home to which the settlers had long been accustomed in their ancestral villages across the sea, and I have seen many such houses in the eastern counties of England and in Holland, giving to the foreign landscape an oddly native air. As contrasted with such Georgian mansions as were being built about the time of Adams's birth, — as, for example, that of his future client, John Hancock, in Boston, — the type marked clearly enough the humble station and lack of wealth of the Adams family, and when in 1751, at sixteen years of age, young John began his studies at Harvard he was graded as fourteenth in a class of twenty-four, the grading being still, as was seating in church, arranged according to social position. As his grandson wrote, even this placing in the class, low as it was, was probably achieved rather from the pretensions of his maternal than his paternal ancestry. The lad, however, showed marked ability, and, when graded according to scholarship, and not social rank, stood among the first three in a rather notable class. Noticed at the Commencement exercises, in 1755, for his evident acquirements, he was at once offered the position of Latin master in the grammar school at Worcester, and about three weeks later he made the trip to his new post, sixty miles, in one day by horseback.

So far, he was but repeating the early stages in the career of his uncle, the third Joseph, whose father had also given him a college education, and who had also temporarily taught school, to become thereafter, for sixty-eight years, the pastor of the church in the small village of Newington, New Hampshire. But from this point the careers diverge. The times, it is true, had altered; but, more important, something, we know not what, had altered in the cells of the Adams brains. For one thing, that insatiable desire to write, write, write, which has been so notable in the family ever since John graduated from Harvard, suddenly makes its first appearance. So far as appears, no member of the family had, from the dawn of creation to November 1755, ever expressed a thought on a written page. From that month and year, generation after generation, for a century and three-quarters, without intermission, they have filled scores of printed volumes and left or destroyed untold quantities of unpublished manuscript. The trait, as curiously persistent in survival as it was sudden in appearance, is but tangible evidence of that abrupt psychological alteration, that "change of phase," as an Adams of a later generation might have termed it, which we have to note in our history of a family.

When John, as yet only nineteen years of age, rode off so incontinently to do his sixty miles to Worcester, in the summer of 1755, the world was before him, but it was a world he would have to conquer unaided, by himself. It was the custom in those days among more humble folk who made sacrifices to give the eldest son a college education, to consider that education as a legacy, and to divide their modest estates among the younger children who had not been given such advantage in the struggle for existence. John, therefore, could not look forward to even a few hundred pounds in a remote future. During the months that the boy taught his band of small and unruly scholars he had ample time for reflection on the problem. He had, of course, been given his education with the expectation that he would become a clergyman, be the respected leader of some small village, and continue to live on that plane of gentility above his farmer father to which his Bachelor's degree had already served as stepping-stone. But John did not, somehow, accept the New England clergy unquestioningly. Among other influences, the war, then in progress, had, as always, done a good deal by its heavy rumblings of one sort and another to unsettle the foundations of old unquestionables. Adams had been teaching only a few months when we read in his *Diary* the laconic but startling entry for a New England Sabbath: "15. Sunday. Staid at home reading the *Independent Whig.*" By "18. Wednesday" we realize, though John did not, that the game is up and that the eldest son of the old Adamses and the founder of the new will never be a New England village clergyman. He writes: "Spent an hour in the beginning of the evening at Major Gardiner's, where it was thought that the design of Christianity was not to make men good riddle-solvers, or good mystery-mongers, but good men, good magistrates, and good subjects, good husbands, and good wives, good parents and good children, good masters and good servants. The following questions may be answered in some time or other, namely, — Where do we find a precept in the Gospel requiring Ecclesiastical Synods? Convocations? Councils? Decrees? Creeds? Confessions? Oaths? Subscriptions? and whole cart-loads of other trumpery that we find religion encumbered with in these days?" Even worse was to follow, which we need not quote.

We may echo John and say, "Where, indeed?" but it was evident that if father Joseph had sacrificed heavily, as undoubtedly he had, to send John to Harvard in the hope of raising up a New England divine, his money was wasted. Uncles and other relations expected the boy to follow the usual path, and it is interesting to note that had the "change of phase" in the Adams brains occurred, say, in 1650 or 1700, instead of 1750, the situation thus developed could have resulted only in worldly failure or spiritual martyrdom. The list of rebels against New England orthodoxy, from the days of the Browns, Anne Hutchinson, and Roger Williams, was long and disheartening enough. If John Adams was never much given to hiding his light under a bushel, neither can he ever be accused of trimming his ideas to any degree whatever of public malignity. Had he, as the first example of the change of phase in his family, been born a century earlier, we should probably have had only a personal tragedy to record, if we had anything at all. It was his good fortune that the change, for which he was not accountable, occurred just at a time when his own consequent personal revolt against old forms of life and thought found itself aligned with the major forces that were driving society along new paths, so that his refusal to accept the opinions of parents, uncles, other relations, and neighbors spelled success instead of martyrdom.

The small colonial world in which young John Adams had to find his way about was in an interesting stage of transition. Elsewhere I have called the decade of 1740 to 1750, which covered the years of his conscious boyhood, "the Great Divide." [1] Even in Puritan New England, there had come about, for various reasons, a marked secularizing of life. During the first century of the colony's history the clergy had held almost undisputed sway as leaders of opinion. They were, of course, for long to remain important, but their primacy was crumbling rapidly. As compared with the political power exercised by a John Cotton or a John Norton in 1650, the lack of self-confidence expressed by even such a clerical-politician as the Reverend Jonathan Mayhew in 1750 is noteworthy. Preaching a political sermon in that year, he felt called upon to half-apologize for it as being possibly "out of character for a Christian minister to meddle with such a subject." Such a hesitating deprecatoriness in a New England clergyman would have been almost unthinkable until the very generation in which John Adams was luckily born. A decade after he graduated from Harvard, two theses submitted there for the Master's degree were on the question, "Ought ministers of the Christian religion to preach politics?" and in both cases the answer was in the negative. When the public subscription library was founded in Albany in 1758 a rule was made that no clergyman could

[1] *Revolutionary New England, 1691-1776*, chap. IX, Boston, 1923.

ever serve as a trustee. The pulpit was to continue as one of the influences in forming opinion, but it was no longer to be the main stepping-stone to power for a young man with ambition and his own way to make in the world.

Business was becoming more and more of a career for those desiring power as well as wealth. There had been a notable enlargement of the scale on which it was conducted, whether it were as a shipping merchant, a timber merchant, a speculator in lands and townships, or even a promoter of combinations such as the spermaceti "trust," as we should call it to-day. The close alliance of the larger business interests and the legislatures was manifest in many ways. We can point to cases at this time in all the New England colonies in which legislation was secured to further the personal interests of groups or individuals. It is true that the overwhelming mass of the population were still farmers, and farming, under the conditions of soil and climate in New England, of necessity was limited to small freeholds which opened no avenue to wealth or power. Such an avenue, however, could be opened by a shrewd combination of business and legislative influence. The time had come when a man could wield genuine power without being in either the pulpit or the General Court.

The secularizing of life and the rapid rise of what we may call, with due regard to the general scale of that day, "big business" both helped to establish the profession of law in a new position. This happened to be an important fact for the rise of the Adams family in its new phase. For some reason, obscure as all the others connected with its sudden alteration, the Adams mind was henceforth to find one of its main lines of action in law — law both in its narrower aspect of a profession and in its wider one of a mode of interpreting human society and the fundamental reality of the universe. As to the former aspect, we may merely note here that of the seven members of the four generations more particularly discussed in this book all studied law and six became members of the bar. The other aspect will become evident as our story proceeds. Were we dealing with a family of erratic mental predilections, producing, perhaps, unpredictably a politician, a merchant prince, a musician, or a blank, the point would have little interest. Considering, however, the persistent preoccupation both with law as a profession and, from John to Henry, with the search for law running through the universe, it is noteworthy that the change in the family mind should have taken place just at the time when law as a profession suddenly became not only respectable but a road to power. The old New England theory of special providences and an arbitrary God also gave way to the theory of natural law.

The rise of the legal profession in America can be clearly dated from John Adams's boyhood. There had always been a few lawyers in the colony. Not only were they, however, as such, of not the slightest importance, but, on the contrary, to be a lawyer was to incur social opprobrium. In 1698, for example, in Connecticut, they were included in discriminatory legislation in company with drunkards and keepers of brothels. In 1730, in Rhode Island, a law was enacted excluding them from membership in the legislature. In that same year the number allowed to practise in the courts of New York was limited to eight, although there were thirty in the city, many of extremely bad reputation. In the very mid-century, however, their rise was rapid. Many of the most eminent men at the Albany Conference in 1754 were lawyers, and with, as I have noted, the development of business on a larger and inter-colonial scale, and with the coming to the front of legal problems in the discussions preliminary to the Revolution, law opened the surest way to reputation, influence, and power. The pulpit gave way to the bar, and the preaching of brimstone was soon to yield to the teaching of Blackstone.

After the upheaval of the French and Indian war, the way was also unusually open to new men. Wealth secured by privateering, smuggling, army contracts, speculation in all forms, had brought a whole new class of men prominently into light. There was a general effervescence and unsettlement. "The most opulent families, in our own memory, have risen from the lowest rank of the people," wrote Colden in New

York, and the statement was true generally. The professional politician was also coming into being, and young John was not many years out of college when he discovered that, instead of Boston being run by "the people," "the Caucus Club" met in "the garret of Tom Dawes," choosing the town officers "before they are chosen in the town." Moreover, the advance of news-sheets, in quality, number, and circulation, opened the way to a new line of influence just at the time that the itch for writing made its appearance in the Adams line.

In other respects, the young school-teacher, casting about for a career, was fortunate in his time and place. The provincial stage on which he was to win his first speaking part was small, but the drama enacted on it was to make world history and create world reputations. In 1755 the population of Paris was well on to a million and that of London perhaps half again as great. Boston, the centre of the world drama in which Adams was to be cast, was a mere village of fifteen thousand. The population of the whole thirteen American colonies was scarcely greater than that of the city of London alone at that time. To-day, a man may be a fairly successful lawyer in New York or Boston and, as far as the public is concerned, remain hidden in complete obscurity all his life. In the big village of 1755 one could not be one of the dozen or so members of the bar without being a marked figure, known to the public as well as to every man of wealth and influence in the town. With John Adams's mind, industry, great ability, capacity for public business, combativeness, and penchant for controversial writing, he would probably have become known at any time and in any community, but the smallness of the community in which he did so made the process far easier and more rapid. Moreover, his great good fortune was, as we have noted, that the small provincial town in which he rose quickly was to become a centre of world interest. At any time in the century and a half preceding his great years, he might have been just as great himself and yet, because the stage remained provincial, have been able to play only a provincial part.

A characteristic of the Adams mind in its new phase was to be its broad sweep, its fondness for generalizations, its dislike of the specific, and its taste for establishing general laws. It was to be a mind that cared little for the individual, either fact or voter. It must work on broad lines, touch the high spots in thought, and be stung into its best action by crises in history. For three generations, the crises were to be provided for it. In historical writing it would have little use for mere antiquarianism; in science for the patient accumulation of facts or laboratory experiment; in statesmanship none at all for politics. Until after the Revolution, in spite of the new men in society, public life was still aristocratic in its basis. The "gentry," the learned, the "best people," still had a great advantage in any struggle for office. In fact, much of the time there was no struggle. With the aristocratic basis of life, and in small communities in which everyone of any pretensions at all was well known to everyone else, positions of public responsibility and trust were more apt to be thrust upon one than to have to be sought after. This situation was also to prove one of John's lucky cards, for it was to be another characteristic of the Adams mind that it instinctively rejected as unworthy the striving for public office, a trait perhaps emphasized in later generations by the self-consciousness engendered by the prestige of the offices already held by the members of the family.

We have spoken of the public stage in 1755 as being small and provincial. It *was* provincial in a way, as undoubtedly as it was small, yet in another way there was less cultural difference in 1755 than in 1925 between the American and European environments. Young Europeans of wealth and position made, of course, "the grand tour," but for ordinary people, without introductions to grandees, Europe held much less then as education than it does now. Landscape, as yet, was but little regarded, in spite of Thomson's *Seasons*, published in 1730. Some progress, perhaps, had been made, since in the preceding century James Howell, Gent., had described the Alps as "high and hideous," "uncouth huge monstrous excrescences of nature" bearing nothing but "craggy stones."

There was no romantic interest in the past. That still awaited the wand of Scott to bring it into being. To most people, Gothic and the Middle Ages were, as were the Alps to blunt James Howell, "uncouth, huge, monstrous." Opera of the day could be heard in Paris and a few other places, but there was no such general opportunity for musical education as is offered to the tourist to-day. On the other hand, there were extremely good orchestral concerts then to be heard in several American cities, and the theatrical season of 1754 in New York could hardly have been excelled, if it was, by that of any European city in the same year. Pictures there were in Europe in plenty, but they were in private hands. The day of museums and public galleries, open to all travelers, had not yet dawned. There was no National Gallery, and merely the germ of a British Museum in London; no Louvre in Paris; no Ryks Museum in Amsterdam; no *Gemäldegalerie* in Dresden; no Pitti or Uffizi in Florence. For most people, books were the main sources of culture, and they could be studied as well in New England as in old. To John in the first Adams generation of the new phase, Europe was an extraneous political force to be reckoned with hostilely; to Henry in the fourth, it was part of the fibre of his spiritual self.

The young schoolmaster, whom we have left in reflection at Worcester while we have been glancing about his world, did not take many months to make up his mind that he was personally unfitted for the Church and that, for the rest, the career for an ambitious young man in 1756 was clearly the rising profession of the law. The family, of course, in its corporate capacity of parents, uncles, aunts, and all the tribe, had to be reckoned with as in any important step taken by any young man. Belonging to the small farmer type, to whom a clergyman was still of God and newfangled lawyers very possibly of the Devil, John's sledding was probably none too smooth, but on August 22, 1756, he records in his *Diary*, with perhaps a sigh of relief, "Yesterday I completed a contract with Mr. Putnam to study law, under his inspection, for two years."

The two years passed pleasantly enough on the whole in the

agreeable and cultivated, if extremely limited, society afforded by the villages of Worcester and Braintree at that early date. His *Diary*, highly introspective, as was the custom of the times and as was to remain conspicuously an Adams trait, gives us ample glimpses of his mind and doings. At twenty, he had already made and noted the all-too-true discovery that vanity was his "cardinal vice and cardinal folly," and he called himself, as did so many others in later life even after he had achieved greatness, "puffy, vain, conceited." If vanity were fatally to shadow his footsteps as closely as the black dog did Faust's, and do much to injure his reputation and career, he was as conscious of it as any critic, and struggled against it with more heart-searchings and burnings than, very likely, did his critics against any private sin of their own.

Scattered jottings here and there show his lighter, and what devotees of the new biography would probably be pleased to consider his more "human," side. He bets "a pair of gloves with Mrs. Willard that she would not see me chew tobacco this month," though he does not record whether he was not to chew or merely not to be caught. When he engages in a long diatribe against the wastefulness of time in playing cards and backgammon we fear a little that, for a boy, he is in danger of developing priggishness, but are relieved when we find him spending an afternoon "cutting and smoking tobacco, and in chatting with Dr. Savil's wife." Indeed, we are struck with something like consternation when we read that he has made a deliberate resolve that "on a Sunday I will read the Enquiry into the Nature of the Human Soul, and for amusement, I will sometimes read Ovid's Art of Love to Mrs. Savil." "This," he says, "shall be my method." The picture of John Adams reading Ovid's *Ars Amoris* to a married lady on a New England Sabbath sets the period in quite a new light. A somewhat later entry includes a "Friday, Saturday, Sunday, Monday. All spent in absolute idleness, or, which is worse, gallanting the girls." He was, he wrote in later life, always of an amorous disposition, and from the age of ten much given to the company of young women, but he was proud to say that

The Adams House and the Old Garden at Quincy

(By permission of the Adams Memorial Society)

they were all modest and virtuous, and that "no virgin or matron ever had cause to blush at the sight of me, or to regret her acquaintance."

We need not take too seriously the frequent self-condemnations for idleness or dawdling found in the *Diary*. Even during his young bachelor days, until his marriage in 1764, he appears to have been incessantly at work reading and writing, with merely such hours off for recreation as any healthy young man would take. Besides his law books, he browsed a good deal in general literature, — Voltaire, Milton, the *Spectator*, Bolingbroke, Virgil, Butler's *Analogy*, — ranging, as we have seen, from theology to Ovid. By 1758 he had completed his two years at Worcester under Putnam and was admitted to the bar in Boston, although he returned to live with his parents at Braintree and there began to practise. Old Jeremiah Gridley had vouched for him to the other members of the bar at the time of his admission, giving him excellent advice on the occasion, among other suggestions being one which Adams never forgot — namely, to pursue the study of the law, rather than the gain of it. The examination appears to have gone little beyond asking the young aspirant what books he had read in Latin, Greek, and French. Although the fledgling lawyer made no effort at first to push his way into the larger opportunity of Boston practice, the small metropolis of the colony was but a few miles away and Adams naturally was frequently there. On one occasion, in February 1761, he was present in the court when Otis made his famous speech against the Writs of Assistance, and the notes which he took at the time form our only report of one of the most celebrated speeches ever delivered in an American court of law.

In May of the same year his father died, John continuing to live with his family in the old homestead, which he bought from his brother thirteen years later, paying for the buildings and thirty-five acres of land £440. Previous to that he had already owned some arable and meadow himself, and, although Braintree was notoriously litigious, the cases and fees were trifling, so that John for some years combined his profession with farming, and we find him chopping wood or tossing hay as readily as he studies Justinian's *Institutes*. He talks much with his friends; reads Coke, Locke, Homer, Horace, Andrews, innumerable books on history and law; wishes he could get hold of a copy of Blackstone; develops a low opinion of all compilers, abridgers, and abstract makers; takes his "science from its fountain in original authors"; condemns the time he spends in "running to the barn, down to meals, and for pipes, coal and tobacco"; puts in a half-day cleaning out the spring; a bright, warm July day after a long rain lures him to a stroll about the country, when he feels he should have been at work in his study; he notes that he has been "guilty of rash and profane swearing" against the characters "of Goffe, J. Russell, lieu-tenant-governor, &c."; is "creating enemies in every quarter of the town"; lays aside the *Institutes* for six months — "Amidst the dissipations of business, pleasure, conversation, intrigue, party, &c., what mortal can give attention to an old Latin Institute of the Canon Law?" And so it goes, a very human picture of a very human man as disclosed in the pages of the *Diary*.

All the time, however, he is making friends, becoming known, moving among very different characters from his farmer an-cestors. Then, on October 25, 1764, he is married. Abigail Smith, the bride, is by far the most distinguished woman who has yet appeared in the annals of the family, a woman who would have been illustrious in the annals of any house. Her father, William Smith, was minister of the church at Wey-mouth, and her mother was Elizabeth Quincy, daughter of Colonel John Quincy, who had been Speaker of the House and a member of the Council. He, in turn, had married the daughter of the celebrated Reverend John Norton, and his mother had been the daughter of Thomas Shepard, one of the most eminent divines at the time of the first settlement of Massachusetts. A distaff should evidently have an important place in the Adams arms. By this marriage the first Adams of the new phase at once found himself a member of a family clan than which none was of a more cultured and scholarly breed. They all had minds of keen quality, well-tempered by education. Moreover, they were people of weight and influence in the colony, and the effect of this was immediately evident in the law practice and income of their new connection. Finally, the bride herself was a woman of such mind and character as could not fail to have a marked and beneficent influence upon the life and career of any man to whose fortunes she should consent to link her own. Her *Letters*, after a century and a half, still maintain their preëminence in that department of American literature, and her knowledge of both belles-lettres and philosophy was remarkable for a woman of that, or perhaps any, day. If Shakespeare, Addison, Swift, Milton, Dryden, Pope, and others were thoroughly familiar to her, so also were the works of Tillotson, Berkeley, Butler, and Locke. Her character was as strong and fine as her mind, yet both were wholly feminine. If she could share her husband's studies, she could also as readily manage the cooking and servants, run the farm in his absence, play the part of wife of the Minister to the Court of St. James's or the President of the United States; and yet remain wholly a woman in her passion and her devotion to husband and children.

We need not here more than mention the local village offices held by John Adams, such as surveyor of highways, selectman, assessor, and so on. They were unimportant in themselves and merely indicative of that willingness to serve the public, in any capacity, small as well as large, that has marked every generation of the family both before and after John. With his marriage and his new position, socially and professionally, we may close the chapter of youth. Within a few months he was to enter upon a larger stage, and the multifold public careers of an American family were to begin.

II

BOSTON

ALTHOUGH Adams continued to live in Braintree until 1768, his interests and career will be centred in Boston for the decade following his marriage. As far as he was concerned, the first crack in the structure of the British Empire, due to the stresses and strains of a century and more of development and change, were to be noticeable at that point. Both the government in England and the governed in America were being brought face to face with the problem of the reconciliation of empire and freedom, a problem as insoluble as that of an irresistible force meeting an immovable obstacle. It can hardly be said to have been solved by the British Commonwealth of Nations as yet, and we assuredly have not solved it in our American empire, in different parts of the framework of which may be found any and every form of "despotism" against which we ourselves protested at the time of the Revolution — appointed governors, taxation without representation, review of legislation, the making of tariffs and other commercial legislation without the representation or consent of the governed, and all the rest of the "tyrannies" of George III with which every school-child is familiar. The problem, theoretically, is, as I have said, insoluble. When we tax the inhabitants of the District of Columbia without giving them a voice in any legislature, they have as much right to cry out as had the inhabitants of Boston in Adams's day. In Alaska we are, to a great extent, repeating the story of eighteenth-century misgovernment by England, to say nothing of the anomalies of our situation in Hawaii, the Philippines, Porto Rico, and our other overseas "possessions." We may express glittering generalities, but governments are confronted by practical situations. Theoretical considerations frequently play very little part until citizens feel themselves too greatly hampered by their practical applications, usually in the economic sphere.

The end of the war in 1763 had left England burdened with a heavy debt of £140,000,000. The maintenance of a peace-time military establishment was obviously necessary for the safety of the Empire in a world full of embittered enemies waiting an opportunity to strike. The English government considered it fair that at least the smaller part of this cost should be met by the American portion of the Empire, which, like the home country, shared the benefits of the military insurance. The colonies were asked to suggest some scheme of voluntary coöperation. They could suggest none. Any representation that might be accorded to them in Parliament would evidently be of as little real value to them in protecting them against misgovernment as is to-day the one representative whom Alaska is allowed to have sitting in Congress without the power to vote. The English government felt that, if they derived benefit from colonial trade, so also did the colonies obtain benefit from the protection of the British army and navy, and that in view of the heavy war debt, which they did not ask the colonies to share, it was only fair that the colonies should bear some part of the permanent establishment. The colonies, on the other hand, could see no way in which they could submit to direct taxation without endangering their liberty. Both parties had reason and justice on their side, but no practical solution of the problem could be suggested by either party satisfactory to the other. The colonies could take refuge in inaction. It was the duty of the British government to devise some means of acting. The history of the Western world for the next two decades is mostly filled with their unsuccessful and certainly none too wise efforts to work their way out of the imperial impasse. The storm and turmoil resulting from this meeting of an irresistible force and an immovable obstacle whirled John Adams from the obscurity of a village lawyer in a remote province to the position of a world-known states-man in Paris, The Hague, London, and Washington. For the rest of the story we must assume in the reader a general knowledge of the background of events.

The English business man knew well enough the value of his individual interest in the colonies, as an American business man to-day knows his in Alaska, Porto Rico, or the Philippines, but paid about as little attention to the political feelings or problems of their inhabitants as does his modern American successor. In March 1765, Parliament, without the slightest suspicion that it was sowing the whirlwind, passed the Stamp Act, taxing the colonies. The crash of the repercussion when the news became known in America is too familiar to need retelling. The characteristic lawlessness of America was at once made manifest in mob violence, to the intense disgust of Adams. He himself took the legal road, petitioned the select-men for a meeting of the town, and at the meeting presented a draft of instructions to the representatives in the General Court. These were presented, published in the Boston news-papers, and immediately adopted by forty additional towns. He at once became a marked man far outside his former circle.

When the time came when legally stamps had to be used, the course of law was stopped, and the courts were closed. As Adams noted, debtors grew insolent, creditors grew angry; but, he added, "the bar seem to me to behave like a flock of shot pigeons; they seem to be stopped; the net seems to be thrown over them, and they have scarcely courage left to flounce and to flutter." For Adams personally, as for many others, the situation was serious. Idleness, he wrote, would make "a large chasm" in his affairs even if it did not force him to fail to meet his financial obligations. He lessened his expenses and complained characteristically. "I was but just getting into my gears," he noted in his *Diary*, "just getting under sail, and an embargo is laid upon the ship. Thirty years of my life are passed in preparation for business; I have had poverty to struggle with, envy and jealousy and malice of enemies to en-counter, no friends, or but few, to assist me; so that I have groped in dark obscurity, till of late, and had but just become known and gained a small degree of reputation, when this execrable project was set on foot for my ruin as well as that of America in general, and of Great Britain." We have no wish to stress weaknesses and foibles, but the note struck in this passage, which could be equaled in many more, of belief in the jealousy and malice of others and of the world being against an Adams, is to be so characteristic of the family, generation after generation, and is to work so much harm both to its own mental outlook and to the world's opinion of its members, that we cannot pass it in silence. This persecution complex, persecution by individuals or society, is so persistent and so strong as almost to indicate a pathological condition, and was to bring its own Nemesis.

A few hours after penning the above entries in his *Diary*, Adams received a brief letter in his Braintree home announcing that the town of Boston had chosen Gridley, James Otis, and himself to serve as counsel before the Governor in Council supporting the town's memorial praying for a reopening of the courts. At once mental depression changed into extreme activity, spurred by interest, ambition, honor, gratitude, and duty, as he lists the motives. The next day, the three argued their case before Hutchinson, Adams grounding his argument both on the invalidity of the Stamp Act, owing to the lack of legal consent upon the part of the colonists to its passage from lack of representation, and on the impossibility of executing it.

Adams was a clear thinker. He could not fail to realize that a government without the power of taxing was no government, that, as Washington was to exclaim long after independence had been won, "influence is not government." He realized, also, that the colonists could never in any worth-while way be represented in a Parliament three thousand miles away in which they must always, from the nature of the case, be heavily outnumbered by the very men whom they considered oppressors. If taxation was essential to government, and if there could be no rightful taxation without representation, and if representation was impossible, then . . . The logical sequitur was plain — independence. How early Adams came to this end of his premises is unknown, but he stuck to the premises until independence was declared. His friend and distant cousin, Sam Adams, had, rather emotionally than logically, arrived at this conclusion at the time of which we are writing. John contented himself for the moment in writing in his *Diary* a string of logical theorems on the closing of the courts, the reciprocal duties of protection and allegiance, and, "in short, where will such a horrid doctrine terminate? It would run us into treason!" The next day, Sunday, the laconic but significant entry is: "At home with my family, thinking"; and, a few days later, on Christmas: "At home, thinking, reading, searching, concerning taxation without consent; concerning the great rest and pause in business." Sam Adams dropped in and congratulated John on having been chosen by Boston as its counsel in the case, hoping that it would make him friendly to that town, increase his practice, and perhaps induce Braintree to elect him to the General Court in the spring.

Adams, however, although his pleading in the law courts case had made him prominent in the colony and partially committed him to the patriot party, continued to devote himself assiduously to the building up of his law practice, accepting only the office of selectman in Braintree, in 1766. The following year, on the eleventh of July, his son, John Quincy, was born, and some months later, in the beginning of 1768, the family moved to Boston, settling in what was known as the "White House" in Brattle Square. His practice was increasing rapidly and he was now becoming a man to be reckoned with. He had not long been a resident of Boston when he was offered indirectly from Governor Bernard the lucrative post of Advocate-General in the Court of Admiralty, which he refused without hesitation, on the score that, his political opinions being what they were, the acceptance of office under government would place him under obligations and restraints to which he could not honorably submit. Although the governor declared that Adams's opinions were well known to him and that he had no desire to influence him by giving him the office, there can be little doubt that, in spite of the ability of the rising young lawyer, the main object in making such an offer was to gather him into the fold.

Adams, however, was not thus easily to be taken, and was soon off on the circuit, attending court at Worcester and Springfield. During his absence the British troops had been landed and on his return he found Boston full of redcoats, the grievances of the colonists having been thus, according to the punster Mather Byles, "red-dressed." "My daily reflections for two years, at the sight of these soldiers before my door, were serious enough," Adams wrote, realizing the probability, sooner or later, of some clash between the people and the military. Writing many years later, 1805, he said that "the danger I was in appeared in full view before me; and I very deliberately, and indeed, solemnly, determined at all events to adhere to my principles in favor of my native country, which, indeed, was all the country I knew, or which had been known by my father, grandfather or great grandfather; but, on the other hand, I never would deceive the people, nor conceal from them any essential truth, nor, especially, make myself subservient to any of their crimes, follies, or eccentricities."

Several points are notable in this extract. One is the complete lack of any sentimental attachment to England, such as was felt by the great majority of the richer and more cultivated colonists of that day. In time, many of the best minds in the colonies found that they had to range themselves in opposition to the mother country, but, for the most part, they did so with sorrow and reluctance. Adams, however, was never touched by any such feeling. Again, we may note a complete absence of any sense of belonging to an imperial system. Imperialism, as an emotion, was, indeed, yet far in the future, but the imperial system, as a complex of duties, rights, demands, and benefits, was well understood. Adams appears to have thought solely in terms of two countries one of which had no right to impose its will upon the other. Lastly, we may note how far removed is his solemn determination as expressed above from the working of the mind of a popular politician.

No Adams, in truth, has ever been fitted or had the slightest

desire to play that rôle.   In these years, John was deeply pondering the path both he and his country would have to follow.
He was reading steadily in the political writers, — Harrington,
Sidney, Hobbes, Nedham, and Locke, — but he had no intention of sacrificing his own intellectual integrity by becoming a
popular leader.   Constantly solicited to attend the town meetings of Boston, the centres of popular political debate, and to
harangue there, he as constantly refused.   It has been said of
him that he was that peculiar but no less genuine product, a
self-made aristocrat.   At any rate, he had all of the aristocrat's
instinctive dislike of the mob, with, at the same time, all of
the aristocrat's sense of public duty and willingness to serve the
State.   Declining regularly to appear at town meetings, he
nevertheless was chosen, both in 1768 and in 1769, to draw up
the instructions from the meeting to its representatives in the
General Court, and did so.

He did not, however, object to influencing the minds of the
people by less direct ways than controversial articles in the
papers.   We find him, for example, attending a dinner of three
hundred and fifty Sons of Liberty, at which, apparently, he
thoroughly enjoyed the singing and drinking, noting in his
Diary that no one got drunk, and that such entertainments,
promoted by Otis and Sam Adams, "tinge the minds of the
people," impregnating them with the sentiments of liberty and
making them fond of their leaders.   The Sunday night following this we find him with Otis, Sam Adams, Davis, and John
Gill, "preparing for the next day's newspaper — a curious
employment, cooking up paragraphs, articles, occurrences, &c.,
working the political engine!"   Sam Adams, who was of a very
different type from his distant cousin John and his descendants,
was a pastmaster in the art of manipulating public sentiment
by propaganda, and he was as familiar with such a scene as that
described as any propagandist in the government service in the
last war, but evidently John writes of it as something amusingly
unfamiliar to him.   At any rate, being a "mixer" at political
barbecues, or "cooking up paragraphs, articles, occurrences,"
late at night for the next day's paper, was foreign to his nature.

He might find it entertaining, for the moment, as the intellectual usually does, to be shown the mysterious inner workings of the machinery of practical life, and to play for an instant the rôle of a "practical man," but controlling events and the course of history in any such fashion was completely alien to his nature, and John had little to do with it.

He preferred to sit in his study, ponder Locke and Sidney and the broad fundamentals of the situation into which imperial relations were drifting, and get on with his law practice. It had become one of the largest in Boston, and in 1768 he secured as a client the richest man in the town, John Hancock. Under the revenue law passed by Parliament in 1764 the wines from Madeira, Fayal, and the other Atlantic islands had been made dutiable in the colonies at the rate of £7 per tun of wine, or approximately six and three-quarter pence per gallon. The duty, though heavy, was not mentioned among the serious grievances, and in general it had been paid, although some of the largest importers, such as Hancock, had preferred to smuggle their cargoes in. The extra profit was a handsome one, though they may have been actuated by purely patriotic motives. However that may be, there had already been serious trouble with the customs authorities when early in June, 1768, Hancock's sloop *Liberty* arrived with wine from Madeira. In brief, a customs inspector was forcibly confined in the cabin while the cargo was unloaded, and threatened with his life if he made a report on what had happened. A few days later, the ship was seized by the customs officials, towed under the stern of the ship of war *Romney* for safety, and mobbing began again in the town. The Commissioners of Customs were driven on board the *Romney* and then took refuge in Castle William. The *Liberty* was condemned in the Admiralty Court and Hancock was sued for a very heavy sum, engaging Adams for the first time to act for him as counsel.

Adams placed the case squarely on the ground that the statute levying the duty was void because it had been enacted without the consent of the colonists. "My client, Mr. Hancock, never consented to it; he never voted for it himself, and he never voted for any man to make such a law for him." For this defense, as for most of the rights-of-man philosophy of the Revolutionary period, it is difficult to find any legal or logical basis. The United States to-day does not hesitate to lay duties on the commerce of its own colonies, enact other trade legislation, and extend the Eighteenth Amendment of the Constitution over them without giving them any of the rights of citizenship under that Constitution. The more one studies the rationalizing of the Revolutionary controversy, the more one comes to realize that it was merely rationalizing a position that the colonists felt strong enough to assume. If the theory of the patriots of that period was sound, then the present course of the United States is indefensible. I do not say it is not. For us, in tracing the rise of the Adams family, the important point is that in fighting for the rights of the unrepresented citizen, legislated for without being represented, Adams in 1768 was leading the most powerful current of thought of his day. If he were devoting himself to the same task a century and a half later, on behalf of our own colonists, his voice would fall on utterly deaf ears, and he would be voted a crank and a nuisance if any attention at all were paid to him. So far from founding a family, he would merely founder himself.

He had, however, taken bold ground and by now was publicly committed to the patriot side. There was, indeed, as yet but slight element of personal risk. Adams had confined himself to legal argument, however unpalatable to the British government. The argument, of course, by any logical sequitur, would lead to the Declaration of Independence, but Adams left that to the intelligence, of which there was none too much, of Parliament. Massachusetts had been defying and thwarting England for a full century and a half, and as yet no one had swung for it. For the rest, among his own friends and neighbors in his own country, "the only country he knew," he had increased his own prestige and popularity by espousing the popular cause, with the richest man in the colony, and almost in the New World, as his mate and client.

The next trial with which his name was to be connected, however, reveals him in another light and lends him imperishable fame. After many ominous minor encounters, the fatal clash between the citizenry and soldiery which he had foreseen occurred. Late on March 5, 1770, a crowd of idle loafers and boys tormented a British sentry, throwing sticks and stones at him and threatening his life. He called for aid and Captain Preston and six more soldiers came to his support. The small crowd of civilians also rapidly grew, and pressed on the eight soldiers, daring them to fire. One of them, who had been knocked down, did so. Whether the others mistook the cry of the mob for an order of their officer, or merely acted in self-defense, is uncertain, but a volley was fired into the crowd, killing three and mortally wounding two others. For a long time ill-feeling had been stirred to a serious pitch by items in the newspapers and stories circulated among the people. Knowing Sam Adams and recalling that evening when John found him "cooking up paragraphs, articles, occurrences, &c., working the political engine," one does not have to seek far for the origins of the "Boston Massacre," as the episode was at once dubbed. The value of the incident for propaganda was clear, full use was made of it, and the wrath of the people was unbounded.

The military authorities made no objection to the arrest of Captain Preston and his seven men by the civil government on a charge of murder. They were promised a fair trial, and the problem at once arose as to who would dare to undertake the odious task, in the eyes of the populace, of defending them. At Preston's request Josiah Quincy, Junior (the first asked), and John Adams were chosen. Both undoubtedly felt that they were hazarding all their popularity and influence with the patriot party, but both, from a stern sense of duty, undertook the unpleasant task. Although Adams wrote that his acceptance "occasioned a great clamor," his courageous action appears, after time for reflection, to have increased his popularity, for before the postponed trial took place he was elected as a Boston representative to the General Court. The trial, when it finally occurred in October, resulted in a complete exoneration of Preston.

Meanwhile, Adams's election to political office in such troubled times gave him much food for thought. Sent for by the town meeting which had elected him, he at once went to Faneuil Hall and accepted, although, as he wrote in his *Autobiography*, he considered that by doing so he devoted his family to ruin and himself to death. "I could scarce perceive a possibility that I should ever go through the thorns and leap the precipices before me and escape with my life," he added. In the evening he unburdened himself of all his gloomiest forebodings to his wife, who broke into tears but approved his decision and expressed herself as willing to share whatever might come. He had at that time, he wrote, "more business at the bar than any man in the Province," and "as bright prospects as any man ever had before him," but in such times ruin stalks before any man, whichever side he takes. Except on the score of his health, which, although he was then only thirty-four, he considered "feeble," or on the assumption that he foresaw the patriot cause doomed to failure, it is difficult to understand his seeing scarce a possibility of escaping death. If he foresaw certain failure for the coming revolt, it may be questioned how far he was justified in helping to plunge a nation into war on such a desperate chance, if any, of success. I think the answer to his forebodings is probably to be found in the extreme apprehensiveness that has lain behind the gruffness of many in the family line. It has never prevented them from taking action in accordance with their consciences, but has often filled them with almost pathological fears, and hampered their careers as it has marred their happiness. One cannot imagine Washington confiding to his *Diary*, though his service was to be on the field and not in the closet, such passages of dire foreboding of certain death on embracing the Whig side of the controversy. Much of the story of the Adams family probably stems from mysteries in the nervous system of which as yet we know little or nothing.

At this period in his life especially, Adams appears to have been so apprehensive about himself as to call forth no little comment. He served but one term as representative in the General Court and then, April 1771, moved back to Braintree, fearing the effect of Boston (a village of fifteen thousand people) upon his health. By November of the following year he was once more settled in Boston, and though only just thirty-seven years of age he speaks of himself as "an infirm man." In a heated encounter with James Otis, Otis upbraided him with being "tired with one year's service; dancing from Boston to Braintree, and from Braintree to Boston; moping about the streets of this town as hipped as Father Flynt at ninety, and seemingly regardless of every thing but to get money enough to carry you smoothly through this world." Adams indulges in a violent outbreak against Otis in his *Diary*, affirming that "there is a complication of malice, envy, and jealousy in this man, in the present disordered state of his mind, that is quite shocking." There has always been in the Adamses a strong tendency toward dramatizing themselves and making themselves imaginatively play the leading rôles in whatever situation they may be found. In indulging in this they exaggerate the elements in every such situation, intensifying in their own minds the odds against which they have had to struggle. A competitor is not merely a competitor; he is a malignant enemy, come from the Devil to destroy the noblest work of God. Circumstances that may oppose their plans are not accidents; they are damnable efforts on the part of society to thwart an Adams. It is not pleasant to dwell upon this aspect of the family mentality, but it is necessary to understand it, for it has been as continuous a trait as has the great intellectual ability displayed by every generation beginning with John, and, in its way, of almost as great an influence upon the family's history. It is a trait that is characteristic of the early New England divines, who felt that any opposition to their own ideas or wishes were assaults of the Devil upon the Kingdom of God. In reading innumerable entries in the *Diaries* of John and John Quincy, as well as the *Autobiography* of Charles Francis and the *Education* of his brother Henry in the last generation, we are reminded of the *Diary* of Cotton Mather, whose vituperative vocabulary was even more copious, whose opponents were always "vile fools," "tools of Satan," and against whom the forces of society and of Hell itself were arrayed when anyone mildly disagreed with him. It is, indeed, an aspect of Puritanism, for if one is the elect of God what must, necessarily, one's enemies be? The inference to be made is of the simplest sort. To identify one's self with God is greatly to complicate one's social relations.

It was another characteristic of Puritanism that, although one might fairly grovel on the ground as a base worm in questioning one's own motives, one would smite with the sword of the Lord anyone else who did so. It was one thing to write, in one's own diary, as John did not so very long before Otis upbraided him: "What is the end and purpose of my studies, journeys, labors of all kinds . . . ? Am I grasping at money or scheming for power? Am I planning the illustration of my family or the welfare of my country? These are great questions. . . . Which of these lies nearest my heart?" But when Otis undertook to tell him, that was quite another matter. There need be no heart-searching over what was so obviously dictated by "malice, envy and jealousy."

Living at Braintree and jogging back and forth to his law office in Boston, Adams was as yet but a well-known citizen of that small town, with something of a reputation throughout the colony. Many years later, he claimed that he had never been a "John Bull" but always a "John Yankee," and he appears rather amusingly as a very provincial John Yankee in these last months before he was unexpectedly to be forced forward on to a wider stage. In June 1771 he takes a solitary journey through Massachusetts and Connecticut for the benefit of his health, and gets as homesick and restless as a modern American business man in Paris. He is "sick of this," he writes in his *Diary*; "I feel guilty; I feel as if I ought not to saunter, and loiter, and trifle away my time; I feel as if I ought to be employed for the benefit of my fellow men in some way or other. In all this ramble from Stafford I have met with nobody that I knew excepting Jo. Trumbull. . . . My wife is one hundred and fifty miles from me, at least, and I am not yet homeward bound. I wish Connecticut River flowed through Braintree." In true John Yankee style, being employed for one's fellow man takes a curiously personal tinge. "The barren, rocky mountains of Braintree are as great a contrast as can be conceived to the level, smooth, fertile plains of this country; yet [how often has one heard this identical strain at the Café de la Paix!] Braintree pleases me more; I long to be foul of Deacon Belcher's orchard; I am impatient to begin my canal and bank, to convey the water all round by the road and the house; I must make a pool in the road by the corner of my land"; and so on, after having just taken the "finest ride in America," as he calls the eight miles from Hartford to Wethersfield. Nothing can exceed its beauty and fertility, he says, but it is the fertility, not the beauty, that appeals to him, as his mind immediately turns to problems of management and dunging. He quotes a statement he has heard that there is no place in England equal to either Hartford or Wethersfield, but he thinks that if he had to take another trip for his health he would go in another direction and perhaps pick up some land for a speculation.

When he had moved from Boston to Braintree he entered in his *Diary*, "Farewell politics," and this is the burden of many subsequent entries at this time. He has sacrificed too much for the people and stood by them "much longer than they would stand by themselves." He will mind his own farm and office. On his return to live in Boston he records his "fixed resolution to meddle not with public affairs of town or Province. I am determined my own life and the welfare of my whole family, which is much dearer to me, are too great sacrifices for me to make. . . . I will devote myself wholly to my private business, my office and my farm, and I hope to lay a foundation for better fortune to my children and a happier life than has fallen to my share." Thus he writes at the age of thirty-six, having risen from obscurity to a position of prominence, from poverty to the largest law practice of the colony, and with perhaps the ablest and finest woman of her time and place as his passion-

ately devoted wife. What she thought of her emotional and
changeable husband is hidden in her woman's breast. But at
times it must have been difficult, as it is for us, to have patience
with him. Yet in a few months all was again to alter and he
was to appear wholly admirable and great on the opening of a
new career. At the moment of his return to Boston, however,
we cannot but think Otis may have had more than a little
foundation for his comment quoted above. A more practical
comment, without a word, was that made by John Hancock,
who, for reasons now known only to himself, withdrew his
legal business from Adams's office. "This day," wrote Adams
on Christmas Eve 1772, "I heard that Mr. Hancock had pur-
chased twenty writs for this court of Mr. S. Quincy. Oh, the
mutability of the legal, commercial, social, political, as well as
material world! For about three or four years I have done all
Mr. Hancock's business, and have waded through wearisome,
anxious days and nights, in his defence; but farewell!" At
this time, Hancock and Sam Adams were no longer friends,
and it was the period when the conflict with England, kept
alive by the more radical agitators, was otherwise in train to
adjust itself. The change of lawyers on Hancock's part may
thus well have had a political reason.

Although vacillating between the open courses of public and
private life, Adams stood staunchly by the patriot party. In
1773 he wrote a series of articles on the question of judgeships
in the *Boston Gazette*, and probably wrote the rejoinder made by
the House in a controversy with Governor Hutchinson over the
fundamental position taken by that body in the quarrel over
constitutional principles of colonial government. The same
year he was elected a member of the Council, but was negatived
by the Governor. A few months later came the publication by
the General Court of the stolen letters from Hutchinson,
Andrew Oliver, and Charles Paxton to a member of Parliament,
setting forth their views as to colonial government and problems,
and which, passing by means yet unknown into the hands of
Benjamin Franklin in England, had been sent by him to Boston.
Franklin had given a pledge that they should not be published,

and the violation of this pledge ruined his reputation and use-fulness in London.   The disclosure of the views of Hutchinson and the Olivers raised a storm in the colonies, and it was evident that the patriots would not consent to the retention of any of them in office.   The problem was what measures, beyond protests to the home government, could be taken to get rid of them.   Peter Oliver, brother of Andrew, was Chief Justice of Massachusetts, and Adams proposed the startling plan to have him impeached by the Council.   That the colonial Council, elected annually by the Lower House of the legislature, pos-sessed the same judicial functions as the House of Lords in England was assuredly a proposition that might have startled anyone, but Adams carried the day; the Justice was duly impeached, and Adams, in spite of his resolutions to the con-trary, had once more come to the fore in public affairs.

He still, however, appears to have considered himself as somewhat aloof from the daily scheming and planning and manipulating of the patriot party leaders.   Unlike many of the best patriots throughout the colonies, he approved heartily of the destruction of the tea when thrown into Boston Harbor, but his comment on the episode in his *Diary* is that of a calm observer of events rather than of an actor in the arena.   "This is the most magnificent movement of all," he writes.   "There is a dignity, a majesty, a sublimity, in this last effort of the patriots, that I greatly admire.   The people should never rise without doing something to be remembered, something notable and striking."   There is a singular detachment about this passage that is worth noting in passing.   There are "the patriots," and "the people," and, from his study watching them to applaud or condemn, John Adams.   "We" is a rare word in the Adams vocabulary.   Its absence, for four generations, though apparently trifling, is of no trifling significance.   We. The leaders begin to toss it carelessly among the people in this decade.   *We.*   It is proclaimed to the world in 1776.   *We.* It rumbles resentfully through every village in 1800.   We.   It rolls from the West like an Indian war whoop behind the lean figure of Jackson in 1828.   WE.   It has become a roar by the fourth generation of Adamses, who have never been able to say it because they have not felt it. They have loved their country as nobly as any; served her as faithfully and ably; made willingly every sacrifice — save that of feeling and saying "we." It is a trait easy to sympathize with, but the pronoun may be used as one of the measuring rods in tracing the family and its background. In 1774 a man could lead the nation who stood foursquare on "I"; by 1874 all power lay in "we," and the man who could not stand on that was lost. We may construe it as a change from aristocracy to democracy, from statesmanship to politics, from unity to multiplicity, — a dozen ways, as we will, — but it was a change fatal to those who still insisted upon being, morally, socially, intellectually, politically, "I." The fourth generation considered the change as a form of degradation. Very possibly they were right. At any rate, they refused to change themselves. John had been "I," and "I" each generation has remained in its own right. The story of the family and its relations with its background is largely the story of how the first has insisted robustly upon a philosophy and an instinct of "I" while the people, in the background, have insisted upon the deliquescence of all individuals, — leaders and led, — into "we," with all the manifold implications of that process.

The Boston Tea Party was followed in due course by the various retaliatory measures of the British Ministry, including the closing of Boston Harbor to commerce and the paralysis of its trade. The business of Adams, as of everyone else, came to a dead stop. "I don't receive a shilling a week," he writes to his wife, then at Braintree, during that summer of 1774. As usual, however, when there is genuine crisis to be met he meets it bravely. He does, indeed, speak of his "infirmities" of health, but as in the same letter he mentions that he rises "at five, walk three miles, keep the air all day and walk again in the afternoon," they could not have caused his wife any great anxiety. His financial situation was more genuinely serious. In another letter to his wife, he writes: "I was first sworn in 1758. My life has been a continual scene of fatigue, vexation, labour and anxiety. I have four children. I had a pretty estate from my father; I have been assisted by your father; I have done the greatest business in the province; I have had the very richest clients in the province. Yet I am poor, in comparison with others. This, I confess, is grievous and discouraging. I ought however to be candid enough to acknowledge that I have been imprudent. I have spent an estate in books; I have spent a sum of money indiscreetly in a lighter, another in a pew, and a much greater in a house in Boston. These would have been indiscretions, if the impeachment of the Judges, the Boston port bill, &c., &c., had never happened; but by the unfortunate irruption of my business from these causes, those indiscretions became almost fatal to me." He might have added the purchase of the family place at Braintree, which he had made only four months previous to his letter. Continuing, he contrasts the ease of making money by law in the country as compared with the town, but the failure to accumulate money by a lawyer with the largest and most lucrative practice in the colony is merely evidence of the absence of that shrewd Yankee business sense in which the family, as a whole, has persistently been lacking. It is another measuring rod, like "I" and "we." Combining the two, we may note that in 1774 "I" might, without money, control power. A century later, "we" might do the same, but for an "I" man to think of doing so without large personal control of what had become the great reservoir of power had become well-nigh impossible. He could not defy at once the political social temper of his age and its reservoirs of stored energy and expect to control its power in high office.

So far, John Adams could take a very solid satisfaction in what he had done for his family. The old line of village yeomen had definitely ended. He might contrast his own modest fortune made from the bar with that of James Sullivan, David Sewall, or John Lowell of Newburyport, "who has built himself a palace like a nobleman, and lives in great splendor," but what Adams before could ever have thought of such a comparison without making himself ridiculous? The advance in the family is indicated by the very fact that such a comparison could be made at all, and if, with his provincial outlook, he could think the Lowell house a "palace like a nobleman," so much the better for his peace of mind.   If he rightfully estimated money at its real value and many other things higher, nevertheless his several references to his having the richest men in the province as clients, quite apart from Otis's unpleasant dig, shows that he was not oblivious, as no sensible man could be, of the advantages of its possession.   He had made a brilliant marriage and had a growing family.   He had attained a prominent provincial position professionally and politically, if not socially.   Had he chosen to join the Tory Party, much more might have been added.   It is no wonder if occasional outbursts of disgust should have punctuated his quiet observation of the growing unrest of the times, due wholly, as he felt, to the tyranny of England, which threatened to destroy all that he had so painfully achieved.   This tyranny, however, although he did not know it, was the strongest card in the hand of his fate.   Thanks already in part to it and in part to the law, he had given a village family provincial rank.   Resistance to tyranny was now to make it nationally known, and the "Adams family" was to emerge from its dull Boston chrysalis.

On June 17, 1774, the General Court, behind locked doors while the Secretary stood outside with an order from the Governor dissolving it, appointed James Bowdoin, Samuel Cushing, Robert Treat Paine, Samuel Adams, and John Adams a committee to attend a Continental Congress from all the colonies, to be held in Philadelphia on the first day of September.   "There is a new and a grand scene open before me; a Congress," Adams confided to his *Diary*.   "This will be an assembly of the wisest men upon the continent."

We may pause a moment to consider this entry of the family upon the stage of national and international affairs.   In the first place, we may note that Adams did not owe his post to popular election.   He had been appointed by an able deliberative assembly to every one of whose hundred and twenty-nine voters he was undoubtedly known by sight as well as by reputation, if not personally. There had been no need to humor an electorate of the mob. In the second place, we may note that the public duty he had undertaken was one of the highest intellectual interest, and, aside from the place which the Congress might one day take in history, it could not but be an honor to be a representative to a body which included among its members such men as Roger Sherman, Cæsar Rodney, Thomas McKean, Edward Rutledge, Christopher Gadsden, Joseph Galloway, John Dickinson, Peyton Randolph, George Washington, Richard Henry Lee, Edmund Pendleton, Patrick Henry, Philip Livingston, and John Jay, to name a few of the fifty-five members, all men of high standing. Debate among such men on the fundamental principles of government in the face of a fatal crisis was bound to be intellectual discussion of the highest order. Lastly, we may note that the instructions to the delegates gave them the widest possible scope for the exercise of their independent judgments. This was politics on the plane of statesmanship, an opportunity and an occasion for the display of the uttermost intellectual and moral integrity and independence. No greater opportunity or occasion could have been offered to a man with the qualities of both mind and character possessed by Adams, and these qualities show at their noblest in the next few years. The qualities of the family in its new phase, beginning with John, required for their best exercise a free hand, even a lone hand, in action at times of crisis.

Bowdoin had declined to serve, and on August 10 the remaining four members of the delegation started their long drive to Philadelphia, where they arrived nineteen days later. The road from Boston, or rather Newburyport, to Philadelphia was the only good one in the colonies and the only one over which commercial traffic passed regularly. Within the previous twenty years stagecoaches had been introduced, but, except for three or four established routes, horseback or, where the conditions of the roads permitted, a private carriage was the only means of land transport. Throughout the journey, but especially in Connecticut, the delegates were received with great enthusiasm and distinction. "No Governor of a Province,

nor General of an army, was ever treated with so much ceremony and assiduity as we have been," wrote the flattered
Adams in his *Diary*, and writing to his wife from Princeton he
added that "we have been treated with unbounded civility,
complaisance and respect." Vanity, however, plays less of a
part in his reflections now than at any other period of his life.
He applies himself with high seriousness to the work in hand
and his own self assumes reasonable proportions in relation to
others.

On the way, the party made short stops at Hartford, New
Haven, New York, and a few other places for rest, and everywhere Adams naturally met the most prominent men of the
several towns. It was the first genuine enlargement his mind
had yet received from travel. The pastoral charm of the view
from the steeple of Wethersfield church is still for him "the
most grand and beautiful prospect in the world, at least that I
ever saw." The city of New York, with its population of a little
over twenty thousand, is a subject of much speculation to him
as he approaches it, and immediately after dining upon arrival
he walks to every part of it, starting with "the ruins of that
magnificent building, the Governor's house," destroyed by fire
the preceding year. He meets all the prominent and wealthiest
inhabitants, but notes that, "with all the opulence and splendor" of the city, "there is very little good breeding to be found.
We have been treated with an assiduous respect; but I have not
seen one real gentleman, one well bred man, since I came to
town." One cannot but smile at this judgment of a village
farmer's son, now a self-made man of thirty-eight, upon his new
acquaintances — the Lows, Scotts, Smiths, Livingstons, Litch-
fields, Jays, Duanes, and Bayards. For the first time, indeed,
Adams had heard in New York the outer world's opinion of
New England. The shock was undoubtedly severe. Perhaps
an inference unconsciously took form in his mind that anyone
who criticized Boston and New Englanders could not be a
gentleman, just as later the family was invariably to infer that
anyone who criticized an Adams must be a scoundrel. Adams
found that one party in New York feared "the levelling spirit"

of New England; another entertained "Episcopalian preju-
dices" against it; by Philip Livingston, "a great, rough, rapid
mortal," "hints were thrown out of the Goths and Vandals;
mention was made of our hanging the Quakers, &c." It was all
extremely irritating to a Bostonian who had just been fêted
through the whole length of the Puritan colonies. Education
by human contact was indeed a rough and unpleasant method.
"Breakfasting, dining, drinking coffee, &c., about the city, is
very disagreeable on some accounts. . . . It hinders us from
seeing the college, the churches, the printers' offices, and book-
sellers' shops." One is not brutally jostled in the world of
print. We can shut up a book with dignity when we disagree
with it, but how shut up a "great, rough, rapid mortal" when
he more than hints that we are no better than "Goths and
Vandals"? If one is going to manage the world, one must
know the world, but it is so much less distressing to learn it
through a book in decency and privacy than in arguing with
these uncouth New Yorkers who simply are not capable of
appreciating Boston.

However, he did succeed in seeing the college, the bookshops,
and the churches before he got away. St. Paul's was then "a
new building, which cost eighteen thousand pounds, York
money," but after examination Adams found that, although
very "grand," it did not strike him, "taken altogether," "like
the Stone Chapel, or like Dr. Cooper's meeting-house, either
on the inside or outside." As one watches the short, round
figure of John standing in front of the new St. Paul's, "which
cost eighteen thousand pounds, York money," contrasting it
with Dr. Cooper's meetinghouse, another short, round figure comes to our mind, standing in front of the cathedral of
Chartres. John Adams contemplating St. Paul's and the
Boston meetinghouse; Henry Adams analyzing Mont Saint-
Michel and Chartres; what an odd lot of measuring rods there
are. But John is on his way to a Continental Congress to
make a nation, and it is time we let him get on with it. Glad,
probably, to be through with New York, he crossed the
Paulus Hook Ferry to New Jersey, then the Hackensack

Ferry and the Newark Ferry, and made Elizabethtown in time for lunch.

By the twenty-ninth of August, Adams and his colleagues had reached Philadelphia, at that time the leading city of the colonies, with a population double that of Boston and half again as large as that of New York. Charleston, South Carolina, the leading centre for music, the theatre, and the other arts, was the only other city on the continent with a population of over ten thousand, and even it was in reality merely a big village of twelve thousand. The first few days were spent by Adams in finding lodgings, looking about the town, and meeting the leading Philadelphians and such delegates to the Congress as had already arrived. Between a third and a half of the members, he found, would be, like himself, members of the bar. The most important work of this first Congress was to enable the leading men from all the colonies to become acquainted with one another and to take the measure of public opinion and its leaders in the colonies other than their own. For this purpose the social gatherings were perhaps more important than the formal sessions of the Congress itself. Of the former there was no lack. Such entries as the following in Adams's *Diary* are typical of those of almost any other day: "Dined with Mr. Chew, Chief Justice of the Province, with all the gentlemen from Virginia, Dr. Shippen, Mr. Tilghman, and many others. We were shown into a grand entry and stair-case, and into an elegant and most magnificent chamber, until dinner. About four o'clock we were called down to dinner. The furniture was all rich. Turtle, and every other thing, flummery, jellies, sweet-meats of twenty sorts, trifles, whipped syllabubs, floating islands, fools, &c., and then a dessert of fruits, raisins, almonds, pears, peaches. Wines most excellent and admirable. I drank Madeira at a great rate, and found no inconvenience in it. In the evening, General Lee and Colonel Lee, and Colonel Dyer, and Mr. Deane, and half a score friends from Boston came to our lodgings. Colonel Lee staid till twelve o'clock, and was very social and agreeable." Or he meets the Marylanders: "A mighty feast again; nothing less than the very best of Claret, Madeira, and Burgundy; melons, fine beyond description, and pears and peaches as excellent. This day Mr. Chase introduced to us a Mr. Carroll, of Annapolis, a very sensible gentleman, a Roman Catholic, and of the first fortune in America. His income is ten thousand pounds sterling a year now, will be fourteen in two or three years, they say; besides, his father has a vast estate which will be his after his father." On another day, Adams writes: "There is such a quick and constant succession of new scenes, characters, persons, and events, turning up before me, that I can't keep any regular account." He is in his element and evidently enjoying it all hugely. Showing that the ill-health about which he had so constantly talked for so long was mainly mental, he now writes, in spite of terrapin, Madeira in quantity, and late hours, that it is excellent, "much more than I know how to account for."

Adams had been warned by his old friend Joseph Hawley before starting from Boston that there was an opinion abroad in the other colonies that Massachusetts men were apt to be vain and self-conceited, "to assume big and haughty airs," and that the Massachusetts delegation should for that reason proceed with great care at the Congress, where they would meet gentlemen "fully equal to yourselves or any of you, in their knowledge of Great Britain, the colonies, law, history, government, commerce, etc." Adams took the counsel in good part and acted with exemplary modesty and caution. Indeed, in these few hurried weeks he appears to have been genuinely made aware of the abilities and virtues in other men. He was himself a man of wide knowledge and great ability. In Boston he could measure himself only against such other men as were leaders of that little community of fifteen thousand persons. A few years later, when his reputation had become international, his ego again inflated, owing to the positions he had held and the genuine services he had rendered, but, suddenly confronted with the need for acting in what he could not help but note as "a collection of the greatest men upon this continent in point of abilities, virtues, and fortunes," his own ability shone without being impaired by his unfortunate vanity.

He himself, by this time, had, in his own mind, completed the unfinished syllogism regarding taxation and representation, and realized that the final conclusion must be independence, but the temper of the Congress was conservative, and he restrained himself. Placed on the committees concerned with drafting a declaration of rights and pointing out wherein they had been infringed, he strove hard, without success, to include an assertion of "natural rights" to serve as the basis of the broader foundation which he foresaw would be called for in the future. The other important formal work of the Congress, the adoption of the non-importation, non-exportation, and consumption agreement by the colonies, did not meet with his approval, and, on the whole, he was disappointed by the progress made when Congress adjourned and he started for home again on October 28, taking his departure "in a very great rain, from the happy, the peaceful, the elegant, the hospitable, and polite city of Philadelphia." This superfluity of generous adjectives must have been caused by delight in the prospect of a return home, for a fortnight earlier he had written that "Philadelphia, with all its trade and wealth and regularity, is not Boston. The morals of our people are much better; their manners are more polite and agreeable; they are purer English; our language is better, our taste is better, our persons are handsomer; our spirit is greater, our laws are wiser, our religion is superior, our education is better." So that was that. Adams was highly emotional and his views of men and cities were apt to go through astonishing and instant changes. He was apt to be away up or away down, sanguine or despairing, happy or extremely irritable, and his views partook of the mood of the moment. On the whole, as he started homeward to see the family to which he was deeply devoted, he could take a lively and just satisfaction in the way he had played his part for the first time on a national stage, and the experience and reputation he had acquired, so that his spirits were evidently bubbling gayly in spite of the "very great rain." He was not to be quite so happy in the second Congress, but there was much to occupy him before that met.

He was almost immediately chosen to represent the town of Braintree in the Provincial Assembly, which kept him busy until its adjournment in December. Through the winter he contributed a series of controversial articles to the *Boston Gazette* under the pseudonym of "Novanglus," until the controversy was abruptly terminated by the battle of Lexington. His articles, however, were reprinted in London the following year.

John Hancock had been added to the Massachusetts delegation to the second Congress, which assembled at Philadelphia on May 5. Adams, who had had a touch of fever, was unable to set out with his colleagues, but, traveling in a sulky with a servant on horseback, overtook them at New York and entered Philadelphia in their company. The progress of events, including the opening of armed hostilities in Massachusetts a fortnight before the meeting of Congress, had naturally created a division of opinion greater in that body than in its predecessor. In the minds of many the inevitability of war and independence loomed larger, while in those of others the need for a cautious and conciliatory spirit had correspondingly increased. Adams, whose opinions were well known, was among the most impatient of the first group and John Dickinson among the ablest of the second. The first serious clash occurred between them when Adams bitterly but unsuccessfully opposed in debate Dickinson's motion to send a second petition to the King. Meeting outside in the yard immediately after, Adams pictures the usual natural rôles of the two men as reversed, and the suave, courteous, amiable Dickinson as upbraiding him like a schoolboy, and Adams answering him coolly. Dickinson was clearly much upset at the constant opposition of New England to any conciliatory measures, and as Adams says that he himself happened to be "at that moment in a very happy temper" the collision may have occurred just as he describes it. In any case, all personal, although not official, intercourse was now ended between the two and Adams had had the first of the innumerable quarrels in his long public life.

It was rendered more serious and permanent by an indiscretion which caused him much trouble and which, although he treats it lightly, was in truth bad enough. Adams was, as we have seen, a creature of moods, and if at times he was almost absurdly timorous, at others he could be rashly impulsive. Several times in his life he distinguished himself by dealing a bold stroke which was as wise as it was unexpected and daring, but often in smaller matters his impulsiveness created endless trouble for him. For many months now he had taken the greatest care to express himself cautiously in both written and spoken word. Suddenly, without any excuse, he exploded a veritable bombshell. An utterly insignificant young man, who wished to go to Boston, asked Adams to let him be the carrier of some letters from him. After much hesitation, Adams suddenly consented and wrote one letter to his wife and another to James Warren. He began the latter with "I am determined to write freely to you this time" — and most assuredly he did! In the two letters he disclosed his ideas as to policy, and berated Congress in general and some of its members in particular in good Adams form. "The fidgets, the whims, the caprice, the vanity, the superstition, the irritability of some of us is enough to . . ." he wrote, and complained bitterly of the position into which Congress had got itself — "between hawk and buzzard" — by its delay and incompetence. Dickinson he described as a "great fortune and piddling genius" who "has given a silly cast to our whole doings."

The bearer of these inexcusable letters, young Hichborn, was intercepted by the British on his way to Boston, and the letters were seized and immediately published. An explosion inevitably followed. Dickinson at once cut Adams's acquaintance, and some of the others shunned him. For the time his popularity was greatly lessened, as was his reputation for ability and good judgment. He himself pretended that the publication of the letters did good by making the people at large argue the question of independence, but we can regard that as merely a spurious balm for a self-inflicted and unnecessary wound.

It is pleasant to turn from this episode to another far more important one, in which Adams displayed that capacity for independent judgment, assumption of sole responsibility, and courageous action which has formed the chief characteristic of the family in placing them apart from mere intellectuals on the one hand or politicians and the lower rank of statesmen on the other, and which, in spite of all too obvious petty personal traits, gave them their hold on popular imagination.

Whatever hopes the loyal and conservative might yet have held of solving the controversy with England by negotiation, that controversy had, *de facto*, entered upon the stage of armed force. General Gage was being besieged in Boston by an "army," although that army had no legal basis for its existence. Adams was not alone in seeing the necessity for the adoption of the nondescript forces outside Boston by Congress if they were to become both legally organized and national. This could be done by Congress taking the army over and appointing its commanding officer. Who should that officer be? The army was a New England, almost a Massachusetts, affair. If a commander were appointed from some other section, would not the resentment felt in New England destroy the whole fragile structure of colonial unity; and, on the other hand, would not the appointment of a New Englander have exactly the same effect through the disgruntlement of the other sections? Intercolonial jealousy had always been the besetting sin of the colonists, and, indeed, in preventing any united action earlier, when the British government had asked for it, was in no small measure responsible for having brought on the whole controversy with the mother country. To make any move toward solving the problem of the army and its command was to risk bringing on such a crisis as would paralyze the bickering colonies in the face of the common enemy.

It was this nettle that Adams, solely on his own responsibility and apparently without taking counsel of anyone, grasped in his own hand. On entering Congress one morning, Adams, with a mere word of his intention to his cousin Sam in passing his seat, proceeded to take the step that not only settled the immediate problem but did perhaps more than any other single act to ensure the ultimate success of the Revolution. Having obtained the floor, he proposed, in a very brief eulogizing speech, that George Washington should be appointed General of the American army. After a few days' discussion, the bold project succeeded, Washington was unanimously elected, and North and South were indissolubly bound in the common cause through the personality of the only man who could possibly have been accepted by all sections. The petty jealousy of Washington's fame which disfigured Adams's later years should not blind us to the greatness and daring of the service which he rendered at this time, and the judgment and courage that he showed in putting the whole colonial structure and its sentiment for unity to the test.

The late summer vacation of Congress gave Adams a chance to be at home once more with his family, which was visited heavily with sickness and death during the epidemic of dysentery which prevailed. In a few weeks, however, he was back in Philadelphia, displaying to the full his enormous capacity to transact business as well as his ability. It is impossible even to catalogue all the committees he was on and the duties he performed. He wrote that he was busy daily from seven to ten in the morning on committees, from ten to four in Congress, and from six to ten again on committees. Naturally, he did a vast amount of work and thinking outside of these formal meetings. Since the preceding session, there had been somewhat of a reaction in Congress and its spirit was rather less ardent and mutually cordial than it had been. New England had lost something of its popularity, and, as the weary months passed, discouragement and exacerbated nerves made teamwork difficult. The comments on his fellows in Adams's *Diary* become almost as bitter and vitriolic as those in the more celebrated one kept a generation later by his son. Nevertheless he toiled stubbornly on.

He was placed on the committee charged with establishing an American navy, a scheme which had seemed absurd to many in its impossibility when first proposed. It was one of the objects nearest to Adams's heart, and so well did he labor that he has been considered the real founder of that branch of our fighting services, and, although the names of the other members of the committee are practically forgotten, there has always been, for a century and a half, and always will be, a ship of war of the United States bearing the name of *John Adams*.   In connection with this work, he had not only to find, equip, and man vessels, but to prepare a maritime code.

He was fast advancing in influence, and in the records of this session his name appears as the chairman of not less than twenty-five committees, and he was a member of many others. One of the most important of these was the newly created Board of War and Ordnance.   The labors of this committee alone were excessive, almost everything having to be created from nothing.   Another important committee was that on establishing relations with foreign governments, which involved creating a foreign policy and the organization of a whole diplomatic service.   Adams appears to have greatly overrated the ability of the colonies to attain their independence unaided by direct military assistance, but had been keen for foreign alliances based on mutual advantages to be gained by trade. The best speech which, in his own opinion, he ever made in Congress was one urging the appointment of ambassadors to France, though it met with much opposition.   In the course of the debates on foreign affairs, he anticipated both Washington's "Farewell Address" and one aspect of the Monroe Doctrine by declaring that we should "separate ourselves as far as possible and as long as possible from all European politics and wars."   If he did not realize the full price that would have to be paid for alliances, and also the extent to which the need for them was later to become apparent, he was, on the other hand, far in advance of the more hesitant portion of Congress, and it is probable that his midway position did more to bring about the later sending of embassies than the more radical demands of men like Patrick Henry, who were willing to make even territorial sacrifices to gain foreign aid.

To his daily exasperation, however, Congress moved slowly, or so it seemed to him.   In reality it was probably moving as fast as public opinion would, in any case, have followed.

Adams himself was intensely impatient for what he saw as the inevitable independence of the colonies to be made an avowed fact. Discussion of it had been worn threadbare, but by the spring of 1776 events were greatly strengthening the hands of the radicals, notable among them being the news of the hiring of German mercenaries by the British government. On May 15, on Adams's initiative, Congress passed a resolution recommending that each colony form a new government, and he immediately improved this opportunity by proposing a preamble in explanation of the resolution, already adopted, which should commit Congress still further. On June 7, Richard Henry Lee brought in a resolution to declare the colonies free and independent, and, although discussion was postponed until July 1, a committee was appointed on June 11 to draft a declaration to have ready when the matter should again come up. The committee consisted of Jefferson, Adams, Franklin, Sherman, and Livingston, the five later appointing Jefferson and Adams a subcommittee to make the draft. This was practically the work of Jefferson, Adams making only a few slight changes. Jefferson, however, although ready with his pen, was helpless in debate, and when that occurred, on July 1, the task of forcing the Declaration through Congress fell almost wholly upon Adams, his leading opponent being John Dickinson, who pleaded for delay.

The passage of the Declaration filled Adams with joy, and to him belongs the chief credit for having, after long struggle, brought Congress to the point of making it. He had not been placed on the committee to prepare a plan of union for the colonies, but his influence, which had now become great, his indefatigable zeal, and his long pondering on the problems of the new constitution were of marked effect on the plan as drawn up and adopted. Although he printed his pamphlet, *Thoughts on Government*, anonymously, he was known to be its author, and it was widely read among the members of Congress, as well as through the country. It is useless to continue a description of his labors until the end of his career in Congress in the autumn of 1777. He himself claimed, at one time, to have been the hardest-working member in that body, and this estimate would appear to be correct. Nor was his merely *hard* work. For constructive statesmanship during this whole period he was unequaled.

Unfortunately, however, he now began to overrate his services, great as they were — or, rather, he failed to realize the difference between his own and those of others, no less essential because different. In a word, at this period began that jealousy of Washington that became the greatest blot upon his own career. The soldier and the statesman were both indispensable, and without Washington Adams's work would have gone for nothing. Adams himself, indeed, might have swung on a gallows instead of living to be President of the United States. This, however, he could never see, and he looked upon Washington as merely a creation of his own. Adams, intensely jealous in any case, had with respect to Washington that form of jealousy, compacted part of envy and part of disdain, that the thinker has for the man of action, the intellectual for the practical.

At one time, in May 1775, he had, for a passing moment, the absurd notion that he himself would go into the army. "Colonel Washington appears at Congress in his uniform," he writes to his wife, and then childishly adds, "Oh that I were a soldier! I will be. I am reading military books. Everybody must, and will, and shall be a soldier." But the mood passed, and some months later he writes that he is "too old, and too much worn with fatigues of study in my youth," to entertain any such thought, though he was then only forty, and over three years younger than Washington. In June 1775, having ridden out from Philadelphia with others to accompany the newly appointed commander-in-chief on his start for Boston, he wrote to his wife, concerning the farewell given to the general, that "such is the pride and pomp of war. I, poor creature, worn out with scribbling for my bread and for my liberty, low in spirits and weak in health, must leave others to wear the laurels which I have sown; others to eat the bread which I have earned; a common case." So common, that we can easily recognize all the symptoms. We cannot but regret that John Adams, in many ways so greatly and so nobly uncommon, should have displayed them. In 1777, after the defeats of that year, he played his part in attempting to create a second army with a chief who might come to be considered as a substitute for Washington, but fortunately he was out of Congress and away from the centre of intrigue before the worst of the efforts to supplant Washington were to be made. Adams, however, became definitely known as belonging to the anti-Washington faction.

During his long, trying, and arduous years in Philadelphia, Adams more than once became heartily sick of the business, but persevered. He writes to his wife in every mood, and she constantly encourages him. She herself bore nobly the responsibilities and anxieties thrust upon her by the times and the absence of her husband. She had the care of the four children and, at a time when labor was difficult to get on account of the war, the duty of carrying on all the farm work. She was the refuge of friends and neighbors in distress. Before the seat of war was transferred from Boston to New York she was living almost on the firing line, responsible for the children and household. "I went to bed after twelve," she writes one day, "but got no rest; the cannon continued firing, and my heart beat pace with them all night." The morning of Bunker Hill she wrote again: "I went to bed about twelve, and rose a little after one. I could no more sleep, than if I had been in the engagement; the rattling of the windows, the jar of the house, the continual roar of twenty-four pounders, and the bursting of shells, give us such ideas, and realize a scene to us of which we could form scarcely any conception. About six, this morning, there was quiet. I rejoiced in a few hours' calm. . . . Tonight we shall realize a more terrible scene still. I sometimes think I cannot stand it."

In August an attack was anticipated on Boston by the British fleet. "All Boston was in confusion," she wrote to her husband, "packing up and carting out of town household furniture, military stores, goods, etc. Not less than a thousand teams were employed on Friday and Saturday; and, to their shame be it told, not a small trunk would they carry under eight dollars, and many of them, I am told, asked a hundred dollars a load; for carting a hogshead of molasses eight miles, thirty dollars. O human nature! or rather, inhuman nature! The report of the fleet's being seen off Cape Ann Friday night gave me the alarm, and, though pretty weak, I set about packing up my things, and on Saturday removed a load." In the same letter she notes that "it is almost thirteen years since we were united, but not more than half of that time have we had the happiness of living together." She adds that when she contemplated leaving all their home and property to destruction, without her husband to console her, she felt almost too weak to bear it, but, she ends, "the hope of the smiles and approbation of my friend sweetens all my toils and labors." In her letters she seeks constantly to strengthen and encourage her husband. Of a passionately affectionate nature, she stifles complaints of her loneliness and gives him, besides the domestic news he craves, all that of a political and public nature that she thinks can be of use to him. She understands his every mood, and gayly pulls him over the rough places.

By November 1777, however, Adams had determined to retire from public life. There is no contemporary record in his *Diary*, but writing thirty years later he gives his reasons for the step at length. "I had been four years in Congress," he wrote, "had left my accounts [at home] in a very loose condition, my debtors were failing, the paper money was depreciating; I was daily losing the fruit of seventeen years' industry; my family was living on past acquisitions, which were very moderate, for no man ever did so much business for so little profit; my children were growing up without my care in their education, and all my emoluments as a member of Congress, for four years, had not been sufficient to pay a laboring man upon my farm. Some of my friends, who had more compassion for me and my family than others, suggested to me what I knew very well before, that I was losing a fortune every year by my absence. Young gentlemen who had been clerks in my office, and others whom I had left in that character in other offices, were growing rich; for the prize causes, and other controversies had made the profession of a barrister more lucrative than it had ever been before. I thought, therefore, that four years' drudgery, and sacrifice of everything, were sufficient for my share of absence from home, and that another might take my place."

He had in truth done his great work in Congress. More than any other man he had laid the constitutional foundations for the new nation, and it seemed as though the work of "carrying on" could be done by others. He had made great sacrifices, and there were duties to his family and himself to which he well might return. On resuming practice he found that his former clients returned to him and that many new ones came. Happily reunited to his wife and children, pursuing his old calling of the law, he had, however, been at home for less than three weeks when a word was whispered to him while arguing a case at Portsmouth that shattered all his plans and in an instant altered his entire career.

III

EUROPE

THE word whispered to him by John Langdon, just back from Philadelphia, was that Silas Deane, because of his complete unfitness for the post, had been recalled from his mission to France and that Congress had appointed Adams in his place. So far was any thought of such a mission from his mind that he did not believe the news until, after jogging back to Braintree on his nag, he found a packet of letters from Congress containing the appointment and instructions, with the further news that he was to sail as soon as the frigate *Boston* could get to sea. The risks, of course, were great. Those of the sea would have been enough had not that of possible capture been added. Adams's habit of foreseeing all possible evils did not enliven the prospect. He pictured himself being captured by a British frigate, landed in the Tower, and there suffering death after having had practised on him "all the cruelties of their punishment of treason." Gloomy forebodings always made a dangerous task more difficult for an Adams, but never deterred him from undertaking it. His wife, as always, encouraged him, and not only urged him to undertake the mission, but wished to accompany him with all their children. This he wisely would not permit, but he promptly made up his mind as to his duty and accepted the offered post.

It was not one that held any great prospects save of serving his country. He had every desire and incentive to resume his private life. He had no wish to visit Europe, and assuredly not in war time and as one of three commissioners who had already squabbled sufficiently among themselves. Benjamin Franklin, Arthur Lee, and Deane had got along together none too well, and now Adams was merely to replace the discredited Deane. Nevertheless, after much delay on the part of the frigate, Adams set sail on February 13, 1778, and in spite of the fears confided to his *Diary* he took with him his young son, John Quincy, then ten years old. If Adams himself should have ended the trip in the Tower instead of Versailles, what he expected to do with the child is an interesting speculation. At any rate, the boy was urged, with true Adams instinct, to keep a record of his experiences, and the most famous diary in American history, that of the second generation of Adamses in their new phase, thus had its first faint beginning. When Adams got on board the boat he found that, unknown to each other and to him, two friends had also confided their sons, lads in their teens, to his care.

The voyage is described at length in Adams's own *Diary* and need not be given in detail here. They had the usual frightful storm; were chased by one English vessel; and captured another. Although the trip was eventful enough, Adams managed to do much reading and make scientific observations on many topics, from the Gulf Stream to seasickness. He failed, however, in one intellectual endeavor, that of learning French on the way over, and most travelers can agree with his reason. "I have often heard," he wrote, "of learning a language, as French or English, on the passage, but I believe very little of any thing was ever learned on a passage. There must be more health and better accommodation." After six weeks of no little discomfort and ample excitement, he landed at Bordeaux on the first of April.

Once in Paris, Adams was soon initiated into the quarrels and incompetency of the triple-headed commission. Franklin complained of Lee and Deane, Lee complained of the others, and so on in a fatal circle of conflicting minds and temperaments. Adams also promptly discovered that "the public business has never been methodically conducted. There never was, before I came, a minute book, a letter book, or an account book." All this, with the striking capacity that the Adamses have always shown for almost incredible labor with pens and clear minds, Adams started in to correct. There is no use, however, in lingering over the details. Of diplomacy at this juncture there was little, although Adams met Vergennes and others, official and unofficial, of the diplomatic and social sets. He tried the opera, but did not enjoy it. He records in words almost identical with his daughter's some years later, "I always wish, in such an amusement, to learn something," and he learned nothing from the opera in Paris.

He commented highly upon Lee, but he had always felt that Franklin was overrated, and now that he was even more closely associated with that gentleman than he had been in the Congresses he noted that, although it was certain that he "was a great genius, a great wit, a great humorist, a great satirist, and a great politician," it was very questionable whether he was "a great philosopher, a great moralist, and a great statesman." In any case, Adams found the affairs of the commission in confusion, and a great deal more money being spent by everyone than there was any need for in his opinion. Unable to write officially to Congress as an individual, he unburdened himself on the situation to his cousin Sam Adams. He advised strongly that Congress should distinguish between ministers and commercial agents; that one of the former would be much more efficient than three; and that a definite salary, strictly accounted for, should be substituted in place of the former lax system of sending in expense accounts.

In this, Adams acted like a high-minded public servant. Lee had been appointed to the Spanish mission, and there was no question, owing to his immense influence and vogue in France, that Franklin would have to be continued in Paris. Adams, as he well knew, was signing his own recall. Congress acted on his informal recommendations in all points except that it forgot to recall him, and left him in an embarrassing position. When Franklin was appointed sole agent, his advice to Adams, in true Franklinian vein, was that he should stay on and enjoy himself in Paris at the public expense. This was obviously not at all to Adams's taste, and as soon as possible, but after much delay in securing passage, Adams at his own expense, and with his young son, reached Boston again, after an absence of nearly a year and a half, on August 2, 1779.

Massachusetts was in the throes of forming a new constitution, and Adams had scarcely got his land legs on again when he was elected to the constitutional convention as delegate from Braintree. The task was wholly congenial, and nothing would have pleased him better than to resume his home life and be thus occupied until he could pick up his law practice once more. He was placed on the committee to draft the constitution, but before the work of the convention was concluded he was once more, unexpectedly to himself, on his way to France. It is impossible, and needless, to go into all the congressional and diplomatic webs that had been weaving in the recent months. Suffice it that it was deemed advisable to have on hand in France a man clothed with full powers to negotiate a treaty of peace and another of commerce with England when circumstances should make such a negotiation possible. It was felt that the time was nearing, and John Adams was chosen as the man. He accepted, and on November 13, accompanied by two of his sons, John Quincy and Charles, he sailed again for France on the same ship which three months before had brought him home, burdened with the greatest responsibility which had yet fallen to his share.

Adams and America were almost equally fortunate in the choice that had been made. His most unbiased and ablest biographer has questioned whether he would have made a good diplomat had he followed diplomacy as a career, believing that his "quickness, pugnacity, want of tact, and naïve egotism" would have proved too much for him. It is quite possible. He himself noted on his first mission to Paris that Sir John Temple said of him that, whatever else he might be, "he is the most ungracious man I ever saw." Graciousness has never been an Adams characteristic. Bitterly as, generation after generation, they were to assail England, they are the most English of all the greater American families. Each generation was to score a great diplomatic triumph, and it is not a little singular that in each case it was to be against Englishmen.

Each Adams and his opponents understood and could appreciate each other. Whether an Adams would have made a success of diplomacy as a career is in any case beside the point. One cannot imagine them as tolerating such a career — indeed, any "career" in the ordinarily accepted sense. It is not in the blood slowly to climb the political or professional ladder, to devote a lifetime consistently to the accumulation of fortune, or to the scholar's tasks. They are not domestic animals. They are rather what the Jardin des Plantes in Paris labels on certain cages, *animaux féroces*.

John Quincy, in the second generation, and Charles Francis, in the third, would have to meet as antagonists only the disliked but understandable British. John had to counter at once the finesse of the French and the more sympathetic bulldog tactics of the ancestral English. The assistance of the French in the Revolution has, utterly without foundation, been the basis for a traditional friendship between the two nations, evaluated realistically in France and romantically in America. France, after long hesitation, came in on the side of the colonies not for any love of them or for republicanism, but to use them as a whip with which to beat its traditional foe, England. The astute French Minister, Vergennes, had no intention of raising up a powerful democracy overseas. Adams himself, in spite of his bitter opposition to England and friendship for France, sensed this, and feared to trust French protestations very far. He may not have been a diplomat, but he was a shrewd Yankee, and he was not long in Paris with his commissions to negotiate a peace and a commercial treaty with his country's foes before he realized where he stood as to his country's friend, France.

Promptly on his arrival, Adams wrote to Vergennes stating that he would take no steps of consequence without consulting him — an intention that, he added, he felt sure would be the wish of his countrymen. He then proceeded to ask the Minister's advice as to making his errands known, both in France and in England. The reply gave the confiding diplomat a severe shock. Vergennes had no wish to see any unnecessary advantages accrue to the new, small state across the ocean which France was helping to establish merely to score against England. He had greatly disliked the thought of the United States negotiating a favorable commercial treaty with England when peace should come, and meanwhile, as to peace itself, he was anxious to hold all the strings in his own hand as long as possible. Secretly, unknown to Adams, he had been trying to get the instructions to negotiate the commercial treaty revoked by Congress through the French agent in Philadelphia, Gérard. With an utter lack of diplomatic courtesy, he replied to Adams that he preferred to give him no answer until Gérard should return, as he would probably bring a copy of Adams's instructions with him, and that meanwhile he advised Adams to conceal the nature of his mission, particularly from the English court.

Adams at once realized the breach of etiquette that Vergennes had so arrogantly committed, and also his object — namely, to get information as to Adams's secret instructions either through his agent or by having Adams fall into the trap and divulge them himself. Adams had not been at all satisfied with his instructions, which he considered relinquished too much on the points of boundaries and the fisheries. In so far, however, as he could twist those instructions to justify him, he had, he wrote in his *Autobiography*, come to an "unalterable determination to insist on the fisheries, and on an ample extension of our boundaries." On the other hand, he at once saw that if Vergennes should learn the exact wording of the instructions he would go to the utmost length, when the negotiations should begin, to make Adams forgo the fisheries and limit the boundaries, and that he would give the British negotiator a hint which would greatly weaken Adams's hand in dealing with him. Adams himself was far too astute to give Vergennes any inkling of what the instructions might be, but the news that the French agent was expected to learn them in Philadelphia gave him much anxiety. "Some alarming ideas," he says, "were excited by the consideration that my sovereign was an assembly of more than fifty members; and fifty incorruptible men, all

capable of containing a secret, was not always to be expected."
He countered Vergennes's letter, however, in a dignified reply,
which showed clearly enough that he understood both his own
rights and diplomatic usage. The Count replied that Adams's
mission to negotiate peace in the future would be published in
the *Gazette of France* when he was presented at Court, but that
his other mission, to negotiate a commercial treaty, should be
kept secret. Adams was somewhat puzzled. He wrote many
years afterward, "I was not clear that I suspected his true
motives. The United States were clearly at as full liberty to
negotiate concerning commerce as concerning peace. In both
they must be governed by their treaties with France, but not
in one more than in the other. However, time brought to light
what I but imperfectly suspected. The Count meditated at
that time, no doubt, what he soon carried into execution with
too much success — his intrigues with Congress, at Philadelphia,
to get my commission to negotiate a treaty of commerce an-
nulled, without renewing it to the five commissioners whom
they afterwards appointed to negotiate peace. It was intended
to keep us embroiled with England as much, and as long as
possible, even after a peace. It had that effect for eleven
years. The United States never had spirit, decision, and
independence, to remove this obstacle to a friendly understanding with England, till 1794, when Mr. Jay sacrificed, and Mr.
Washington diminished his popularity, by a treaty which excited the insolent rage of France without a color of justice."
Had Adams's hatred of the English been somewhat less
unreasoningly virulent, he might have understood the selfish-
ness and duplicity of the French policy somewhat more clearly.
He ought, at least, in view of his correspondence with Vergennes,
who continued to delay publication of even Adams's character
as a peace negotiator, to have been extremely careful in his
dealings with the Minister.

Unfortunately he was not, and managed to get himself into as
unnecessary an imbroglio as diplomat ever snarled himself in.
Franklin was, of course, the only accredited American Minister
to the French court. Adams merely held commissions to

negotiate with England at some future date when negotiations should have become possible. Both discretion and courtesy obviously called for his holding himself strictly aloof from all which did not concern the object of his mission. Unfortunately his temper was more restless than discreet. One cannot help feeling that his intense Puritanic earnestness here played him a shabby trick. He might have had both a happier life and an even greater career had he not believed in the moral necessity of improving every moment of his time. But such speculations are futile. He would not then have been John Adams. Once in a while he gives us a glimpse of what he might have been had he not been so stern a Puritan. "The cookery and manner of living here," he writes to his wife from Paris, "is more agreeable to me than you can imagine. The manners of the people have an affection in them that is very amiable. There is such a choice of elegant entertainments in the theatric way, of good company, and excellent books, that nothing would be wanting to me in this country but my family and peace to my country, to make me one of the happiest of men. John Bull would growl and bellow at this description. Let him bellow if he will, for he is but a brute."

This note, however, is rare. As a rule, his Puritanism and also his lack of any æsthetic appreciation are marked. "The public buildings and gardens, the paintings, sculpture, architecture, music, etc., of these cities have already filled many volumes," he writes to his wife. "But what is all this to me?" he adds. "I receive but little pleasure in beholding all these things because I cannot but consider them as bagatelles, introduced by time and luxury in exchange for the great qualities, and hardy, manly virtues of the human heart. I cannot help suspecting that the more elegance, the less virtue, in all times and countries." "I could fill volumes," he writes in another letter, "with descriptions of temples and palaces, paintings, sculptures, tapestry, porcelain, &c., &c., &c., if I could have time; but I could not do this without neglecting my duty. The science of government, it is my duty to study, more than all the other sciences; the arts of legislation and administration and negotiation, ought to take place of, indeed to exclude, in a manner, all other arts. I must study politics and war that my sons may have liberty to study mathematics and philosophy. My sons ought to study mathematics and philosophy, geography, natural history and naval architecture, navigation, commerce and agriculture, in order to give their children a right to study painting, poetry, music, architecture, statuary, tapestry and porcelain." It is evident enough that all these things meant nothing to Adams, that they counted as nothing in his mental or spiritual development, but were merely things to be toyed with by people not engaged in serious work. Had it been otherwise, had he realized that they were essential instruments for developing a higher type of mind or character, his sense of duty would have made him find time for them. It was a pity that he neglected them at this juncture for the dangerous art of negotiation when there was nothing to negotiate.

Insisting upon employing himself, as he thought, usefully, and driven by the new urge in his family for writing, he wrote a series of articles intended to dispel the abysmal ignorance of the French on American affairs. These he published, after having them translated, in a prominent Parisian newspaper. There they came under the observation of the wily Vergennes. That gentleman requested that Adams should furnish him with any information about the United States that might occur to him as being interesting or important. Nothing could have been more pleasing to Adams, who had an insatiable desire to impart information and express his views. He began also to write home to prominent men and addressed long letters to Congress. When he should have been discreetly inactive publicly, he began to be most busily industrious. In May (1780) he wrote to Arthur Lee that "with nothing at all to do, I am as busy as ever I was in my life." Among other things, he noted that "I have undertaken to inform congress a little more particularly than they are wont to be informed, of some things that have passed in Europe, which will ultimately affect them." This, of course, was a direct slap at Franklin, our

Minister to France, upon whose preserves Adams, indeed, was now having a glorious romp.

Early in the spring, Congress had recommended to the several states the redemption of the Continental money at the rate of two and a half cents in silver for a dollar in paper — in other words, repudiating $97\frac{1}{2}$ per cent. Adams received a letter from his brother-in-law on the subject, which he promptly sent to Vergennes, overlooking entirely the existence of Minister Franklin. Vergennes replied with a stinging rebuke on the lack of good faith in the American government in thus repudiating its payment of foreign debts. Adams attempted to defend the indefensible and became more and more involved in his correspondence. Vergennes replied that Adams's details had not changed his opinions and that "all further discussion between us on the subject will be needless."

Adams at last remembered that the United States had a Minister to France and sent the correspondence to Franklin with suggestions that that gentleman had better get busy. Indeed, it was time that someone did, for Adams had lost his head completely and made matters ten times worse by writing Vergennes a long letter (filling nine pages of close print in his "official correspondence"), urging a great increase in the naval effort made by France in American waters in order to prove her sincerity under the treaty of alliance, and rising near the close to a genuine eagle screech with: "The United States of America are a great and powerful people, whatever European statesmen may think of them." Considering that Adams's sole mission was to negotiate a peace with England when the time came, and, in order to facilitate that, to keep on the best terms possible with French statesmen, we can only look on bewildered as we watch diplomacy thus running amok. Adams, however, was not through yet. He chose this tempestuous moment to renew his demand that Vergennes should agree to his making known his mission to the British court. The Minister replied with a long and contemptuous analysis of Adams's letter. Two days later, Adams wrote again, reopening the naval question, and, in spite of his incomprehensible blundering and

Vergennes's flat statement that he wished to hear no more, said that, convinced of the necessity of more communications between "his Majesty's ministers and the ministers of Congress," he was "determined to omit no opportunity of communicating my sentiments to your Excellency, upon everything that appears to me to be of importance to the common cause." Adams in his madness had fairly invited Vergennes to crush him, and the Minister stepped on him much as he would have on an annoying insect. Acknowledging his letter, the Minister added, "To avoid any more of the kind, I think it my duty to inform you that, Mr. Franklin being the sole person who has letters of credence to the King from the United States, it is with him only that I ought and can treat of matters which concern them." Moreover, he sent the entire correspondence to Franklin with the request that it all be transmitted to Congress in order to allow them to judge whether Adams possessed the qualifications "necessary for the important and delicate business with which he is entrusted." This was done, but, fortunately for Adams, Congress, well knowing both him and his great services, contented themselves with passing a mild rebuke, followed up some months later with a letter expressing satisfaction with his conduct.

No two men could be more different in every respect than were Franklin and Adams, and Adams had by now come both to mistrust and bitterly to hate the easy-going philosopher. The feud lasted as long as life and thirty years later Adams was still rancorously attacking Franklin's ability, morals, and even patriotism, and raking over the yet glowing coals of this Paris quarrel of 1780. He had always been jealous of Franklin's reputation, which he had thought undeserved. In Paris he felt that Franklin was doing his work most inefficiently, and, without a shadow of diplomatic right, he undertook to do the work himself and to supplant the accredited Minister. The only result was to bring on a most unfortunate quarrel between America's two leading citizens abroad and to anger the French government. Even Adams could see that his usefulness at the French court was over for the moment. The incident has been related somewhat at length because it displays clearly both the strength and weakness of more than one generation of the new family. Conscious of his own great ability and of his services in forming the new nation, Adams could not stand aside and watch what in his opinion was Franklin's carelessness in serving the interests of that country. Mixed with this motive was probably not a little, unconsciously, of that jealousy and depreciation of other men and their motives, and that censorious judgment of their views and habits of life, that were a continuing strain in the Adamses. On the other hand, seeing the situation as he did, Adams did not hesitate to assume the whole responsibility himself and, backed by the enormous industry which has been another family trait, place himself, as he thought, in the breach. Infuriated by what he considered Franklin's faults, he failed to see his value. Moreover, Adams's bull-headed tactics, which when directed against the English had their success, were by no means the methods to employ against a man like Vergennes. For three generations, the family's diplomatic successes were to be solely against the English. They were never, after Vergennes, pitted against the subtler brains of the Latin. They understood the English because they were so thoroughly English themselves.

Adams, discomfited, sore, and somewhat bewildered, now determined to turn to a new field. It had been made severely plain to him that he was not a Minister to France, and the French government had bluntly told him that they wished to hear no more from him. In fact so greatly had he incensed the French Minister that it was evident that that official was on the warpath to take Adams's diplomatic scalp. For a considerable time, Adams had been considering the possibility of gaining help from Holland, especially in the form of a loan. If that could be done, it would not only help to establish the position of the new nation internationally, but would to some extent lessen the sole dependence upon France. He now determined to go to Holland and examine the ground. Expecting to be absent only a few weeks, he was to remain a whole year and effect one of the greatest triumphs of his career.

During the stormy months of his Paris sojourn, his two boys had been attending a school at Passy, the same which John Quincy had attended on his previous visit. Adams took them both with him to Holland and in September placed them in the Latin School at Amsterdam, transferring them in December to the University of Leyden, there to continue their Latin, Greek, and other studies. We shall have more to say of the older lad's further European career in this period later, and here need only note that Charles, whose health suffered in Holland, became homesick and so set his heart on going home that his father wrote the mother "it would have broken it to have refused him." "I desire," he added, "I may never again have the weakness to bring a child to Europe. They are infinitely better at home." In December 1781 the boy was sent home under the care of friends by way of Bilboa.

In Holland, Adams found the same ignorance of America that he had encountered in France, and, seeing the need of laying a foundation, he at once began to make personal acquaintances in the right quarters and to use the press. While thus engaged, he received a commission from Congress regulating his position and authorizing him to negotiate a loan from the Dutch government. Unfortunately, that government became embroiled with England, the English having captured some papers which they considered placed the Dutch in a hostile light. The Dutch were in a panic and in no position to involve their position further by a loan to England's revolted colonies. At this juncture, Adams received two new commissions from Congress, one of which gave him authority to sign the Armed Neutrality and the other to act as Minister to Holland and to negotiate a treaty of alliance. In view of the relations with England, however, he could make but slow progress. Patiently he set to work. Besides his writings in the newspapers, a series of articles were published by him under the title of *Twenty-six Letters upon Interesting Subjects respecting the Revolution of America*, and in personal intercourse he made a great impression upon the leading Dutch statesmen and bankers. He also sent Memorials to the States-General. We

need not here enter upon a description either of the complicated government then existing in Holland or of the complex
political situation of the moment. We may note, however,
that in his efforts Adams had to encounter the opposition of
France, which had no wish to better the position of America
either in the approaching general peace negotiations or after.
Vergennes persistently attempted to have Adams recalled from
Holland and to have him placed under the authority of Franklin.
Suddenly, he sent for Adams to return to Paris on urgent
business.

Arrived, after a hurried trip, Adams found that the occasion
of calling him was the necessity of replying to offers of mediation by Austria and Russia. Four articles had been suggested
as a basis, of which Vergennes communicated only three to
Adams, concealing the fourth. Adams, of course, was also
unaware that Vergennes was doing his utmost to have him
superseded and to have Congress place all the negotiations in
French hands. In that Vergennes was not to be wholly successful, but he did so far influence the now rather spineless body
in Philadelphia as to induce them to revoke Adams's powers
to negotiate a treaty of commerce with England, and to substitute a commission of five, consisting of Franklin, Jay,
Jefferson, Laurens, and Adams, in place of Adams as sole peace
envoy. This last change, a rather wise one, Adams never
objected to. He was not, however, to learn of it until subsequent to his return to Holland after giving his reply to Vergennes with regard to the points submitted to him. By
this time, Adams had come clearly to perceive that the French
Minister was far from being the generous friend of America
which he had always pretended to be, and the Minister's
personal discourtesies, and even threatenings, could add nothing to what Adams already knew, what indeed he should have
known long before.

Once more back in Holland, he decided to push for recognition by that country of the United States in spite of the opposition of the French, and in January 1782 he made a series of
visits to each city, requesting from the authorities a categorical

answer which he could transmit home as to whether they were in favor of recognizing the new country or not. As a result of his daring and understanding handling of the political forces then at work in the States of Holland, Adams's efforts were finally completely crowned with success and the States-General acknowledged the United States to be an independent nation and received him as its accredited Minister. Subsequently the Dutch bankers made loan after loan to Congress through Adams until his return to America in 1788. The conception and carrying through of this brilliant diplomatic stroke were entirely Adams's. Throughout the long-drawn-out negotiations he had shone at his best — independent in judgment, patient, tactful, courageous, enormously industrious and resourceful.

Meanwhile, various diplomatic "balloons" had been sent up by England with intent to discover the possibilities of a peace. Vergennes was also ready. He had succeeded at last in dictating almost word for word the instructions that Congress gave to its peace envoys, who were told to take no step without both the knowledge and concurrence of the French, and to govern themselves by the advice of the King's Minister, Vergennes. France was no longer an ally, but a suzerain, and the subservient Congress had placed the interests and the destiny of their country in the hands of the French Minister. Adams, stung to the quick both in his personal and national pride, was held back only by his patriotism and sense of duty from throwing up his commission. Jay, then Minister to Spain, asked that someone be appointed in his place, but events were now moving so swiftly in England, owing to political changes, that no substitutions were possible. Laurens had declined his appointment and Jefferson remained in America, so that the negotiations devolved upon Franklin, Adams, and Jay. After some fencing as to recognition of the independence of the United States preliminary to negotiating, which Adams settled to the satisfaction of all by having the English commissioners appointed to treat with "the commissioners of the United States," he, while still in Holland, received a note from Jay urging his immediate appearance in Paris. He set off from The Hague on October 17, 1782, and, after having noted, for him, an unusual number of pictures and churches en route, arrived in Paris on the twenty-sixth.

There he found that the early stages of negotiation, the feeling out of one another's position and views through official and unofficial sources, were over, and that the real negotiations were in progress. Adams was at once confronted with a serious decision. The instructions of Congress were clear. The commissioners were to take no step without consulting the French and receiving their approval. Franklin, who had been having a delightful time in Paris for some years, and who had been flattered and cajoled to the top of his bent, by statesmen, men of letters, distinguished ladies, and even by the populace, was more than willing to obey the natural instinct of any envoy to adhere strictly to his instructions. On the other hand, Jay, who, as a descendant of French Huguenots, could place no faith in the Bourbons, and whose term at Madrid had opened his eyes to the intrigues going on between the French and Spanish courts, which, to say the least, did not have the welfare of America as their object, was bitterly opposed to having the enemy-friend, Vergennes, guide and limit America's negotiations with England. In this supremely important decision, Adams had to take sides at once. His attitude toward his two colleagues is clearly shown in an entry in his *Diary* the day after his arrival at Paris. "Between two as subtle spirits as any in this world," he wrote, "the one malicious, the other, I think honest, I shall have a delicate, a nice, a critical part to act. Franklin's cunning will be to divide us; to this end he will provoke, he will insinuate, he will intrigue, he will manœuvre. My curiosity will at least be employed in observing his invention and his artifice. Jay declares roundly, that he will never set his hand to a bad peace. Congress may appoint another, but he will make a good peace or none." It is needless to point out that Adams's hatred of Franklin made him unfair in his judgment. Having given his own vote for proceeding without consulting Vergennes, Franklin quietly acquiesced with his two colleagues, and there is nothing afterward in the *Diary* to indicate any effort on Franklin's part to sow discord.

Adams's decision to ignore Vergennes, which in view of the opposing opinions of the other two members of the commission was a casting vote, was a characteristically courageous one. Knowing all we now do of the French Minister's intrigues and plans, inimical to the best interests of the United States, the decision to negotiate without him was eminently wise, but much that is known now had to be surmised then, and it required a high degree of character and independence deliberately to go counter to clearly worded instructions, the disobeying of which could only be condoned by winning a marked success.

The Americans were all three much abler men than the two English envoys, Oswald and Strachey, and England had at last come to be sincerely desirous of making peace. In those respects, the cards that the Americans held were good. On the other hand, America was exhausted and the rebellion would have failed long before had it not been for foreign aid. Now that a general pacification was in process, America could no longer count on such assistance, and, so far from wishing to see the United States make a good peace, Vergennes exerted himself as far as he could to minimize the advantages that might accrue to her. Adams notes one day that the situation of England and America is like that of an eagle which had seized a cat thinking her a hare. Once in the air, "the cat seized him by the neck with her teeth, and round the body with her fore and hind claws. The eagle finding himself scratched and pressed, bids the cat let go and fall down. No, says the cat, I won't let go and fall; you shall stoop and set me down." This little fable, which sounds very like Franklin, had a good many elements of truth. On the whole, however, the eagle showed more inclination to stoop and let the cat loose at any cost than might have been expected.

Jay proved an admirable negotiator and won the rare distinction of even Adams's hearty praise. The French, of course, turned their battery of compliments on Adams as on others, and in his *Diary* he naïvely records some of those received, among others that more than one person told him he was *le Washington de la négociation*. "A few of these compliments would kill Franklin, if they should come to his ears," he rather maliciously adds, but a few weeks later he records that the man who really deserves the title of "le Washington" of the negotiations is Jay and not himself. This praise and modesty both indicate what an extraordinary impression Jay's ability must have made upon him. Adams, however, played a large part in the work of the commission. It is unnecessary to follow the negotiations in detail. We may note, however, that one of the points in the treaty which contributed largely to rendering it acceptable to the British later was due to Adams. When the question of debts due British merchants and compensation due to the Loyalists was broached, Adams at once pointed out that the question was in reality two, and suggested that a clause be inserted stipulating that Congress should use its influence to prevent the States placing any legal impediment in the way of a collection of just debts. Franklin had approached the problem in the spirit of a haggling trader, but Adams, with the feeling of a man of honor, felt that the American merchants should pay any debts that were just and had been contracted in good faith on both sides. Although the clause was unfortunately not worth much, it did prove of great help in enlisting the whole British merchant class on the side of accepting the treaty — a point which, in forecast, the British negotiators readily seized, and which greatly facilitated the general negotiation.

On another point Adams bore the brunt of the discussion. As an American, and more particularly as a New Englander, he was insistent that the treaty should confirm in the most liberal terms possible that right of the United States to the fisheries off the northeastern and Newfoundland coasts which it had always enjoyed. There was some British hesitation, and, in addition, the French were using their influence to have this point left in such a way as to be productive of as great possibilities of future ill-feeling and conflict between the English and

Americans as might be, on the ground that any source of trouble between rival nations would inure to France's benefit by weakening them. At last, however, agreement was in sight, when an unexpected obstacle was met. "Mr. Strachey," wrote Adams, "proposed to leave out the word 'right' of fishing, and make it 'liberty.' Mr. Fitzherbert [who was now added to the other two Englishmen] said the word 'right' was an obnoxious expression." Nothing could be better calculated to stir Adams's righteous indignation. The group had been seated around the table, but Adams at once rose from his seat, and one would give much to have been able to watch the short, impassioned American as he thundered at the Englishmen, "Gentlemen, is there or can there be a clearer right? In former treaties, — that of Utrecht and that of Paris, — France and England have claimed the right, and used the word. When God Almighty made the banks of Newfoundland, at three hundred leagues distance from the people of America, and at six hundred leagues distance from those of France and England, did he not give as good a right to the former as to the latter? If Heaven in the creation gave a right, it is ours at least as much as yours. If occupation, use, and possession give a right, we have it as clearly as you. If war, and blood, and treasure give a right, ours is as good as yours. We have been constantly fighting in Canada, Cape Breton, and Nova Scotia, for the defence of this fishery, and have expended beyond all proportion more than you. If, then, the right cannot be denied, why should it not be acknowledged, and put out of dispute? Why should we leave room for illiterate fishermen to wrangle and chicane?" The American commissioners, including Laurens, who after the death of his son had joined them in Paris, all stood firm behind Adams.

The rest of the treaty, involving the questions of boundaries, navigation of the Mississippi, and all other points, had by this time been settled, and as the English yielded, after some hesitation, on the fisheries, the copies of the treaties were signed the end of November and "we all went out to Passy to dine with Dr. Franklin." In reality, although Adams calls them so in his *Diary*, the papers signed were not treaties. Owing to the prior treaty of alliance with France, America was bound not to sign any separate peace with England until peace had also been made with France. What the Americans had agreed upon with the English was a paper embodying the terms of a treaty that should be signed by both parties whenever a peace treaty was also signed between England and France. The English had been also negotiating with Vergennes, and as the negotiations had been proceeding satisfactorily, and as he had been kept informed to some extent by Adams of what was going on, he had made no pointed objection to the Americans, who were scrupulously observing the French treaty although not their own instructions, doing their work without him. Suddenly, however, he changed. Apparently neither the English nor the French were sure that the Americans meant to keep faith under the treaty of alliance. When the preliminary treaty or agreement was actually signed, Vergennes feared that, having got all they wanted, the Americans might attempt to gain even more by turning on France. He wrote bitterly to Congress about the breach of faith upon the part of the envoys. As a matter of fact, Vergennes and the British Ministry soon came to terms, signing the preliminary treaty of peace in January 1783, although it was September 3 before all the definitive treaties were in shape to be signed, during all of which time the Americans were kept waiting. As early as February, a repercussion of Vergennes's anger had reached them in the shape of a letter of rebuke rather than congratulation from Congress on the completion of their labors. Congress, indeed, wished practically to apologize to Vergennes for what the commissioners had done! Adams wrote bitterly in the *Diary*, "I have been injured, and my country has joined in the injury; it has basely prostituted its own honor by sacrificing mine. But the sacrifice of me was not so servile and intolerable as putting us all under guardianship. Congress surrendered their own sovereignty into the hands of a French Minister. Blush! blush! ye guilty records! It is a glory to have broken such infamous orders. Infamous, I say, for so they will be to all posterity. How can such a stain be washed out? Can we cast a veil over it and forget it?" Fortunately it was too late for Congress to undo the good work its agents had accomplished.

How different were Adams's own feelings from those of the supine representatives of his country at home is shown by his interview with the English agent, Hartley, one day in April. They were discussing the possible treaty of commerce to be negotiated later between the countries. "I told him," said Adams, "the Comte de Vergennes and I were pursuing different objects; he was endeavoring to make my countrymen meek and humble, and I was laboring to make them proud; I avowed it was my object to make them hold up their heads, and look down upon any nation that refused to do them justice; that, in my opinion, Americans had nothing to fear but from the meekness of their own hearts; as Christians, I wished them meek; as statesmen, I wished them proud; and I thought the pride and meekness very consistent. Providence had put into our hands such advantages, that we had a just right, and it was our duty to insist upon justice from all courts, ministers, and nations; that I wished him to get his commission as soon as possible, and that we might be ready to discuss every point." If Adams had not been utterly lacking, like most of the family, in a sense of humor, we might suspect it when he adds, "I am not fond of talking; but I wanted to convey into his mind a few things for him to think upon." In September he received a commission from Congress to act with Franklin and Jay in negotiating the commercial treaty that he had long had at heart, and his oft-deferred hopes of a return home were again dashed.

The separation from his family had been cruelly long. His wife and three younger children were at Braintree. Early in 1781, when only fourteen, John Quincy had left his studies in Holland to go as secretary to Francis Dana, who had been appointed Minister to Russia, and had remained at St. Petersburg until the late autumn of 1782. There, under private tutors, he studied German and continued his Latin and Greek.

He already spoke Dutch and French, understanding the latter so well, indeed, that his father wrote to him that he was mortified to find that his son wrote better in a foreign than in his mother tongue. The experience was of great interest and value to the boy, but having, as we shall note again later, an extraordinarily sane view for a lad of what was for his own good, he wisely decided after a year to return to his studies at Leyden. He left the Russian capital October 30 in company with Count Greco, an Italian acquaintance, and on account of the badness of the roads did not reach Stockholm until November 25. He remained there, by himself apparently (he was then fifteen), for six weeks, writing that he preferred Sweden to any other country he had yet found in Europe. Leaving Stockholm alone on December 31 for Copenhagen, he was detained in a small Swedish village for a fortnight by a heavy fall of snow, and did not reach Copenhagen until February 15. His father in Paris was greatly worried as to what was happening to the youngster, but the fact that he was allowed to make such a journey alone under the conditions of the time is certainly a great tribute to him in every way. He tried to get from Copenhagen to Hamburg by water, but after waiting three weeks for a favorable wind the harbor froze and he had, after all, to go overland, reaching Hamburg the eleventh of March. He finally got himself safely to The Hague by April 21, 1783, where after his six months' winter Odyssey he settled down calmly to his studies. As soon as John Adams could get away from his duties at Paris, he went to The Hague himself, brought the boy back with him, and employed him as private secretary.

Meanwhile, although Mrs. Adams had repeatedly offered to cross the ocean in order to be with him, Adams had refused to let her, partly on account of the danger and discomfort, and partly from the hope, from month to month, that he might be allowed to return to America. Their correspondence had been constant, but at best it could be but a broken affair. In April 1783 his wife wrote to him that "at length an opportunity offers, after a space of near five months, of again writing to you. Not a vessel from any port in this State has sailed since January. . . . I have written twice by way of Virginia, but fear the letters will never reach you."

The years had indeed been lonely for the harassed and homesick Adams. He would give a million pounds, he writes, to be home once more and for good, and such is the burden of letter after letter. His financial affairs also troubled him sorely. "Not a line from Congress, nor any member," he wrote his wife in 1780, "since I left you. My expenses through Spain were beyond all imagination, and my expenses here so exorbitant, that I can't answer any bill from anybody, not even from you, excepting the one you have drawn. I must beg you to be as prudent as possible. Depend upon it, your children will have occasion for all your economy. Mr. Johannot must send me some bills. Every farthing is expended and more. You can have no idea of the unavoidable expenses. I know not what to do." Again he writes, "You must be frugal, I assure you. Your children will be poorly off. I can but barely live in the manner that is indispensably demanded of me by everybody. Living is dear indeed here. My children will not be so well left by their father as he was by his. They will be infected with the examples and habits and tastes for expensive living without the means. He was not. My children shall never have the smallest soil of dishonor or disgrace brought upon them by their father, no, not to please ministers, kings or nations. At the expense of a little of this, my children might perhaps ride at their ease through life, but dearly as I love them, they shall live in the service of their country, in her navy, her army, or even out of either in the extremest degree of poverty, before I will depart in the smallest iota from my sentiments of honor and delicacy; for I, even I, have sentiments of delicacy as exquisite as the proudest minister that ever served a monarch. They may not be exactly like those of some ministers."

During the weary months of 1783, waiting to sign the definitive treaty and be appointed by Congress to negotiate the commercial one, he still opposed his wife's coming over. He even sent his resignation to Congress. But by September his patience was exhausted and he wrote her to come over with her daughter, leaving the two boys at school.

If Adams suffered in Paris during the many years since he first left home, even more did his wife, left with the responsibilities of the farm and family under conditions that would have taxed the resources of the strongest man. Snow-bound in the small farmhouse in midwinter, she writes, "How lonely are my days! how solitary are my nights! secluded from all society but my two little boys and my domestics. By the mountains of snow which surround me, I could almost fancy myself in Greenland." The rapid fall in the value of the paper money made living an almost insoluble problem with the small means that she possessed. "Goods of all kinds are at such a price that I hardly dare mention it," she writes again. "Linens are sold at twenty dollars a yard; the most ordinary sort of calicoes at thirty and forty; . . . molasses at twenty dollars per gallon; sugar four dollars per pound; bohea tea at forty dollars; and our own produce in proportion." It is little wonder that, in spite of her courage, she wrote that "in contemplation of my situation, I am sometimes thrown into an agony of distress. Distance, dangers, and O! I cannot name all the fears which sometimes oppress me, and harrow up my soul."

In June 1779 she wrote that "six months have already elapsed since I heard a syllable from you or my dear son." Two years later, when the boy was in Russia, she wrote her husband: "Do you know I have not had a line from him in a year and a half? Alas, my dear, I am much afflicted with a disorder called the *heartache*, nor can any remedy be found in America. It must be collected from Holland, Petersburg, and Bilboa." Adams's nature, sternly Puritan and repressive, rarely overflowed into expressions of love and tenderness even in such letters as he wrote to his lonely wife on the farm at home, and occasionally an outburst from her shows how deeply she craved for tenderness. "In the very few lines I have received from you," she writes in one letter, "not the least mention is made, that you have ever received a line from me . . . but I cannot take my pen, with my heart overflowing, and not give utterance to some of the abundance which is in it. Could you, after a thousand fears and anxieties, long expectation, and painful suspense, be satisfied with my telling you, that I was well, that I wished you were with me, that my daughter sent her duty, that I had ordered some articles for you, which I hoped would arrive, &c., &c.? By Heaven, if you could, you have changed hearts with some frozen Laplander, or made a voyage to a region that has chilled every drop of your blood; but I will restrain a pen already, I fear, too rash, nor shall it tell you how much I have suffered from this appearance of — inattention."

"Who shall give me back time?" she writes again in another mood in December 1782, when the second separation had lasted almost four years. "How dearly have I paid for a titled husband? Should I wish you less wise, that I might enjoy more happiness? I cannot find that in my heart." And again, the same month, speaking of her heart, she adds: "The early possession you obtained there, and the absolute power you have ever maintained over it, leave not the smallest space unoccupied. I look back to the early days of our acquaintance and friendship, as to the days of love and innocence, and, with an indescribable pleasure, I have seen near a score of years roll over our heads, with an affection heightened and improved by time; nor have the dreary years of absence in the smallest degree effaced from my mind the image of the dear, untitled man to whom I gave my heart. I cannot sometimes refrain from considering the honors with which he is invested, as badges of my unhappiness." Yet when asked by someone whether, if she had known how long the separation was to become, she would have let him go to France she replies: "If I had known, Sir, that Mr. Adams could have effected what he has done, I would not only have submitted to the absence I have endured, painful as it has been, but I would not have opposed it, even though three years more should be added to the number (which Heaven avert!). I feel a pleasure in being able to sacrifice my selfish passions to the general good, and in imitating the example, which he has taught me to consider myself and family but as the small dust of the balance, when compared with the great community."

Adams's return was delayed even after the definitive treaty of peace was finally signed. There was the commercial treaty to be negotiated, and after that he was really seriously ill with a long fever and protracted convalescence, which latter he spent in England. He was scarcely recovered from that when he was called upon to return to Holland for complicated financial transactions regarding the government loans, and while there received further commissions from Congress to negotiate commercial treaties with any powers willing to make them. Meanwhile, it had been decided that his wife and daughter should come over, and they arrived in the summer of 1784, after a distressing and dangerous voyage. They reached England while Adams was held fast in Holland, and John Quincy was sent to meet them and bring them over. On receiving the news of their safe landing, Adams wrote his wife: "Your letter of the 23d [July] has made me the happiest man upon earth. I am twenty years younger than I was yesterday." After joining him in Holland they all settled to housekeeping at Auteuil, a suburb of Paris.

The reunited family was a happy household, and we get many glimpses of the life they led. To the daughter, who was eighteen, her father was practically a stranger when they met again, and in the journal which, like a true Adams, she was induced to keep, she wrote of him: "I discover a thousand traits of softness, delicacy, and sensibility in this excellent man's character. I was once taught to fear his virtues; happy am I that I find them rather to love, grown up into life unknown to him, and ignorant of him. I had been taught to think him severe, and as he would demand my obedience, I found him far otherwise; he never demanded of me even an acquiescence to his wishes, but left me to follow my own, in the most important concerns of life." In the last point, she has noted a marked trait of the family; the children were always left free and never forced into conduct or career against their wishes.

A remarkable instance of the result of this treatment, at

least as its effects were shown in the Adams family, occurred
at this time.   In February 1785, Adams was appointed Minister to England, the first to represent his country there after
the independence, for which he was himself so largely responsible, had been won.   John Quincy was then but seventeen
years old, but it will be recalled that he had already had a
remarkable career.   He had been private secretary to the
Minister to Russia and to his own father in Paris; knew Greek,
Latin, Dutch, French, and German; had traveled widely on
his own responsibility; and had an extraordinary social
acquaintance among the leading men of his day.   In a letter
to Dr. Waterhouse, his father wrote of him that "if you were to
examine him in English and French poetry, I know not where
you would find anybody his Superiour; in Roman and English
History few Persons of his Age."   In speaking of his knowledge
of mathematics, Adams said that "in the course of the last Year,
instead of playing Cards like the fashionable world, I have
spent my Evenings with him," and that he had taught him
geometry, trigonometry, conic sections, and the differential
calculus, adding that "he is yet but a Smatterer like his Father."

The boy, already so unusually well equipped, was now offered
the opportunity of going to England as the son and secretary of
the American Minister.   A new and extremely interesting scene
was thus opened to him.   Entirely on his own responsibility,
however, although his *Diary* shows how much he appreciated
the new opportunity, he decided to return alone to America,
become a schoolboy again, graduate from Harvard, and begin
the study of law.   He admitted to himself that, with all the
experience and freedom he had enjoyed, with the knowledge of
the world and men he possessed, it would be infinitely hard to
submit himself to the dull routine of classroom work with
unformed boys, with the prospect of some years after that
before his ambition could begin to have scope.   He realized,
however, that his father's small fortune had suffered, that
eventually he would have to look to his own exertions for his
future, and he was determined to be dependent upon no one.
As he himself noted his ambition, it is likely that he wished,

laudably, to make a career of his own. It will be interesting to note his grandson, almost a century later, confronted by almost the identical problem. Henry did not go home, but John Quincy did, and, finding that he was deficient in one or two subjects required by Harvard, set himself to school at Haverhill for a few months, and then, entering the Junior class at Harvard, graduated in 1787. His two brothers were also in the college at the same time, so that Minister Adams wrote that it would almost be cheaper for him to go home and educate the lot himself.

Mrs. Adams had advised her husband against accepting the English mission and modestly felt that she herself would be "an awkward figure." She need, of course, have felt no such hesitation, for Abigail Adams, quite apart from Mrs. John, would have been a distinguished figure anywhere, and she quickly understood, although she did not always admire or approve, the manners of society in the two European capitals. It is interesting to note, however, how she emerged in some ways from the provinciality and strictness of Puritan Braintree. In Paris, the ballet at the opera, she says, at first "shocked me; the dresses and beauty of the performers were enchanting; but, no sooner did the dance commence, than I felt my delicacy wounded, and I was ashamed to be seen to look at them. Girls, clothed in the thinnest silk and gauze, with petticoats short, springing two feet from the floor, poising themselves in the air, with their feet flying, and as perfectly showing their garters and drawers as though no petticoat had been worn, was a sight altogether new to me." Quite. As Adams had said of Philadelphia, it was not Boston. Yet the lady continues: "Shall I speak a truth, and say that repeatedly seeing these dances has worn off that disgust, which I at first felt, and that I see them now with pleasure?" Still she cannot refrain from moralizing on the lives and characters of the ballerinas. Apparently the Massachusetts Puritans had neglected their seaside, for Mrs. Adams was introduced to sea bathing for the first time in England, and *that* amusement certainly need have shocked no one. "The places," she writes, "are under cover.

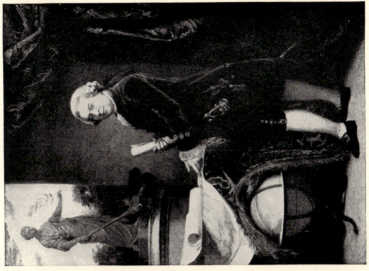

Gilbert Stuart

J. S. Copley

ABIGAIL AND JOHN ADAMS

(By permission of the Adams Memorial Society)

You have a woman for a guide, a small dressing-room to your-self, an oil-cloth cap, a flannel gown, and socks for the feet." But we must control the desire to quote indefinitely from these most charming of all American letters.

Adams himself was engaged in writing of a more serious sort. Both as a patriot and as representative of his country abroad, he was deeply disturbed by the weakness and confusion reigning in both the state governments and the Confederacy at home. Adding new research to his years of study of the principles of government, he wrote a long treatise on the subject, in three volumes, to which he gave the name of *Defence of the Constitutions of the United States of America against the Attack of Mr. Turgot*, which was published in 1787, the first volume reaching America while the Federal Convention to draft a new constitution was in session.

Adams's English mission was a trying and unhappy one. No one could have been better qualified for it, but he was apprehensive of ill-feeling, and, in truth, the English could hardly have been expected to receive any ex-rebel with open arms. Moreover, the country he represented was at that time in a rather despicable state. Congress was at its lowest ebb in mind, ability, and character, and the Union was in almost daily danger of disruption. When Adams attempted to insist upon the English carrying out all the terms of the treaty, he was met by the query as to why the Americans did not do so on their part, to which there was little to answer. The first meeting with King George, dramatic enough in the abstract, went off with simple dignity on both sides, but there was no social pleasure to be obtained by a stay in England for the representative of a revolted State which was expected to break to bits at almost any moment. England had no disposition, immediately upon sheathing the sword, to hold out the olive branch. Adams, in his vision of a future with mutual commercial privileges and restored friendship between the two English nations, was much more statesmanlike than the English in their sullenness, but friendly coöperation at once was too much to hope for. He realized that there was nothing to be gained by remaining on indefinitely, and resigned from his post in 1788 and sailed for home in April. It is rather an odd fact that not only were the heads of the Adams family for three generations Ministers to England, but that in each case they represented America there at a time when, as it happened, English feeling was most bitter against their own country.

IV

AMERICA

THE America to which Adams returned was in some respects very different from that which he had left nearly a decade earlier. "The increase in population is wonderful," he wrote to a London friend; and it was indeed, for it had increased by over a third and was now little short of four millions. Although there had been a serious depression a few years before, business was now booming and many people were rapidly becoming rich. The political changes were equally great. The people, Adams wrote in the same letter, had "discarded from their confidence almost all the old, stanch, firm patriots, who conducted the revolution in all the civil departments," and had "called to the helm pilots much more selfish and much less skilled." He attributed this change, rather naïvely, to some extent to the fact that many of his "brother patriots have flattered the people, by telling them they had virtue, wisdom, and talents, which the people themselves have found out that they had not," and that that had disgusted them with their flatterers. I think the truer reason was that the people had indeed been flattered and promised, but had found, when the war was won, that they were not to enter on the fruits of victory.

The Declaration of Independence had been a trumpet call to the entire people, the lowest as well as the highest. The resounding phrases had been mouthed and echoed in every nook and cranny of the land — "all men are created equal"; "they are endowed by their Creator with certain inalienable rights"; governments derive their only "just powers from the consent of the governed"; and so on through the whole gorgeous preamble. "No taxation without representation" had been the rallying cry of the revolutionists. But when the war was over and won, a very different tune was played. There was not, and never had been, a single one of the revolutionary leaders, not even the most radical of all, Sam Adams himself, who believed in the people. What they believed in, with varying degrees of extension, was the people who had money, talents, or social position. John Adams, whose fundamental theory of government had been adopted in practically all the state constitutions and also in the Federal one, during his absence, was of the same mind.

What he had stood for, briefly, and what, mainly due to him, had become the established form of American constitutions, was a republican government with an executive, legislature, and judiciary independent of one another; complete freedom of conscience and of speech; and, in his oft-quoted words, "a government of laws and not of men." He was often accused of being a monarchist, but there is no reason to doubt his as often reiterated denial. "I am a mortal and irreconcilable enemy to monarchy," he wrote to Dr. Rush in 1790, denying that he had altered his opinions since 1776. "I am no friend to *hereditary limited* monarchy in America. This I know can never be admitted without an hereditary Senate to control it, and an hereditary nobility or Senate in America I know to be unattainable and impracticable. I should scarcely be for it, if it were. Do not, therefore, my friend, misunderstand me and misrepresent me to posterity." If, however, he was no friend to monarchy or aristocracy, neither was he to the rule of the people as understood in later times and expressed in universal suffrage. With all his voluminous writings, he never gave his views any great precision of statement on this point, but he did always lay great stress on the three factors of birth, wealth, and talents, which he claimed formed a natural aristocracy, and denounced an unchecked democracy as "the most ignoble, unjust and detestable form of government." His division into three balanced branches was to check aristocracy and democracy alike.

Other leaders were even more emphatic, and the common people who had fought an eight years' war for what they had

been led to believe were the rights of man were soon disillu-
sioned. When the constitution of Massachusetts was adopted
the property qualification was made double what it had been
under British rule, and the Convention declared that those who
did not possess the requisite amount were either just beginning
life, living on their parents, or had failed to accumulate property
owing to their "idleness of Life and profligacy of manners."
By 1786 over 40 per cent of the state taxes were levied on polls.
Before Adams got home, Shays's Rebellion had come and gone,
Sam Adams himself having come out strongly for the rights of
property above those of men, and for the right of a majority
to do as it pleased regardless of the minority. When John
Adams had left for France, there had been but one party, that
of the patriots. When he returned there were two, the embittered common people who had been denied the suffrage and the
defenders of the rights of property. The latter had a powerful
central group known as the "Essex Junto," composed of such
men as George Cabot, Timothy Pickering, Fisher Ames,
Theophilus Parsons, and others, who were extremely able
politicians, but obstinate, overweening, tenacious of maintaining all power in the hands of the "rich and well-born,"
holding the reins of party organization determinedly in their
own hands. They were in time to be among the chief organizers
and controllers of the national Federalist Party. As yet,
however, although during the discussions over the adoption of
the Federal constitution people had split on the question of the
form and powers of the national government, it cannot be said
that parties, certainly in the later sense, had arisen, though
men were known as Federalist or Anti-Federalist in opinion
as they had advocated or opposed the adoption of the Constitution and its principles.

Owing to delays of Congress, difficulties of communication,
and unfamiliarity with the workings of the new governmental
machinery, the first election held under the Constitution was a
clumsy and bungled affair. In five states, because of lack of
time, the electors were not chosen by the people but by the
legislatures. Owing to a deadlock in the legislature of New

York, that state chose no electors at all. Various odd methods were used in other states. At last, however, such electors as had been chosen met in their respective states to elect a President and Vice-President. A few weeks before, in December 1788, Adams had written to his friend Brand-Hollis in England that he did not expect to have any place in the new government, but this could hardly have been his secret belief. It was universally conceded, indeed, that Washington should be elected to the first place, but Adams was evidently the man for the second. If the President were to come from the South, the Vice-President would obviously have to be chosen from the North. Hancock, then Governor of Massachusetts, Samuel Adams, General Henry Knox, and others were mentioned, but the great services and eminent positions he had already occupied clearly pointed to John Adams — facts of which he could not have been oblivious. There was some question as to whether his known opposition to Washington might make the latter unwilling to have him as second in office, but when consulted on the point Washington declined to interfere beyond suggesting that a Federalist should be elected, and on that score Adams's writings in defense of the Constitution removed any objection in the absence as yet of parties based on anything more than private opinions held.

Alexander Hamilton, owing to his brilliant ability and his great work in securing the adoption of the Constitution, could be ranked as the leading Federalist of the country, but in the first place he was under age for the Vice-Presidency, and in the second he had played only a minor part in the Revolution, and the older generation of Revolutionary statesmen were clearly entitled to the honor of office in the new state that the Revolution had created. He was, however, somewhat distrustful of Adams, whose weaknesses of vanity and temper had impressed him most unfavorably. He wrote, nevertheless, that he had decided to throw the weight of his influence in favor of Adams's election. Under the system of that time, the electors did not vote for President and Vice-President, but the man who received the highest number of votes automatically became President and the man receiving the next highest Vice-President. Unfortunately, Hamilton determined to arrange matters so that, although Washington should be unanimously elected, Adams should be elected with as small a lead over his competitors as possible. He therefore sent word to each of the states advising that although the electors should give every vote to Washington they should scatter the votes for the second candidate. It has been claimed that his motive was to ensure the election of Washington to the highest office, but this is obviously absurd. There was never any doubt that he would receive the unanimous vote of all the electors, whereas it was certain that at least a few votes would be given to others than Adams. His object was clearly to cut down the evidence of popular support and approval of Adams, — whether it was done to lessen that gentleman in his own or the popular esteem, — to make him more amenable to control, to lessen his influence as a leader so as to open the way more easily to Hamilton's own advancement later, or for some other reason.

Whatever the real reason may have been, Hamilton's ill-advised interference had eventually the most disastrous results. When the electoral votes were counted it was found that, whereas Washington had received the entire sixty-nine, Adams had received only thirty-four, the remaining thirty-five being scattered between ten other candidates, none of whom were really serious opponents and none of whom had anything like Adams's claims to the office. The services that Adams had rendered to his country had been second only to those of Washington, although so different that it is difficult to evaluate them both in commensurable terms, and as yet his genuinely great career had been only slightly marred by the faults that from now onward were seriously, at times, to blemish it. He justly felt a strong resentment against Hamilton who had thus interfered to prevent his receiving the full measure of popular approval to which he was indubitably entitled. Hamilton henceforth was to prove his evil genius, and the antipathy between the two leaders, deepening with the years, was to have profound influence upon the careers of both, upon their party and the nation. The unfortunate jealousy that Adams felt for Washington, whom he considered as not at all a statesman but merely a military hero who had owed his career to Adams himself, would in any case have made it difficult for him to accept complacently the lower position in the government, but when, in addition, he felt that the only reward for his services that he had ever asked — a clear expression of public approbation — had been withheld from him through the intrigue of Hamilton, he entered upon his new career at home an embittered man. The full effect, however, of the mutual dislike between him and Hamilton was not to be visible for several years.

Washington and Adams were duly notified at their homes of their election, and each made a triumphal progress thence to New York, which had been decided upon as the temporary capital. On April 21 Adams was introduced to the Senate and took his seat as its presiding officer. As all forms and precedents had to be established, there was much discussion, often apparently trivial and not seldom amusing, over each point as it was raised. Adams realized that forms are by no means empty, and his sense of their real value as well as of his own dignity, combined with, it must be confessed, his rapidly growing vanity, all led him to insist upon them to an extent little relished by many of his more democratic colleagues, earning from Izard the nickname of "his Rotundity," by which, or the more good-humored one of "Bonny Johnnie," he was frequently known.

For a man conscious of his own intellectual power, quick in temper, ardent in debate, the position of presiding officer must have been an exceedingly difficult one. Adams, however, did his duty sternly and acceptably throughout the eight years of his two terms as Vice-President. During the first one, owing to the evenly balanced opinion of the Senate on a great number of questions, he was enabled to exert a much more immediate and direct influence upon the votes than has been the case with any other presiding officer since. No Adams has ever been a party man. Soon after his election, John Adams wrote to Richard Price saying that "I have never sacrificed my judg-

ment to kings, ministers, nor people, and I never will." He
certainly never did, nor has any Adams after him. This
integrity of self, often demonstrated in face of the strongest
temptation, has been a continuing trait, but in an America
demanding more and more that a man shall conform to the
majority it is a trait that has more and more made it difficult if
not impossible for the family to serve in elective office. As we
look over the list of the early leaders of the republic, Washington,
John Adams, Hamilton, and others, we discern that they were
all men who insisted upon being themselves and who refused to
truckle to the people. With each succeeding generation, the
growing demand of the people that its elective officials shall not
lead but merely register the popular will has steadily undermined the independence of those who derive their power from
popular election. The persistent refusal of the Adamses to
sacrifice the integrity of their own intellectual and moral
standards and values for the sake of winning public office or
popular favor is another of the measuring rods by which we may
measure the divergence of American life from its starting point.

If John Adams, however, was not a party man, and always
denied that he was, we find him throwing his important and
decisive casting votes on the side of what was now rapidly
emerging as the Federalist Party. This was a natural result
of his opinions on the nature of government. Both from
theory and from temperament he was in favor of a strong
Federal government. He had had ample experience of the
slackness and weakness of the old Federation, and realized that
although power must be controlled by checks and balances it
must also be genuine. It assuredly could not have given
Adams any pleasure to vote over and over again on Hamilton's
side, and that he did so is ample evidence of the honesty of his
judgment, and we may here note that whatever mistakes he
made, and they were numerous, no one can question the utter
honesty of his entire public and private career. The steady
course that he pursued on the Federalist side led Hamilton to
temper somewhat his own personal dislike, and when, after
four years, a presidential election again came round, Hamilton,

whose word had become law in the Federalist Party, was in favor of Adams for the second place. The Anti-Federalists had also by this time coalesced into a party organization under the name of Republicans, and although both parties united on Washington for President the Republicans strove to elect George Clinton of New York as Vice-President. The result was 134 votes for Washington, 77 for Adams, 50 for Clinton, 4 for Jefferson, and 1 for Burr. A year after his first election Adams had written: "I wish heartily that a change of Vice-President could be made to-morrow. I have been too ill-used in the office to be fond of it; — if I had not been introduced into it in a manner that made it a disgrace. I will never serve in it again upon such terms." In his second election, although the Federalists worked loyally in his support, there was a certain bitterness, taking everything into consideration, in the fact that Washington was obviously the choice of the nation whereas Adams was that of a party. Parties, however, had developed, and it was clear that when Washington should retire the choice of a party would be the only stepping-stone to either of the two highest offices.

There is little that need be commented upon in Adams's second term. He had far fewer opportunities to participate in legislation by his casting votes, and possibly one of the most important elements in these four years, in its influence upon him, was the fact that he had to be the target of most of the abuse of the now strongly organized opposition party. Washington, being above party, was to a great extent, though not wholly, immune from attack, but there was no shield for Adams. He had clearly been elected by a party, but playing, as all the Adamses have, a lone hand with no devoted band of political followers, he had no defense or defenders against the attacks of the Republican press. It was the period of the French Revolution. American political passions, swayed largely by foreign affiliations, were strong and bitter, and Adams, owing to the peculiarities of the situation, was the conspicuous target at which all the discontent and opposition could be aimed. For a man not only sensitive but touchy, not only properly conscious of his ability, integrity, and purity but also more weakly vain, desirous of rising about party but supported and attacked by parties, the eight years he spent as Vice-President could hardly fail to emphasize all his most unfortunate faults and to be the worst possible preparation for his undertaking the duties of a yet higher position. Throughout his life he was hampered by not being able to understand all the motives that influenced other men, or the effects of his own acts and words upon them.

During the years thus spent, partly in New York and partly in Philadelphia, he lived at first in a house with his wife, who left Braintree to join him; but later, owing partly to the public demand for an absurd simplicity in the living of the officers of government which had already begun to characterize the small-minded American electorate, and partly in order to economize, Adams settled in lodgings and Mrs. Adams went back to the farm. Meanwhile, John Quincy, the eldest son, had already entered upon his own career. He had, as we have seen, re-turned to Massachusetts in order to study law. Graduating in 1787 with high standing, he entered the law office of The-ophilus Parsons in Newburyport, and after three years' appren-ticeship was admitted to the bar in 1790. It was just at a time when popular prejudice had again turned against lawyers and the legal profession, owing in part to unpopular enforce-ments of debts and contracts in the troubled business of recent years and in part to a decline in the quality of the members of the profession themselves. Contemporary opinion and the comment of historians have probably underrated the profes-sional quality of the lawyers, who were at least college-bred men, which meant far more then than now, and, the Adams standard both of mind and virtue being exceptionally high, we may perhaps discount John Quincy's verdict, in a letter to his father when considering where he should settle, that there were not, in Boston, many "whose characters are remarkably formidable from their respectability." The young man de-cided, however, to settle there, though, like most Adamses, he did not like "the manners of the town."

The second generation no more than the first could be content with the mere routine of a provincial law practice. The years already spent abroad and in public service, the breadth of his experience and outlook, and a laudable ambition to make a career, soon brought the young man before the public. In 1791, when his year-old law practice must have been of the slenderest proportions, he undertook to answer in a series of articles in the Boston *Centinel*, signed "Publicola," the pamphlet on *The Rights of Man* recently published by Thomas Paine. So ably did he do the work that both at the time and for long afterward the articles were persistently attributed to the pen of his father. The itch and ability to write, however, that had so suddenly appeared in the family with John, was now to be permanent in the strain, and the younger Adams soon followed his reply to Paine with a series of articles, also in the *Centinel*, under various signatures, on the problems of American neutrality arising from the conditions produced by the French Revolution and more particularly the actions of the French Minister Genet.

The younger man had never concealed his ambition to enter upon a public career, but in all the steps leading to it he showed the same remarkable balance of judgment that he had displayed when he had left Europe to return home and become a school-boy again. A letter to his father in April 1794 displays both his judgment and that insistence upon keeping himself free of the opinion and influence of others, whether king or American people, that we have already commented upon as characteristic of the family. "You recommend me," he writes in answer to his father's letter, "to attend the town-meetings and make speeches; to meet with caucuses and join political clubs. But I am afraid of all these things. They might make me a better politician, and give me an earlier chance of appearing as a public man; but that would throw me completely in the power of the people, and all my future life would be one of dependence. I had rather continue some time longer in obscurity, and make some provision for fortune, before I sally out in quest of fame or of public honors." Thus at twenty-six the young man declares that come what may he must be him-

self and independent of any electorate or party. He will enter
public life upon no other terms than such as will leave him free
and untrammeled.

He did not have long to wait. On his twenty-seventh birth-
day, he received notice that Washington had appointed him
Minister Resident at The Hague and that the Senate had
unanimously confirmed the appointment. Young Adams
accepted the office with considerable misgiving, which his
biographer calls "unexplained doubt." A letter to his father
explains it clearly. He had not yet, he says, become financially independent. He had just got well started in his law
practice, which in a few years might be expected to place him
in such a position as to enable him to enter upon a public
career without being solely dependent upon the salary of office.
A diplomatic post could be expected to last only a few years at
most. To return and make a fresh start at law after another
long delay would be extremely difficult, and would again post-
pone by some years laying the foundation for his real career.
Nevertheless, he felt he could not decline to serve, and the last
day of October found him at his post at The Hague, which he
already knew well and where his father had achieved the greatest success of his own career. The following six years were
spent in various parts of Europe, and we must leave the young
man for the present in order to continue the story of his father.

In the summer of 1796 it became definitely known that
Washington would not accept a renomination, and the way
was therefore open for a party contest for the Presidency.
The Republicans decided upon a ticket of Jefferson and Burr,
and the Federalists upon Adams and Pinckney. The only two
other Federalists who could be considered — Hamilton and
Jay — were both ineligible because of their unpopularity
among the people at large, Hamilton on account of his financial
policy and Jay on account of the treaty that he had negotiated
with England. Hamilton, however, was unquestionably the
most powerful politician in his party, and it was recognized
that he could make a President even though he could not secure
the office for himself. The tactics which he adopted in doing

so precipitated the most fatal and bitter quarrel in the annals of American political history.

Although Pinckney was an able man, much better fitted for the office of President than many who have subsequently held it, Adams from his ability, position, and public services was unquestionably entitled to be considered the choice of the party. Hamilton, however, not only disliked him, but knew that he would be intractable to any dictation, and Hamilton wished to remain the real power behind the throne. He could not openly avow this as a reason for opposing Adams, and he therefore resorted to a subterfuge. He sent out word that all electors should cast their votes equally for Adams and Pinckney, on the ground that the defeat of Jefferson was more important than the question of which of the two Federalist candidates should receive the higher vote. By doing so he was in reality working for the election of Pinckney while avowing public support to Adams. There would seem to be no room for dispute as to this, for he himself wrote some years later, when he publicly broke with Adams, that his "plan would have given Mr. Pinckney a somewhat better chance than Mr. Adams; nor shall it be concealed that an issue favorable to the former would not have been disagreeable to me; as indeed I declared at the time in the circle of my confidential friends. My position was that if chance should decide in favor of Mr. Pinckney, it probably would not be a misfortune; since he to every essential qualification for the office added a temper far more discreet and conciliatory than that of Mr. Adams."

As the plan had a certain surface plausibility, Adams did not at once realize the sharp practice that Hamilton was indulging in, but when he did come to understand the whole intrigue it resulted in an embittered and settled hatred of the man whom he had then come to consider as attempting on every critical occasion to thwart and destroy his career. Hamilton on his part, though not vindictive as a rule, also developed an unusual animosity toward Adams, as the latter not only declined to submit to Hamilton's dictation, but, it must be confessed, went much too far in showing his resentment.

When the electoral votes were counted it was found that Adams had received 71, Jefferson 68, Pinckney 59, Burr 30, and the rest were scattered among nine minor candidates. Owing to the method of election, the Federalists had thus elected the President and the Republicans the Vice-President. It is interesting to note how, even thus early, the theory of electors had broken down. It had not been the intention of the framers of the Constitution that the people should elect the President, but that the members of the electoral college, being able and distinguished men, should make a choice in which the body of the people would willingly acquiesce. This was the case in the first two elections, but by 1796 the formation of party machinery had so far progressed that the electors were considered to be instructed. In one case, that of Samuel Miles of Pennsylvania, who acted on his independent judgment, as the Constitution had contemplated, a condemnatory letter in the *United States Gazette* showed clearly how the theory had become altered. The writer angrily said that he chose an elector "to *act*, not to *think*." It was one of the notable turning points toward that theory, common to all democracies with wide suffrage, which has become more and more disastrous in our modern world, — that a public man should be a rubber stamp instead of using his knowledge and judgment to the best of his ability, — and which has more and more deterred men of intellectual power and integrity from submitting themselves to the dictation of the mob and making their own intelligence subservient to the ignorance of the multitude.

It is obviously impossible to discuss the details of the various episodes of Adams's term as President within the limits of a few pages, nor is it needful in a book like this, which is neither history nor biography, but an interpretive sketch of the rise of an American family.

He had long been looking forward to the possibility of his being elected to the position he now held. A year before he had written to his wife saying, "I am weary of the game, yet I don't know how I could live out of it. I don't love slight, neglect, contempt, disgrace, nor insult, more than others."

Yet, he added, he believed he had the firmness to bear it if the country should pass him over.   On the day of his inauguration, Washington, as retiring President, occupied the centre of attention instead of the incoming one, for the only time in American history.   It was clear why it should be so, but it was a bit hard on Adams that he should have to play a subordinate part on the day when every other President-elect has been the figure to which the whole nation instinctively turned.   However, in a few days it was all over.   Washington had courteously taken leave, retired to Mount Vernon, and Adams was at last the head of the nation.   At least, he had every right to deem himself so, and it dawned on him only slowly that another disputed that claim.

During Washington's administration the situation had been peculiar.   Had it not been for his singleness of purpose and the strength and nobility of his character the country would never have emerged successful from the war.   All officers and soldiers of the Revolutionary army are considered by their descendants to have been heroes and patriots.   In fact a vast number of them were neither, and it was, in the main, what we call the "personality" of Washington that kept any army in the field at all.   In the almost equally great crisis of launching the new national government it was wise — indeed, essential — to place at its head the commanding figure of "the father of his country."   Washington, however, neither was, nor pretended to be, a great statesman.   The problems of his terms of office were not those incidental to carrying on the government and a national policy, but in reality to create both.   That under the circumstances he should rely greatly upon the brilliant constructive ability of Hamilton, who was for six years his Secretary of the Treasury, was wholly natural.   The ablest members of the cabinet gradually resigned, probably for the same reason that made it impossible to find men of the same calibre to take their places: namely, the niggardly salaries which they were paid, — Hamilton got only $3500 a year, — and on which they could not even pay their living expenses in Philadelphia. Adams himself as Vice-President had received only $5000, and he and his wife had had to exercise the greatest frugality. At the latter end of his term, Washington turned for advice constantly to Hamilton, who had had to resign, rather than to the lesser men who actually formed his cabinet. When Adams was elected the custom had not yet been formed of a complete change of official advisers on the accession of a new President, and Adams retained the entire Washington cabinet.

It would have been far better had he made a clean sweep, but in the first place there was the difficulty of getting any men at all to serve at that period, and in the second Adams did not at the beginning realize the position in which he was placing himself. That position briefly was that Hamilton expected to continue to direct the policy of the government and that the leading members of Adams's cabinet felt that their loyalty was owed to Hamilton and not to the President. Had Adams been a weak man, glad to hold the appearance of power while secretly it was exercised by others, the situation might have been worked out with a minimum of friction. Adams, however, was not weak. On the contrary, he was a man of oaken character, of great ability, of vast experience, and one who all his life had refused dictation from any quarter — king, statesman, or public opinion. The story of his administration is in the main the story of his awakening to the facts that he was expected to reign and not to rule, that Hamilton intended to be the party leader while Adams was but President, that the cabinet was disloyal; and of the growing bitterness of the struggle between him and Hamilton, a struggle in which both lost their dignity, self-control, and judgment, and which ended in the ruin of both Adams's further political career and the Federal Party. The statesmanship displayed by Adams during his term was on the whole sound and wise. Twenty-five years earlier, in the Continental Congress, he could succeed as a statesman without being a politician. By 1800 conditions had changed. It was beginning to be a question whether there could be a place for a statesman who was not a politician. In another quarter of a century, the question was to be put to the test by the second generation of Adamses. By still another quarter, and by a third generation, the question had been settled in favor of the politicians. By the fourth generation it was accepted as beyond dispute. John Adams, however, was caught in the first swirl of the new tide.

Almost from the formation of our national government until after the close of the Napoleonic wars and our own war of 1812, American domestic as well as foreign politics were largely dominated by our relations with England and France. It is difficult to determine, during the whole of that shameful period, which nation, England or France, treated the newborn and weak nation overseas with the most high-handed disregard of its rights or insulted it the more frequently. Men might have differed on the question then as now, regardless of party, had it not been that England was a monarchy, whereas by the Revolution France had become a republic. For this reason the Federalists, who believed in a strong government, became the friends of England, while the Republicans, who professed sympathy with the common people and the French Revolution, became the friends of France. When Adams became President the international situation was critical. No one could have been chosen who would have been more impartial, and it was in the field of foreign relations, as so frequently in the history of his family, that Adams rendered his greatest services.

In spite of the outrageous attacks that had been made upon him in the course of the campaign, he was not a monarchist. He believed in a government of balances by which both the upper and lower classes should be held in check against undue usurpation. His years of diplomatic service in both countries had shown him clearly that, if England was no friend to his country, neither could France be counted one. He had no sympathy with either country, and his judgment told him that no more was to be gained by suffering insults from the one than the other. I think there is no reason to question the statement of one of his biographers that he was at that time the most even-minded man in the United States, and it is fortunate that he was at the helm. The pressing problem was whether we could keep peace with either country under the provocations offered.

France, however, demanded the more immediate attention. The first task of Adams was to decide what to do in view of the fact that that nation had just refused to receive our envoy, General Pinckney, or to allow him to remain in the country, and had issued more repressive decrees than England with regard to our commerce. Calling a special session of Congress, he urged an increase in our armed forces, especially the navy of which he had been the founder, and also accepted the idea of a mission of three men to make a new attempt at negotiation — an idea which, as it happened, coincided with Hamilton's opinion. Adams therefore secured the approval of the leading three members of his cabinet, Pickering, Wolcott, and McHenry, the Secretaries, respectively, of State, Treasury, and War. When it came to the point of the personnel of the mission, however, there was difficulty. Adams wished to make it bi-partisan, and indeed he wrote long after that he had asked Madison to serve, with the intention of appointing Hamilton if Madison would serve, which he declined to do. If this is so, it shows remarkable forbearance on Adams's part. When he finally decided to appoint General Pinckney, John Marshall, and Elbridge Gerry, both Pickering and Wolcott disapproved strongly of Gerry as not being a good Federalist, and Adams, again showing for him an unusual forbearance, agreed to name Francis Dana, but on Dana's declining he overrode his cabinet members and appointed Gerry. The facts are interesting as showing that, in spite of his hot-headedness, Adams was doing his best to be conciliatory, and that he did not lose his head until he had been repeatedly goaded into half-madness by his opponents.

The story of the mission in France is well known. The French government, through Talleyrand, refused to receive them unless they would pay heavy bribes to the French officials and agree that America should make a large loan to France. When the news reached Adams he sent two messages to Congress stating the failure of the mission and urging preparation for, though not declaration of, war with France. In the course of the warm debate that ensued a demand was sent to the President that all the papers be laid before Congress, and Adams, well pleased, sent the dispatches of the commissioners, telling about the demand for bribes, with no change except the substitution of the initials X., Y., and Z. for the names of the Frenchmen who had acted as go-betweens. The publication of the "X.Y.Z. letters," as they were at once and have always been called, threw the country into the wildest excitement, in which Adams kept perfectly cool. Unfortunately in another message to Congress, after the return of Marshall from France with the latest news, Adams allowed his too facile pen to run away with him and declared that he would not send another Minister to France until that nation should have given assurances that he would be received in a fitting manner. Even more unfortunately, he allowed himself to sign the Alien and Sedition bills as they were passed by a panic-struck Congress.

Out of the French imbroglio emerged an episode in which none of the participants can be considered to have been without fault and which had an unfortunate influence upon Adams's career. The addition to the armed forces of the country called for the appointment of officers. Washington was inevitably named as the commanding general, but as one of the conditions of his serving he insisted upon the right to name his general officers. This obviously had to be conceded, and he named Hamilton, Pinckney, and Knox. Adams sent the nominations to the Senate in the same order and they were promptly confirmed. Subsequently, however, when the question of precedence arose among the three new major-generals, Adams was unwilling to concede the first place to Hamilton, who had had practically no military experience, as against Knox, who had been a general in the Revolution. Immediately an intrigue was set on foot, in which the two leading members of the cabinet, Pickering and Wolcott, sided secretly with Hamilton against their official chief, Adams. Carrying the matter to Washington, they induced him to insist upon Hamilton's being given the precedence. Adams could not stand out against

Washington, but as the appointments were within the province of the President, who was commander-in-chief, and not within that of the general or of a lawyer in private practice in New York, Adams felt a strong and just resentment at thus having his hand forced against his will. He now clearly recognized his position.

At the end of October 1798, Adams, in view of the situation then existing with regard to France, asked his cabinet for their advice as to whether war should be declared with France or whether in his message to Congress he might not suggest keeping open the channel of negotiation by appointing a new Minister, provided the French would agree to receive him properly and appoint a Minister of equal rank and powers to the United States. The members of the cabinet consulted with Hamilton, Pinckney, and, it is said, Washington, and others then in Philadelphia, and as a result of the consultation prepared the draft of a message for the President to send, in which it was said that the dispatching of a new Minister would be an act of humiliation. This did not at all agree with Adams's own view of the needs of the situation, which was of a far more statesmanlike character than that of the party leaders. He accepted much of what had been prepared for him, but on this one point, the kernel of the whole matter, he sent in an entirely different recommendation to Congress, widening yet further the breach between him and the party leaders. The question was clear-cut and was whether the President or a group of party leaders, not elected by the country nor responsible to it, should dictate the national policy. The party leaders would evidently decide one way. John Adams, and any man who insisted upon being himself and shouldering the responsibility, would as unequivocally decide the other. It may well be claimed, as our form of government has since developed, that party organization is essential to its working, and that for party organization party discipline is essential, but the further question offers, which is more difficult of solution: how can a man of intellectual integrity serve as a public official when he has to subordinate his own judgment to that of the party and carry out policies which he believes to be unwise? The answer would appear to be in no way uncertain, but it opens the further question of what is bound to happen if men of firm decision and intellectual integrity cannot serve in public office? In the last two years of his term, Adams's policy was, as events proved, undoubtedly wiser than that of his party, but by forcing it through he wrecked the party.

For various reasons that we need not enter upon here, the Federalist Party had by now come to insist upon war with France, in which Hamilton had hoped to play a grandiose part in the conquest of the Southwest. Adams's policy was to avoid war if it were possible with honor. Through Vans Murray, Minister at The Hague, Adams had kept informed of the progress of opinion in France, and when he received from him a dispatch in which he enclosed an official note from Talleyrand to the French Minister in Holland stating that if the United States should send a Minister to France to terminate the differences subsisting between the two countries he would incontestably be received with the regard due to the representative of a free, independent, and powerful nation, Adams felt that the time had come to act.

Should such an official, albeit indirect, overture be taken advantage of or not? If Adams did not avail himself of it, would not war be the likely result, and with what chance of success would a war be waged which was opposed to the wishes of the entire Republican Party, and which would probably alienate the sympathy of all the moderates of the Federalist Party should it be found that it had been brought on in the face of overtures for a peaceful settlement of all difficulties? Yet Adams knew by this time that the leaders of his party and the members of his own cabinet would oppose any advance to take the proffered olive branch. The Constitution required only that the members of the cabinet should give their advice when asked; not that the President was bound to seek it. Adams resolved on one of those sudden and bold steps which, like his nomination of Washington as commander-in-chief in the Continental Congress, required a man of supreme courage, one who could assume absolutely to himself the responsibility of a decision vital to the national welfare. The Federalist leaders were caught utterly without warning. On February 18, 1799, while the debate on preparations for war with France was being carried on in the Senate much to the complacency of the Federalist members, a message was received from the President announcing the appointment of a Minister to that country. The cabinet had not been consulted. No one had. Adams considered that the time for consultation with those whose opposition was a foregone conclusion had passed. He simply took action. That action fell on the Federalists like a thunderbolt, and their rage was unbounded. In a moment all their plans had crashed. They had seen Hamilton as the conquering hero who might have added Louisiana, perhaps Mexico, to the nation, and who would come back with a more shining glamour than Washington's own. Not only were all such dreams dispelled, but the party itself was riven in twain. Its main stock in trade had become antagonism toward France, and now the Federalist President held out the hand of peace. There have been few more dramatic episodes in American history; none in which a single individual assumed a greater personal responsibility or took a more momentous decision without counsel than did Adams.

Although Adams soon changed the single commissioner to a mission of three, the Senate did its best, almost to the extent of unconstitutional methods, to block Adams's project before confirming his nominations. The cabinet also was obstructive. In the heat of the summer Adams had gone to his home in Quincy, the new town set off in 1792 from old Braintree and including the Adams lands. At the end of July, Pickering was still writing to him trying, in the light of new events of minor importance, to prevent him from carrying out his intentions. Adams sent back word to prepare the commissions at once. The recalcitrant cabinet member did not obey the order for nearly five weeks. Further delays were interposed until on October 10 Adams arrived at Trenton, then the temporary seat of the government. Hamilton was also there, and the Federalist junto was still fighting hard for time in the hope that events in Europe would so shape themselves as to make Adams's plan unworkable. Adams said nothing and at a cabinet meeting held on the evening of October 15 gave no indication of taking immediate decisive action. Early next morning he gave orders that the commissions be prepared without a moment's delay and that a frigate be got ready to take the envoys to France within two weeks. They sailed November 5. From that day it was war to the death with Adams on the part of the Federalist leaders.

Events now followed rapidly. Adams, unable to stand the treachery of his cabinet any longer, dismissed Pickering and McHenry, as he should have done long before. Oliver Wolcott was retained, only to perform a deeper act of treachery than either of his dismissed colleagues, for some months later, when Hamilton was preparing his attack on Adams, he asked Wolcott, from the intimacy of his official relations with Adams, to supply him with any information that might be of use in an attack upon the President, and Wolcott complied. There have been few if any instances of deeper treachery in American public life than this of a trusted cabinet officer using his confidential relations with his chief, to whom he owed the whole of his allegiance unless he chose to resign, to gain damaging information to hand over to that chief's bitterest enemy. Adams, however, was unaware of what was going on.

When the approaching election of 1800 made the choice of candidates again necessary, the Republicans selected Jefferson and Burr. The Federalists were in a quandary. Hamilton made a trip through New England to explore public sentiment, and found that, although the few chief leaders of his party were opposed to Adams, the lesser ones and the rank and file of the party were so strongly for him that the party could have no chance were he thrown over as a candidate to succeed himself. Adams was not the type of man to inspire devoted personal friendship or a popular personal following. The fact that in spite of this and of the determined hostility of the party chiefs they felt that he alone could be a candidate to win victory at the polls certainly raises the question as to whether he and not they really represented the spirit and opinions of the party at large and whether he and not they should have been considered the party's leader.

Finally the party chiefs reluctantly adopted a ticket of Adams and Pinckney, and when the previous plan of giving Pinckney more votes than Adams was suggested, Pinckney, with a higher sense of honor than the leaders, declined to consent to his being thus elected over Adams. The contest between Adams and Jefferson promised to be close, but the probable chances were considerably in Adams's favor, in spite of the dissension in the party, until the publication of Hamilton's famous letter. There had been occasions during Adams's term when the hostility between the two men had led each of them, Adams no less than Hamilton, into breaches of etiquette and the ordinary rules of courtesy that can only be considered as blots upon the career of each. In fact the feud appears to have made all the men most closely connected with it, Adams, Hamilton, Pickering, McHenry, Wolcott, and others, so completely mad as to perform acts which in any other relation they would have considered far beneath them and which are out of keeping with their characters as manifested in all other portions of their careers. None other, however, was quite so mad as the blow prepared by Hamilton.

Making use not only of facts that could have legitimately come to his knowledge, but also of those which his spies in the cabinet had supplied him with, Hamilton wrote a long and extremely bitter attack upon the President, attempting to show that there were "irrefragable proofs of his unfitness for the station of Chief Magistrate" and that there was real cause to apprehend that the government had been undermined by him and "might totter, if not fall, under his future auspices." Yet Hamilton ended this extraordinary attack upon the candidate whom he had chosen for his party by the incredible conclusion that he intended to vote for him in spite of his unfitness. The attack was so insanely injudicious that even Hamilton's closest friends tried to persuade him not to publish it. He printed it, however, and Aaron Burr, having secured a copy, at once gave it to the public. The result was disaster. It is impossible to find a parallel to such a proclamation by a party's leader that the party's candidate was unfit to hold office. Jefferson was triumphantly elected and Adams's career was at an end.

Adams was justly infuriated. Such an ending to such a lifetime devoted to the highest services to his country was as unjust as it was undeserved. Adams, until the end, never realized the full malignity or treachery of his enemies. It is useless to argue whether he or they destroyed the Federalist Party. I think it certain, however, that if he had had at every step a full vision of what was in store for him he would have done exactly as he did. There can be no defense for some of the personal resentment he showed toward Hamilton at moments, but every public act had been performed according to the dictates of his judgment and of disinterested public service. From these he could not have been swerved by any thought of personal advantage. Although his acts with regard to our relations to France had been the chief causes of his downfall, he wrote, long years afterward, that they were "the most disinterested and meritorious actions of my life" and that "I desire no other inscription over my gravestone than: 'Here lies John Adams, who took upon himself the responsibility of the peace with France in the year 1800.'" He has been upheld by the verdict of history, which I think is unanimously agreed that his foreign policy was as unquestionably right as that of his opponents, they of his own household, was unquestionably wrong.

Of the last weeks as Chief Magistrate little need be said except to note one act that perhaps was as pregnant with consequences as any other of his life. At the last moment, before his power was gone for good, he appointed, along with many minor judgeships, John Marshall to be Chief Justice of the Supreme Court of the United States. The Constitution of the country to-day is almost as much the creation of Marshall's interpretation as of the work of the original drafters. By his nomination of Washington as commander-in-chief, Adams had made a nation possible. By his nomination of Marshall he gave, for centuries following, the fundamental law to that nation. Having performed this office, giving full rein to his wrath and disappointment, he rode out of the capital refusing to greet his successor or to perform the courtesies that belonged to his own high office. It was the last gesture of his public career and the only one that was unworthy of him, although one later President also refused to be present at the inauguration of his successor.

During much of his term, Adams had had to live alone, as Mrs. Adams, partly on account of her health, remained for long intervals at Quincy. The cost of living was also extremely high in Philadelphia, and Adams was rather aghast when he contemplated the necessary expense of his needful way of living as President. "I hope you will not communicate to anybody the hints I give you about our prospects," he wrote his wife in February 1797, "but they appear every day worse and worse. House rent at twenty-seven hundred dollars a year, fifteen hundred dollars for a carriage, one thousand for one pair of horses, all the glasses, ornaments, kitchen furniture, the best chairs, settees, plateaus, &c., all to purchase, all the china, delf or wedgwood, glass and crockery of every sort to purchase, and not a farthing probably will the House of Representatives allow, though the Senate have voted a small addition. All the linen besides. I shall not pretend to keep more than one pair of horses for a carriage, and one for a saddle. Secretaries, servants, wood, charities which are demanded as rights, and the million dittoes present such a prospect as is enough to disgust anyone. Yet not one word must we say." The change of the seat of government to Washington did not take place until the very end of his term, but on November 1, 1800, he became the first occupant of the White House. Writing to his wife at Quincy, who was to come and join him, he ended his letter with a prayer to "heaven to bestow the best of blessings on this house, and on all that shall hereafter inhabit it. May none but honest and wise men ever rule under this roof!" At this same time he wrote to her: "Oh! that I could have a home! But this felicity has never been permitted me. Rolling, rolling, rolling, till I am very near rolling into the bosom of mother earth."

He was now at last to have one, from which he scarcely stirred for the twenty-six years still left of life. At sixty-five he retired from the world of affairs, and after his long wanderings — Paris, The Hague, London, Washington — he settled down once more on his farm at Quincy. Writing to Samuel Dexter in March 1801, he says: "I left Washington on the 4th, and arrived at Quincy on the 18th, having trotted the bogs five hundred miles. I found about a hundred loads of sea-weed in my barnyard, and, recollecting Horace's

Et genus et virtus, nisi cum re, vilior alga est,

I thought I had made a good exchange, if Ulysses is an orthodox authority in this case, which I do not believe, of honors and virtues for manure." A few weeks later he wrote to another friend: "The only consolation I shall want will be that of employment. Ennui, when it rains on a man in large drops, is worse than one of our north-east storms; but the labors of agriculture and amusement of letters will shelter me. My greatest grief is that I cannot return to the bar. There I should forget in a moment that I was ever a member of Congress, a foreign minister, or President of the United States. But I cannot speak."

We shall tell in due place of the quarter of a century of retired life that was still to be meted out to the old statesman, but must turn now to pick up the thread of the second generation of the family in its new phase. Many an American family has sprung from obscurity to prominence and then carried on its new sphere owing to inherited wealth. John Adams, however, had no wealth to bequeath. That the family, instead of slipping back, maintained itself in its new phase was due to no inheritance of possessions, but to one of intellect and character. That sudden, mysterious something that had occurred in the family strain with John, that had made the son of genera-

tions of village yeomen one of the half-dozen greatest men that
America has yet produced, was to continue in his descendants.
It is that which gives to the family its peculiar interest and
significance, the continuance, once begun, of the combination
of exceptional intellect with exceptional character.   Before we
once more carry our story overseas to young John Quincy, let
us listen a moment to his father ruminating over his closed
career with his old friend Dr. Rush.   "I do not say when I
became a politician," wrote the old man of seventy, "for that I
never was.   I cannot repent of any thing I ever did conscien-
tiously and from a sense of duty.   I never engaged in public
affairs for my own interest, pleasure, envy, jealousy, avarice,
or ambition, or even the desire of fame.   If any of these had
been my motive, my conduct would have been very different.
In every considerable transaction of my public life, I have
invariably acted according to my best judgment, and I can
look up to God for the sincerity of my intentions."   Nor was
this self-flattery.   "Disinterested as the being who made him"
was Jefferson's appraisal, as it has been that of history.

THE SECOND GENERATION
JOHN QUINCY ADAMS

JOHN QUINCY ADAMS

I

EUROPE

THE young American Minister of twenty-seven, John Quincy Adams, had been ordered by Washington to proceed to his post at The Hague by way of London so as to carry certain important dispatches to John Jay, then Minister to the Court of St. James's. Just outside London an attempt to steal these dispatches by cutting the straps which bound the trunks to the back of his coach gave the young man an extremely bad fifteen minutes, but he finally reached his lodgings with his baggage intact, and hastened out at once to deliver his troublesome trust. London was already familiar to him; in fact, the yeomen line having been suddenly transmuted, London was to be as familiar to generation after generation of the family in its new phase as was the village of Quincy itself. When the young man, with his still younger brother Charles, who had gone to Europe with him, attended a performance of *Henry the Eighth* at Drury Lane with Mrs. Siddons as Queen Katherine, he could write critically of her as compared with her acting in 1783 and contrast her acting with that of Mrs. Yates in the same part. There were more plays, — *Romeo and Juliet*, and others, — the renewing of old social acquaintance, the making of new, and then he proceeded to his post in Holland.

It was not an arduous one, but Adams devoted himself to a severe course of study in addition to the business of his office, beginning his day by three hours' reading between six and nine. He studied Italian, and read a staggering list of works in English, Dutch, French, and Latin, including much drama and poetry. Noting one day having finished *Paradise Lost*, he adds, "the admiration of which increases in my mind upon every perusal." In 1795 he was commissioned to exchange ratifications of the Jay Treaty with England, which again took him to that country. Various unavoidable delays, however, prevented his reaching London in time to act as commissioner in the matter of the treaty, which was possibly just as well, in view of the extremely unpopular character of that document in America. He had, however, more need of caution and diplomacy than would have been called for by the mere ratifying of the treaty, as certain business of a less formal nature, which he had to transact with Lord Grenville, detained him in London long enough to enable the English Foreign Office to attempt to draw him on in matters which were outside the scope of anyone except the accredited Minister to that country, Pinckney, who was then absent. Young Adams showed no little skill in steering a course which would neither irritate the persistent officials nor entangle himself.

He was at the same time engaged in another and very important affair. On September 14, 1797, the Boston *Independent Chronicle* announced to its readers that "Young John Adams' Negotiations have terminated in a Marriage Treaty with an English lady, the daughter of one Mr. Johnson, on Tower-Hill. It is a happy circumstance that he has made no other Treaty." The marriage, in fact, had taken place on July 26, but the *Chronicle* was in error as to the lady's nationality. Her mother, Catherine Nuth, was indeed English, but her father, Joshua Johnson, was a Marylander serving as United States Consul in London (where the daughter, Louisa, was born), and brother of Governor Thomas Johnson of Maryland, a signer of the Declaration of Independence and later Judge of the Federal Supreme Court. When the Revolution interrupted Johnson's duties as consul and made England an impossible place of residence, he took his family to Nantes, where they remained until the end of the war. The child Louisa, with an American father and an English mother, had thus spent all her early life in France. More than a century later, her grandson, Henry, was to write of her that she "was charming, like a Romney portrait, but among her many charms that of being a New England woman was not one." The defect, he points out, was serious, and the future mother-in-law, Abigail, feared lest the young girl with the Romney face should not be of stuff stern enough to weather the Boston climate and mate with John Quincy. The climate and Adams's career were both to prove stormy enough, but the bride survived through it all, though her health did not, and the marriage proved happy and lasting in spite of forebodings.

Shortly before his wedding, Adams had been appointed Minister to Portugal. He had gone to Europe reluctantly and had no wish to remain there. A few months earlier, in writing to his father with regard to the Portuguese appointment, he had expressed himself as very anxious to return to America as soon as his duties would allow him honorably to do so. He had no wish to return to the bar, where he would have to begin over again at the bottom, but on the other hand he wished to preserve his independence, financial and other, entire. "If I can return to *leisure*," he wrote, "I am determined that it shall not be to idleness. But the Americans have in Europe a sad reputation on the article of literature, and I shall purpose to render a service to my country by devoting to it the remainder of my life." Throughout his life, consonant with one of the qualities of the new phase of the Adams mind, he was to be a most voluminous writer. When one considers his other activities and the fact that in those days nothing was either typed or dictated, the mere mass of words which he left behind him is appalling. It was as well, however, that his fate was to lead him in other directions. Neither his poems nor other writings can be held to have added anything to the reputation of American letters. The desire to return home, however, was constant. In February he had written to Louisa Johnson that "it is not at a distance like this from America, out of sight and out of hearing of his countrymen, that an ambitious American is to rise."

His appointment to Portugal, dated eight days later on the seventeenth, gave him concern also of another sort. His sensitiveness and pride rebelled at holding office under his father, President-elect of the United States. The situation was, indeed, a delicate one. He had, of course, been brought into the service by Washington, to whom John Adams turned when the problem of a new appointment, this time to Berlin, came up. Replying, Washington expressed a "*strong hope* that you will not withhold merited promotion from Mr. John [Quincy] Adams because he is your son. For without intending to compliment the father or the mother, or to censure others, I give it as my decided opinion that Mr. Adams is the most valuable public character we have abroad, and that there remains no doubt in my mind that he will prove himself to be the ablest of all our diplomatic corps. If he was *now* to be brought *into* that line, or into any other public walk, I could not, upon the principle which has regulated my own conduct, disapprove of the caution which is hinted at in the letter. But he is already entered; the public more and more, as he is known, are appreciating his talents and worth; and his country would sustain a loss, if these were to be checked by over delicacy on your part." It may be noted that Washington signed this letter not only with "sincere esteem" but with "affectionate regard." For various good reasons, young Adams's station had been changed from Lisbon to Berlin, but his scruples were never assuaged. With regard to the new office, he wrote to his mother that "I never acted more reluctantly, and the tenure by which I am hereafter to hold an office is of such a nature as will take from me all the satisfaction, which I have enjoyed hitherto in considering myself as a public servant." The Lisbon appointment had at least been given him by Washington, whereas that to Prussia was bestowed by his father, and although the latter wrote him that his belief in any impropriety in accepting was without foundation, the young man was far from convinced or happy.

In December, however, he proceeded to Berlin, accompanied by his wife and his younger brother, Charles, who seems to have spent a good part of the preceding year at Paris and The Hague. The journey from London to Berlin, now made comfortably in a trifle over twenty-four hours, took the young people about three weeks, and was one of great hardship. The sea trip from London to Hamburg, owing to storms and rough weather, occupied eight days, and the "journey at land," Adams wrote his father, "from the badness of the roads and of the drivers was worse than the voyage at sea." The young wife was taken seriously ill, and it was with great relief that the thirty-year-old diplomat at last reached his post at the Prussian capital, after having been detained at the gate of the city by a lieutenant who had never heard of the United States.

Although Adams had also been commissioned to negotiate treaties with Sweden, he had but little official business on his hands during the four years he was yet to remain abroad. Various delays, including the death of the Prussian king, prevented until July 1799 the signing of a treaty the negotiations for which had been proceeding leisurely. Of Louisa Adams, at this time, Henry later wrote that "whether she was happy or not, whether she was content or not, whether she was socially successful or not, her descendants did not surely know; but in any case she could by no chance have become educated there for a life in Quincy or Boston." In fact, she never did become so educated, and to the end of her life remained an exotic in the American climate, and to some extent in the family. A half-century later, when Henry could dimly recall her, she was "hardly more Bostonian than she had been fifty years before, on her wedding day, in the shadow of the Tower of London." An historian, not Boston bred, had best content himself, perhaps, with merely chronicling the fact, holding it to be the part of wisdom and modesty not to attempt to fathom the recondite enormity of it.

Her husband realized that he also was not preparing himself for Boston, either as a town or a state of mind, but he busied himself as always with books and observations. Among other trips he made a long one through Silesia, getting as far east as Breslau, and wrote accounts of his travels in a series of letters which he permitted one of his brothers to print in the *Port Folio*, a Philadelphia magazine in which that brother was interested. The letters were subsequently pirated by an enterprising London publisher and published there in 1804 in a volume of nearly four hundred pages, somewhat to Adams's discomfiture owing to certain personal allusions to Englishmen contained in them. Adams, while in Berlin, also wrote a translation of Gentz's treatise on the American Revolution, which likewise appeared in the *Port Folio*, and made a metrical translation of Wieland's *Oberon*, still unpublished among the Adams manuscripts.

At home, events had been moving rapidly in the family circle. John Quincy's brother, Thomas Boylston Adams, had moved to Philadelphia to live, and Charles, who had returned to America, married, and settled in New York, died in 1800. That year also marked the terrible conflict in the Federal Party and the staggering defeat of John Adams for the Presidency. The men of the Adams family, as we have found Abigail complaining, have never been given to expressing any tenderness of personal affection and emotion, in this respect resembling the English whose characteristics they have so incessantly belabored. Under the shell of Puritan repression, however, there has always been a great sensitiveness. Although John Quincy's letters to his father were excessively stiff and formal, reading almost like diplomatic reports, he was deeply troubled for the old man's welfare when the news came of his political overthrow. Knowing the man's pride, touchiness, and irascibility, the son feared, as he wrote his brother, T. B. Adams, for his permanent happiness. Writing to his brother, with a curious personal detachment in pronouns, he indicated his worries. "Were I not therefore acquainted with the genuine energy of your father's character, and the pure magnanimity of his soul, my keenest feelings at this time would arise from concern at what the effect of this event would be upon his mind." After further consideration of this he passes to another point. In reading what he wrote we must recall that his personal property was extremely small, that he was looking forward to a career in which financial independence was essential to him, and that he had a young wife and an infant child, recently born in Berlin. Continuing his thought for his father, he wrote: "I am not without some apprehensions on this occasion arising from another source. Although his principles of economy are as rigorous as can consist with a mind which appreciates money at its true value, and

his practice has always been conformable to his theory, to keep
his estate free from serious and permanent embarrassment, yet
he has been so far from growing rich in the service of the public,
that it is not improbable he may in his retirement have occasion
for money.   I therefore authorize and direct you to consider
all and every part of my property in your hands, whether of
principal or interest, as subject at all times to his disposal for
his own use.   If you are certain (as you have means of information which I cannot at this distance possess) that he will have
no occasion for this, you will not mention to him that I have
given you this instruction, for I wish not to make a show of
offering service where it is not wanted; but unless you are thus
sure, let him know I have given you this order, and that it is my
most urgent request that he would use it whenever it may
suit his convenience."

Adams's stay in Berlin was now rapidly drawing to an end.
He had himself long wanted to return to America.   He was,
indeed, as Washington had pointed out, our ablest diplomat
abroad, but, apart from his own disinclination to remain there,
if he did so, it was evident that he should in fairness be advanced
to a higher post.   Aside from the fact that Rufus King was filling that at London acceptably, the election at home had been
vindictively bitter, and with the change of party it could hardly
be expected that Jefferson would not merely retain but advance
the son of John Adams.   If it has been the principle of the
Adams family, unswervingly adhered to, not to seek public
office, it has equally been theirs not to decline it on personal
grounds if they are called to public service.   It had been a sufficiently hard and delicate position for John Quincy to hold office
of his father.   To have asked him to hold it at the hands of
his father's inveterate foes would have been to create an impossible situation.   There was not a little likelihood, indeed, that
he would be recalled by those foes.   There was no urgent business, hardly any business at all at the moment, in Berlin.   As
the father faced the end of his term in the White House he
determined to recall his son himself, and on January 31, 1801,
he ordered John Marshall to prepare the necessary papers.

It is by no means needful to ascribe this, as has often been done, to irascibility or pettiness of temper. I fail to see how the coolest judgment could have found a better way out of the difficulty, with its complex points of honor, than John Adams chose. The letter of recall reached John Quincy in Berlin April 26, and on September 4, after a passage of fifty-eight days from Hamburg, he, his wife, and his small son, George Washington Adams, landed at Philadelphia, the latter two going for a visit to the wife's family in Washington.

AN AMERICAN INTERLUDE

A FEW weeks after his return to Quincy, Adams wrote to Rufus King in London that the appearance of "our country has very much improved since I left it in 1794. I find everywhere the marks of peace within our walls, and prosperity within our palaces — for palaces they may truly be called, those splendid and costly mansions which since my departure seem to have shot up from the earth by enchantment." The United States was indeed becoming wealthy and had recovered amazingly from the financial crash of 1791. Its population was well over five millions, or about a third that of the British Isles and one-fifth that of France. The government was well established. One did not, like John Adams in England in 1784, have to put up a bold front to hide inner fears and apologies.

As John Quincy looked about him on his return he could little have dreamed that a grandson of his, Henry, would write the best analysis of the conditions which his grandfather was investigating that has been written of any period of American history. But if at first he was much impressed, even fresh from European capitals, with the new architecture, he was, in the years to come, to be even more so by other aspects of the scene. As his grandson was to write, "the same bad roads and difficult rivers, connecting the same small towns, stretched into the same forests in 1800 as when the armies of Braddock and Amherst pierced the western and northern wilderness, except that these roads extended a few miles farther from the seacoast. Nature was rather man's master than his servant, and the five million Americans struggling with the untamed continent seemed hardly more competent to their task than the beavers and buffalo which had for countless generations made bridges and roads of their own." If America, like Europe, was to rely upon water communication, sea, lake, or river, for its heavy traffic, "a single republican government must meet extreme difficulties," as the valley of, say, the Ohio had nothing more to do with the valleys of the Atlantic-flowing rivers than had that of the Danube with those of the Rhine, Po, or Elbe. This question of physical transport, of the physical character of the continent in relation to government, was to weigh heavily on the grandfather as upon the grandson, and we shall have important occasion to refer to it later — long later.

In the Boston to which Adams returned, the houses were of wood, the streets and sidewalks, paved with round cobblestones, were unlighted at night, and there were no police. Wealth was largely concentrated in the hands of a few merchants, who, with three mails a week to New York and an occasional one, mostly in the summer, from Europe, had ample leisure to consider their ventures while sipping their Madeira. Throughout the state the vast bulk of the population pulled along on amazingly small incomes. The Reverend Abijah Weld, for example, of Attleborough, managed to bring up a family of eleven children and to dispense charity and hospitality on a salary of two hundred and twenty dollars a year. Unfortunately we have not Mrs. Weld's version of this bit of domestic economics, but we do know that five hundred dollars was an excellent income for a clergyman of that day.

The city of Washington, although the White House had been completed in time for John Adams to spend a few unhappy days in it, was otherwise almost nonexistent, and the roads south of Baltimore can, perhaps, best be left to be described, imaginatively, in the oaths of those who had to drive over them. In the seaboard states, which were all that as yet counted politically, political thought was conservative, and the French Revolution had tended to make it almost reactionary. Society was still, in the American sense, aristocratic, and the influence of "the rich, the wise and the good" — considered almost interchangeable terms — was just beginning to be dangerously questioned. In Massachusetts, under severe property qualifications for the franchise, there were about forty-five thousand voters, of whom about twenty thousand were despised Republicans, followers of Jefferson, — Democrats, as we should say to-day, — and the rest, forming the majority, were Federalists, made up of the wealth, social position, and religious leadership of the state.   Boston was poor in intellect (such names as Jeremy Belknap and Jedediah Morse are among the best it can show), and even poorer in science.   A few Bostonians could read and even speak French, but when Germany, hitherto practically unknown, was brought to their attention by Madame de Staël in 1814, George Ticknor could not find either a German teacher or a German dictionary in the city, nor a single German book in any of its shops or libraries, not even at Harvard.   It was to such a town that the American Minister Plenipotentiary to Prussia, with a wide acquaintance with European languages and thought, familiar with the highest society and the courts of half a dozen or more European capitals, from London to St. Petersburg, returned to earn his living and to make a career.

For the purpose of achieving the latter if not the former, it was fortunate that he had spent the last ten years in Europe, far from personal participation in the bitter quarrels that had marked American political life.   Both the spirit and the machinery of party were developing rapidly.   Political management there had always been, the sort of management that old John Adams had caught a glimpse of in Tom Dawes's garret thirty years or so earlier and which can readily be traced back to the days of John Winthrop.   But there had been no party machine that had extended to the people at large.   The town meeting had been the starting point of political advancement, and as late as 1798 a writer complained that the country people never prepared their minds before they attended the meetings and so easily fell under the control of "their most influential and learned men."   By 1800 town caucuses became very common, but the Federalist leaders, "the rich and the well-born," acting largely through their adherents, the Congregational clergymen in all the towns, did much less to perfect popular political machinery than did their opponents, the Jeffersonian Republicans, or, as we should say, Democrats, who as an opposition party had to storm the citadels of power. In a letter written to Jefferson in 1801 by a group of local New England Democrats, the future of our political life was clearly foreshadowed. After advising the President to dismiss certain Federalists from office and replace them by "deserving Democrats," the letter continued: "The season has now arrived when it is necessary for us to organize and adopt measures for conveying to our People just sentiments respecting the motives, measures, and objects of the present administration and to obviate the false impressions which the federalists and federal papers have made and are making upon their minds. This organization' which will consist of a General Committee, of County Committees, and of Sub-committees in the towns of the State, must be conducted with great fortitude and perseverance, through much labor and expence to an end difficult to be attained but highly important to a republican administration." It was evident that a new period was beginning. The rich or the good or the able or learned man, who, known first to his neighbors in the town, then to the county, then to the state, had been able to rise to leadership with independence of mind, would have to begin to think about this machinery of committees in the background. Besides his voice and reputation in the open, there would now be a numerous hierarchy of political plotters working underground and in the dark for or against him among the people in inn and cottage and at street corner. The modern system had not yet been completed, but it was in the making.

It was to be a system in which no Adams, insisting upon independence of judgment and action, could ever feel at home. To sacrifice intellectual or moral integrity at the call of party allegiance would forever remain unthinkable for them. When Adams returned from Prussia, party issues were still somewhat confused. In the main he would obviously rank himself with the Federalists rather than the Democrats. Not only had his father served twelve years as Vice-President and President in that party and he himself held office for ten years under it, but its tenets were more in line with his own. On the other hand, it was not easy to say just what the Federalist Party was. It had been split wide open into two bitter factions through the quarrel between his father, with his followers, and the Hamiltonians.

In the atmosphere of European culture, Adams had determined to devote himself to literature rather than go back to the drudgery of legal practice, but once back in the American atmosphere the fantastic impossibility of such a career in America evidently became apparent, and the dream, if he still held to it, quickly evaporated. Some years before, old Jonathan Trumbull, when combating his painter son's desire to devote his life to art, sternly bade him remember that "Connecticut is not Athens." John Quincy promptly discovered that Boston was not Paris. A few weeks after his return home he had taken a house and opened an office for the practice of law, though, four years later, he wrote to his father that "the bar is not my element" and that he expected to derive little either of honor or of financial profit from it.

In the Massachusetts of that day, however, it was evident that, bitterly as old John Adams was hated by many of his fellow citizens, young John Quincy, the son of a President, himself an ex-foreign minister and one of the ablest men in the state, could not be ignored politically. As soon as he started practice he was appointed a commissioner in bankruptcy by the judge of the district court, but was removed from this office, after a short tenure, by Jefferson. John Adams and Jefferson had become completely estranged by the campaign of 1800, and in the heated atmosphere of those days this act of Jefferson's was considered as a petty insult to the Adams family. In 1804, when Jefferson's daughter died, Mrs. John Adams, in spite of intense feeling against Jefferson, wrote him a note of condolence, which led to several other letters in which various acts of Jefferson considered inimical to the Adamses were discussed, among them the removal of John Quincy. Jefferson then wrote that in 1801 the law had been changed and the appointments of bankruptcy commissioners had been placed in the hands of the President, and that in making the new appointments he had not inquired as to who the former incumbents of office were, and declared on his honor that Mrs. Adams's letter contained the first information he had ever had that her son had held one of the offices. This may seem almost incredible. On the other hand, it is equally incredible, with all his faults, that Jefferson was such an unprincipled blackguard as to state in writing on his honor what he knew to be a falsehood, and I think we must accept his statement. As was natural in a wife, Mrs. Adams's feelings against Jefferson were the most implacable in the family. John Adams became reconciled with him a few years later, and John Quincy had never allowed his own feelings to be swayed by his father's personal animosities. As we have seen, he had named his eldest son George Washington, and after his removal by Jefferson his mother wrote that she had never heard "an expression from him of censure or disrespect" toward Jefferson in consequence of it. John Quincy's invective against those whom he believed had wronged him *could* be scurrilously withering, and in later life he was to turn against Jefferson for quite other reasons.

In April 1802 he was elected by the Federalists of Boston to represent them in the State Senate, and at once showed himself independent of party. A few weeks after election, at a Federalist caucus he proposed that the Republicans should be allowed a minority representation in the Council, which was immediately construed as treason to the party. On the only strictly party vote at the spring session, he felt it his duty to vote with the Republicans, and in the winter one he again felt constrained to cast his vote with them on two important questions. One of these, a bill to create a bank, which was favored by all the moneyed men, and which Adams opposed, did much to lessen his popularity with the party leaders, who, as Fisher Ames wrote to Gore, began to consider him "too unmanageable." Writing many years later of his one term in the State Senate, Adams noted that it was "the noviciate of my legislative labors, during which I was not able to effect much good, or to prevent much evil. I wanted the authority of experience, and I discovered the danger of opposing and exposing corruption." One of the best deeds of the year he considered to have been an address he made before the Charitable Fire Society, which he thought had done much to shame "the Bostonians out of their inveterate fondness for wooden houses" and to have contributed to rebuilding the city in stone.

In spite of his lack of party discipline, he was nominated for Congress, but was defeated by a few votes. The newspapers attributed this to the fact that the day was very rainy, but Adams attributed it rather to the lack of energy on the part of the Federalists. The party was indeed so split by the feud between Hamilton and John Adams that the son of the latter could hardly command whole-hearted support. However, on February 3, 1803, he was elected by the Legislature as United States Senator. His biographer thought this rather handsome of the Hamiltonians, as Timothy Pickering was very keen for the office,[1] but Fisher Ames probably explained it when he wrote that Adams was chosen "in consequence of a caucus pact, that if Col. Pickering should not be elected on two trials, then the Feds. would combine and vote for J. Q. A. This happened accordingly." The other Senatorial seat falling vacant soon afterward, Pickering was elected to fill it, and was to prove a jealous and most uncomfortable colleague, during the five years, until his resignation in 1808, that Adams remained in Washington.

That city was not easy to get to. When Abigail Adams went there in 1800 to join her President husband, she wrote that you saw nothing but woods all the way from Baltimore, and, the road to the capital being nothing but a dirt path, the party were lost for hours and rescued by a stray Negro. After describing to her correspondent the city, or rather its absence, she added a caution not to quote her, but "say that I write you the situation is beautiful, which is true." There was, in truth, little except the "situation." Woods and malarial swamps extended in every direction. There were few buildings of any sort, and scarcely one between the White House and the Capitol, along what is now Pennsylvania Avenue. The streets were

---

[1] J. T. Morse, Jr., *John Quincy Adams*, p. 30.

mere mud ways in which even ambassadorial carriages would get mired to the hubs and have to be abandoned by unhappy diplomats. Congressmen, mostly without their families, huddled together in unkempt boarding houses. It is needless to say there was no library. Indeed, there was practically nothing, not even a single church of any denomination. The city, as Gouverneur Morris wrote, was wholly "in the future." It was certainly not on the banks of the Potomac.

Up to this period of John Quincy's life there had been manifest only slightly that bitterness of spirit and invective that were later to be so characteristic. The ablest of all his race, before or since, his psychological position was perhaps the best. His father, eminent as he was, had been a self-made man, with all the psychological disadvantages of that character. John Quincy was not, in the same sense, self-made. He had been brought in contact from earliest childhood with what was best and most stimulating, socially and intellectually, in Europe and America. On the other hand, he had not behind him that long family record and tradition that we shall find, to some extent, paralyzing the career of, say, Henry. He touched earth, the soil, with his grandfather. But with his Washington life he was to be made aware of two inimical forces, the enmity against his father and the new spirit of party.

The first three years of his term were, indeed, a sort of martyrdom. Anyone who has lived long abroad, even in these days of easy communication and millions of cabled words of news, realizes how remote the pressures and passions of American life come to appear. It was impossible that John Quincy, at The Hague or Berlin, could have fully sensed the virulence of the feeling against his own father. At home in Boston or Quincy, there were so many friends that there was little sense of public enmity. In Washington, however, Adams was alone, even his colleague from his own state belonging in the house of his enemies. It has been said of the Senate in those years that "the Republicans trampled upon the Federalists, and the Federalists trampled upon John Quincy Adams."

He was unpopular because he was the son of his father;

because he was unbending, unconciliatory, a poor "mixer"; and because he could not and would not sacrifice his independence and integrity to party. He was in no doubt as to what such a refusal would mean to him. "The country," he wrote at the end of his first Senatorial year, "is so totally given up to the spirit of party, that not to follow blindfold the one or the other is an inexpiable offence. The worst of these parties had the popular torrent in its favor, and uses its triumph with all the unprincipled fury of a faction; while the other gnashes its teeth, and is waiting with all the impatience of revenge for the time when its turn may come to oppress and punish by the people's favor. Between both, I see the impossibility of pursuing the dictates of my own conscience without sacrificing every prospect, not merely of advancement, but even of retaining that character and reputation I have enjoyed. Yet my choice is made, and if I cannot hope to give satisfaction to my country, I am at least determined to have the approbation of my own reflections."

Before continuing to speak of his political career at this time, we may note two events of a personal nature that occurred during his first year in the Senate. If he was made happy by the birth of a second son, in Boston on the fourth of July, who was named John, he was also plunged into great unhappiness by the failure of a commercial house in London, with which he had deposited a considerable part of his father's property as well as some of his own. His own finances were severely strained by the failure, but, as he wrote in his *Diary*, "its effects in diminishing the comforts of my father's age have been among the most painful things that ever happened to me. I have in some degree shared in the loss, and have done all in my power to alleviate its evils to him. But it has been and remains a continual source of uneasiness to me; nor have I any prospect that it will ever be removed."

It was said of Adams that he considered every measure to be voted on as he would a proposition in Euclid, utterly divorced in solving it from any thought of party. In fact, by the end of his service, he was acting more frequently with the Democrats than with the Federalists. He was very early brought into collision with the latter, nominally his own party, by feeling called upon to vote for the acquisition of Louisiana, though opposing the constitutional method of making it a state. It is well known that in all the troublous years leading up to the war with England, and during that war, the New England Federalists were strongly opposed to any break with that country, albeit the war when it came was ostensibly, though not really, waged in defense of that section's commerce and "sailors' rights." Adams, from the first, was strongly opposed to any encroachment on American rights by the British, and throughout his life he was a staunch upholder of the dignity and rights of his own country against any other country whatsoever. His introduction of resolutions condemning the British claim to the right of seizure of neutral vessels, his vote in favor of Jefferson's Non-Importation Act in 1806, and the whole of his subsequent course in defending the rights and honor of America made the breach with the New England Federalists unbridgeable. Adams was not only independent in judgment, but combative in disposition and one of the hardest fighters in American public life. When, after the attack of the British ship *Leopard* upon the American *Chesapeake*, he heard John Lowell, a prominent Federalist of Boston, justifying the attack, he was, as he wrote later, alienated forever from the counsels of the Federalist Party. He spoke at Faneuil Hall, and although, when he drafted strong resolutions on the outrage, the Federalists had to some extent to fall in with him, they never forgave him. When in the autumn of 1807 he voted in favor of Jefferson's Embargo, the party wrath against him was unbounded. On June 2/3, 1808, the Massachusetts Federalist Legislature, anticipating the end of his term by nine months, insulted him by electing a successor and adopting resolutions against the Embargo. On the eighth, Adams resigned his seat.

He had become, so far as he could ever be said to have belonged to any party, a Republican. In the Senate itself his influence had been steadily growing. It was an influence dependent solely on character and intellectual integrity. In no way springing from the strength of party affiliation, it was not even helped by eloquence. Adams, as he records himself, was not an eloquent man. In extemporary debate, he says, his manner was "slow, hesitating, and often much confused." "In tracing this deficiency to its source," he added, he found it "arising from a cause that is irreparable," a "slowness to grasp the whole compass of a subject in the mind at once with such an arrangement as leaves a proper impression of the detail — and an incapacity to form ideas properly precise and definite with the rapidity necessary to give them uninterrupted utterance." The day was to come, many long years later, when he would be heard as the voice of a prophet, but it would be due to the utter selflessness and intensity of the opinions to which he would give utterance rather than to the rhetoric in which they would be clothed. Toward the end of his Senatorial term, however, he had been made professor of rhetoric at Harvard, and delivered his lectures, afterward published, before the students there.

Adams had perfectly well realized his fate as a Senator, though not the insulting form which that fate was to take. On the last day of each year he was accustomed to enter in his diary reflections upon his life during the term just ended. On December 31, 1807, he wrote: "On most of the great national questions now under discussion, my sense of duty leads me to support the Administration, and I find myself of course in opposition to the federalists in general . . . as my term of service draws near its close, I am constantly approaching to the certainty of being restored to the situation of a private citizen. For this event, however, I hope to have my mind sufficiently prepared. In the meantime, I implore that Spirit from whom every good and perfect gift descends to enable me to render essential service to my country, and that I may never be governed in my public conduct by any consideration other than that of my duty."

When, a few months later, the legislature of his state took the action described above, it was not the election of a successor so far ahead of the usual time that called forth Adams's resignation, keenly as he resented the action, but the passage by

that body of instructions for his voting on the guidance of its
Senators — a notable beginning of our newer theory of representation that has tended to turn representatives into mere
machines to record the public's will, ignorance, or passion.
"As to holding my seat in the Senate of the United States
without exercising the most perfect freedom of agency, under
the sole and exclusive control of my own sense of right, that
was out of the question," Adams wrote to Giles. Two theories
of government had come into collision. The rising tide of
democracy had rushed for a moment up over the rock of intellectual integrity. Adams's resignation was inevitable.

In December, following that event, Adams wrote to Orchard
Cook, who had intimated the possibility of an appointment
under the new Madison administration to begin in March,
describing his attitude toward public office. It always had
been, and continued to be, he wrote, "that which philosophers
teach us should guide our views of death — never to be desired,
never to be feared." There is no doubt that Adams always
greatly craved high office, but to the last day of his life he would
never lift a finger or relax a muscle of his face to obtain it.
He had not, however, long to wait.

In Washington at the time of Madison's inauguration, in
connection with legal business before the Supreme Court,
Adams received a note from the President on March 6, asking
him to call at the White House at once. When he reached
there, Madison offered him the post of Minister to Russia, asking for an immediate answer, as the nomination had to be sent
to the Senate in less than thirty minutes. Adams accepted,
although he told the President that he thought confirmation
of his name by the Senate would be uncertain. The surmise
was correct, and the Senate voted that a mission to Russia was
unnecessary. In June, however, when Madison again sent the
nomination to that body, it was confirmed, Pickering voting on
both occasions against Adams.

During these unhappy Senatorial years, Adams's home in
Boston had been in a wooden house on the corner of what are
now Tremont and Boylston Streets, and there, on August 18,

1807, had been born his third son, with whom our story will have much to do. He was baptized in due course Charles Francis — the Charles in memory of John Quincy's deceased brother, and Francis for that Judge Dana with whom Adams had made his first essay in diplomacy when he went to Russia in 1781. The boy Charles Francis was now in turn to pass his own most impressionable years at the court of that same country, so far removed from any predictable orbit for the childhood of Bostonian youths.

III

EUROPE ONCE MORE

It must have been with very mixed feelings that Adams embarked, August 5, 1809, on the ship *Horace*, which was to make a direct voyage from Boston to St. Petersburg. It had been reported to him that Colonel Pickering, although he had voted against the appointment, had remarked that probably the best thing to do with him was to send him out of the country. Ezekiel Bacon had written to him that the post was "somewhat like an honorable exile," and Adams himself had long believed that foreign duty was hindrance to an American career. The possibility of such a career, however, had now become problematic. There was little hope for a Republican in Federalist Boston, and, with his unbreakable sense of public duty and his theory of public office, Adams would probably have buried himself in Timbuctoo if he had been appointed to any office there the discharge of the duties of which might accrue to the benefit of his country.

On the other hand, although he was passionately devoted to that country and also felt deep personal grief at leaving his now ageing parents and his two elder children, who were to remain at school in Boston, Europe had far more attraction for John Quincy in the second generation of the family than it had had for John in the first. He appreciated to the full the varied advantages of that European society in which he had moved easily from his earliest boyhood, and he had also acquired tastes that his father had not. "I had always," he wrote at this time, "an eager relish for the pursuits of literature [which his father had also had], and [which his father did not] acquired at an early period of life a taste for the fine arts," a taste which, he noted, had been bred in him by the opportunities he had had of seeing the best of sculpture, painting, architecture, landscape, and drama, and hearing music, in Europe in his impressionable youth. If Europe were, for a time, "honorable exile," it would be an exile mitigated for him as for few other Americans of his day. John had made the family international politically; John Quincy had become international impressionably. Still sternly Puritanical in facing moral problems for himself and others, his nature was both a deeper and a more maturely civilized one than that of the self-made John. Art for him was not a toy which earnest men could have no time for. It was a beneficent and moulding influence to which the spirit should be submitted. In balanced judgment, probably the little Charles Francis, a less than two-year-old baby about to be carried aboard the *Horace*, was to become in time the most notable of the family line, but that distinction must be given to John Quincy when we are considering the balance between the moral, intellectual, and æsthetic in character.

The Minister Plenipotentiary's party, as it left his Boston house in carriages that August noon to take ship at "Mr. William Gray's wharf in Charlestown," was a numerous one. Besides the Minister himself, there were his wife, the baby Charles Francis, his wife's sister, his nephew, who was to act as private secretary, two volunteer secretaries going at their own expense, his wife's maid, and a black manservant for himself. The boat slipped out from the wharf as the church bells of Boston and Charlestown rang one o'clock, and Adams, who had taken leave of his parents "deeply affected," found on the ship a farewell letter from his mother, Abigail, "which would have melted the heart of a Stoic."

The long voyage — they did not reach St. Petersburg until October 23 — was Adams's fourth to Europe and we need not dwell upon it. Arrived at the Russian capital, he found himself in the usual disagreeable predicament of every American diplomat, from his day to our own, who is not possessed of ample private means and who has to live on the beggarly salary provided by a government whose roots are in Main Street. The difficulty was much emphasized at St. Petersburg, where the cost of living was excessively high and the extravagance of the court and diplomatic sets beyond all reason. Economy was considered disreputable, and the scale of living of everyone with whom Adams was perforce brought into social and official relations made his situation a trying one. The form of the Russian ménage called for a horde of servants. There were a steward, a cook, two scullions, a porter, two footmen, a man to make fires, a chambermaid, housemaid, and laundress. Three of the menservants were married, and their families expected to live in the house. The household supplies had to be bought by the servants, who first robbed Adams on the cost and then pillaged the larders and wine cellar. It was the custom of the country, and Adams was in despair over his accounts. He dismissed some of the servants, remained in the city during the summers when the rest of the diplomatic corps, like all of society, were in the country, and as far as possible declined all invitations because of financial inability to return civilities. He had been helped with small allowances from his father until he was twenty-six, but after that had kept absolutely within the limits of his own income, though, in his public life, it had been "at the price of uncommon sacrifices of consideration and a reputation which, in the spirit of this age, economy cannot escape." In Russia, however, he wrote that the temptation in his position to do otherwise amounted almost to compulsion, though he held steadily to his resolution. His duty to his country required him to appear in a society which otherwise he could have shunned, but to do so in a condition of what was almost poverty contrasted with the extravagance of all their acquaintance must have sorely tried both him and his wife.

How different the social requirements of the society to which American Main Street had sent him was from that of that thoroughfare itself may be glimpsed in an account of a dinner at the French Ambassador's which he wrote to his mother as a sample of what all were like. As a glance backward into a society now gone for good, the description may be quoted at perhaps undue length. "At half past four," he wrote, "I went to the ambassador's hotel, at the outer door of which stood the

J. S. Copley

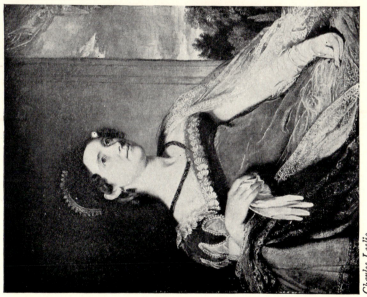

Charles Leslie

MR. AND MRS. JOHN QUINCY ADAMS

(By permission of the Adams Memorial Society)

porter, or *Swiss*, in full dressed livery, deeply bordered with gold lace, a three-cornered hat, also gold laced, a broad girdle of cloth passing over from the right shoulder to the left side, bordered with gold lace and worked with gold embroidery, and a large thick staff about five feet long, and headed with silver. He opened the folding doors and I stepped from the carriage into the house. As my style here is altogether republican, I went only in a chariot and four, attended by two footmen in livery, and driven by a coachman on the carriage box, and a postilion, between boy and man, on the right side horse of the leading pair. My own footmen followed me about half the way up the stairs, when I threw off and gave them my *shoop*, a large outside fur garment, fit only for wearing in a carriage. . . . On the steps of the staircase stood a line of twenty footmen, reaching from the bottom to the top of the stairs, all in the same livery as the Swiss, excepting the girdle, staff and hat, and in silk stockings instead of boots. They stand there from the time the company begins to come, until all the guests are arrived. They stand like so many statues, and are there merely for the magnificence of the show. At the top of the staircase, at the folding doors of the first antichamber, stood two *chasseurs* with pea green liveries, as deeply laced with silver as those of the footmen with gold, and with each a hanger suspended at the thigh by a leathern baldric passing over the shoulder. These like the Swiss were in boots. In the second antichamber was a line of eight upper servants, above the rank of footmen and chasseurs, in uniform dresses embroidered in gold, but of the same colors with the liveries. They were all in silk stockings, and stood like the footmen, merely to be seen by the company. In the third antichamber, the guests were received by the Ambassador's secretaries and by the French consul. The Ambassador himself stood in the saloon, near the door of entrance, both folds of which were wide open, and there received and returned the salutation of each guest as he arrived." It is not necessary to follow the further description of the dinner itself, of the beautiful damask, the magnificent service of Sèvres porcelain, the French cooking, and the rare wines in great variety. The difficulties of a Minister and a high-spirited, proud gentleman who was forced by his position to live in such a society and yet who was determined to live within his total income, official and private, of a few thousand dollars a year, are obvious enough.

Although the Russian was then, perhaps, the gayest of all great capitals, the years spent there must have been far from gay for the wife of the American Minister. Her heart longed for the two little boys she had been forced to leave at home. An infant daughter, born in St. Petersburg, could not survive the rigor of the climate and was buried under the Russian snows. The effort to run so alien a household, and to appear decently in society with preposterously insufficient means, must have been wearing in the extreme.

To a considerable extent Adams solaced himself by satisfying his insatiable intellectual cravings with study. When in Washington he had noted that the habit of reading had become a passion and that he found little in life when severed from his books. For a while, he devoted four or five hours a day to the education of Charles, but later the boy was sent to an English boarding school in the city. The education of the child, who was only seven when he left Russia, was rather desultory, but, as it happened, both his parents, from residence in France in youth, spoke French almost as a native tongue, and the language was also that universally used in Russian society, so that Charles came to speak it more readily than English, and, in fact, preferred it throughout his life. It was to be an extremely useful tool to him when he in turn became a diplomat. Adams also took a lively interest in the education of the boys he had left in America, writing to George, then ten years old, not to forget his French, and sending to him a series of letters on reading his Bible that were afterward twice published as a small volume. It was his own invariable custom, which he never allowed travel or other preoccupations to interfere with, to read the Bible completely through once every year, and while in St. Petersburg he did so twice in English and once each in French and German. He was far, however, from thinking of his boys only in terms of intellect. Writing to his brother Thomas about them, he urged that they be taught drawing and fencing and the use of firearms, and asked him to take the small George out hunting with him. "Let him have as much relaxation and sport as becomes his age," he wrote, "but let him be encouraged in nothing delicate or effeminate. Seize every possible occasion to give him hardihood, inure him to fatigue; let him if there be an opportunity begin to mount on horseback. If he goes into Boston to see a play, make him walk for it rather than ride in a carriage. Let him learn to skate this winter, and if he has not already begun, let him by all means learn to swim next summer. In everything of this kind I know there is danger, but it is a world of danger in which we live, and I want my boys to be familiarized as soon as possible with its face, that they may be the better warned and guarded against it."

He met the Czar, Alexander, frequently, often quite informally, and in many ways the society, with occasional birds of passage like Madame de Staël, was agreeable enough. As the Napoleonic wars were raging, sweeping even into Russia and burning Moscow, the post of observation was an interesting one. The United States, of course, was also at war with England, and the chief point of diplomatic interest during Adams's stay was the offer of the Czar to arbitrate in that conflict. The United States accepted, and even, too hurriedly, sent three commissioners to act with Adams in possible negotiations, but, as England declined the offer, nothing came of it. Finally, however, England did express a willingness to negotiate direct, and Adams received orders to proceed to Gothenburg as one of the American commissioners for the purpose of making a treaty of peace. Having spent nearly five years away from home, he was most anxious to return, and, indeed, had recently applied for a recall. In 1811 he had been offered an appointment on the Federal Supreme Court, which, much to his surprise, had been unanimously confirmed by the Senate, but had declined it on the score of his utter unfitness, in his own mind, for a judicial post. Now, however, instead of the recall, came, first rumors, and then the definite notice, of his appointment on the peace commission. It was a duty much to his liking, and he hoped that immediately afterward he would be allowed to go to America. As he wrote to his mother, after five winters in Russia he had no wish to expose his family to the climate any longer, and there seemed to be no matter of public business that required him to make further sacrifice. He had not, however, definite knowledge as to whether he would be relieved, and, as it was the worst possible season for crossing the gulf between Russia and Sweden, he left his wife and son in St. Petersburg and proceeded alone, with a manservant, to Stockholm by way of Reval. There he awaited news of the appointment of English commissioners, and found that Gothenburg had been abandoned as the place of meeting and Ghent decided upon in its stead. In fact, although Gothenburg is now a delightful and extremely interesting city, it is somewhat difficult to understand why it should ever have been selected for such a purpose in 1814. On account of ice and adverse winds, it had taken Adams from the twenty-eighth of April to the twenty-fifth of May to get from St. Petersburg to Stockholm, a journey that can now be made in a single day, and he was by no means pleased at the change in meeting place. Henry Clay, another of the commissioners, had actually reached Gothenburg, and the other two, Gallatin and Bayard, were in England, as were, of course, the English representatives. Jonathan Russell, American Minister to Sweden, was also a commissioner, and he and Clay, at Gothenburg, agreed to the change of place if the proposal came entirely from the English. Adams received the news when thirty miles on his way from Stockholm to Gothenburg, and after reaching that city spent another three weeks in reaching Ghent, venting his irritation in a letter to his wife. He had, however, a fondness for Holland and recovered his equanimity when he reached that country, where he found the "traces of the Napoleon family" being removed "as fully as the convenience of the moment would admit." In the Stadthouse a large unfaded space of the damask wall-covering showed where a large portrait of the Emperor had hung during the last few hectic years. He found, however, the Dutch thrift strong

as ever.   On a square of window glass in the palace was still the
inscription, written with a diamond, "Vive Louis Napoleon
Roi de Holland."   "To remove it would cost a new square
of glass, and why should that expense be incurred?"   When
Adams reached Ghent, on June 23, British troops were stationed
at Antwerp and Brussels, and it was rumored a British garrison
would soon be in Ghent itself, and Adams had no desire to
negotiate a peace at the muzzle of a British gun.   However, he
accepted what had become a *fait accompli* without consultation
with him.

He was not a little pleased at finding that he was first on the
spot, but by July 12, the other American commissioners —
Bayard, Gallatin, Clay, and Russell — also arrived, and the
five took a house together.   It was a curiously assorted group
to be thus suddenly made not only colleagues but intimate
members of one small household.   When they first met they
were, as Adams wrote to his wife, "all in perfect understanding
and good humor with one another," and perhaps the chance of
remaining so would have been better had each had his own
lodgings to which to retire.   They did, indeed, soon learn to
go their several ways after sitting regularly together over dinner
from four until six.   Adams usually went for a three hours'
walk, which appealed to none of his colleagues.   They preferred, he wrote, "the coffee houses, the Reading Rooms, and
the billiard tables."   Adams occasionally played chess or whist,
and on one occasion even danced until three in the morning,
but for the most part he went to bed at nine o'clock.   He had
no objection to playing cards for money provided the stakes
were so small as not to constitute gambling.   Clay, however,
"soon grew weary and impatient" of such low play, for he had
the genuine gambler's passion.   Adams was an early riser as
well as retirer, and we soon begin to find such entries in his
Diary as "Just before rising I heard Mr. Clay's company retiring from his chamber.   I had left him with Mr. Russell, Mr.
Bentzon and Mr. Todd at cards," or "There was another card
party in Mr. Clay's chamber last night, and I heard Mr.
Bentzon retiring from it after I had risen this morning."

All his life Adams was keenly fond of the theatre, but the only company in Ghent was, he wrote to his wife, "without exception the worst I ever saw." The only tolerable male singer had "a figure like Sancho Panza" and the only female one "was sixty years old and had lost her teeth." In spite of this the other members of the American mission became constant attendants and "in a manner domesticated behind the scenes," having become intimately acquainted with the whole troupe. Adams, in spite of his love of the theatre, had made it a rule never to make the acquaintance of an actress, and went only once a week to hear the orchestra, which was tolerably good. The popular conception of the man is of a cold, stern Puritan, given in his old age to volcanic outbursts of rage, but a letter written to his wife in 1822 on this topic of theatrical acquaintance is worth quoting here as helping to make the reader understand the very human nature that lay beneath his moral restraint. Writing to her of his boyhood forty years earlier, he said that "the first woman I ever loved was an actress, but I never spoke to her, and I think I never saw her off the stage. She belonged to a company of children who performed at the Bois de Boulogne near Passy, when I lived there with Dr. Franklin and my father. She remains upon my memory as the most lovely and delightful actress that I ever saw; but I have not seen her since I was fourteen. She was then of about the same age. Of all the ungratified longings that I ever suffered, that of being acquainted with her, merely to tell her how much I adored her, was the most intense. I was tortured with the desire for nearly two years, but never had the wit to compass it. I used to dream of her for at least seven years after that. But how many times I have since blessed my stars and my stupidity that I never did get the opportunity of making my declaration. I learnt from her that lesson of never forming an acquaintance with an actress to which I have since invariably adhered, and which I would lay as an injunction on all my sons."

Adams was ruthless and unsparing in his self-analysis and well knew his own weak points. During the seven months that the five commissioners were destined to work together, there were many explosions of temper, due mainly to the wholly anti-pathetic natures and, later, views of Adams and Clay, although Adams was also frequently piqued by the constant and minute criticism of his drafts of documents indulged in by his colleagues. Russell, a younger and much less able man than the others, took little part in the proceedings and was practically negligible, but Gallatin found his most trying and perhaps most useful work in keeping the peace between the Americans rather than in making it with the British.

Adams was fully aware of the characters and rôles of all, including himself, and at the end of the conference, in December, wrote what is perhaps the fairest commentary on them all in a letter to his wife, and which we may quote here at the beginning. Addressing her as "My Best Friend," he writes: "This appellation reminds me of an occurrence on Monday last, which I may tell you exactly as it happened, and which will show the sort of tone which my colleagues observe with me, and I with them. We had been three hours in conference with the British plenipotentiaries, and it had been perhaps the most unpleasant one that we have held with them. We had returned home, and were in a session conversing together upon what had been passing in the conference, when Mr. Clay remarked that Mr. Goulburn [British] was a man of much *irritation*. *Irritability*, said I, is the word, Mr. Clay, irritability; and then fixing him with an earnest look, and the tone of voice between seriousness and jest, I added, 'like somebody else that I know.' Clay laughed, and said 'Aye, that we do; we all know him, and none better than yourself.' And Mr. Gallatin, fixing me exactly as I had done Mr. Clay, said emphatically, 'that is your *best friend*.' 'Agreed,' said I, '*but one*' — and we passed on in perfect good humor to another topic. There was, however, truth in the joking on all sides. Of the five members of the American mission the Chevalier [Bayard] has the most perfect control of his temper, the most deliberate coolness; and it is the more meritorious because it is real self-command. His feelings are as quick, and his spirit as high as those of anyone among us;

but he certainly has them more under government. I can scarcely express to you how much both he and Mr. Gallatin have risen in my esteem since we have been here living together. Mr. Gallatin has not quite so constant a supremacy over his own emotions; yet he seldom yields to an ebullition of temper, and recovers from it immediately. He has a faculty, when discussion grows too warm, of turning off its edge by a joke, which I envy him more than all his other talents, and he has in his character one of the most extraordinary combinations of stubbornness and of flexibility that I have ever met with in man. . . .

"The greatest diversities of sentiment and the most ani-mated mutual oppositions have been between [Mr. Clay] and *your* best friend. They are unquestionably the two members of the mission most under the influence of that irritability which we imputed to Mr. Goulburn; and perhaps it would be difficult to say which of them gives way to it most. Whether Mr. Clay is as conscious of this infirmity as your friend, whether he has made it as much the study of his life to acquire a victory over it, and whether he feels as much regret after it has passed every occasion when it proves too strong for him; he knows better than I do. There is the same dogmatical, over-bearing manner, the same harshness of look and expression, and the same for-getfulness of the courtesies of society in both. An impartial person judging between them I think would say that one has the strongest, and the other the most cultivated understanding; that one has the most ardency, and the other the most experi-ence of mankind; that one has a mind more gifted by nature, and the other a mind less cankered by prejudice. Mr. Clay is by ten years the younger man of the two, and as such has perhaps more claim to indulgence for irritability. Nothing of this weakness has been shown in our conferences with the British plenipotentiaries. From two of them, and particularly from Mr. Goulburn, we have endured much; but I do not rec-ollect that one expression has escaped the lips of anyone of us that we would wish to be recalled." One cannot know Adams only from that famous *Diary* which he used as a safety valve to let off the steam of his passions. One can get the true figure of the man only by reading the letters to his family.

The American commissioners were, as he says, to be called upon to endure much at the hands of the British. Those three gentlemen, if, indeed, they could all be called such, Admiral Lord Gambier, Dr. Adams, and Mr. Goulburn, did not arrive until August 7, the delay much exasperating Adams, who felt that the change in meeting place and other delays had all been purposely made by the British in the hope of something turning up in their favor before the negotiations began. In Parliament itself Lord Castlereagh was asked on July 20 "whether the persons sent to Gothenburg for the American government were quite forgotten by His Majesty's Ministers, or whether any one had been appointed to treat with them?" The English were all inferior to the Americans in ability, and, as it developed, they had been sent to act less as diplomats than as transmitting clerks for the British government in London. Whereas the Americans had to decide all questions themselves and assume entire responsibility, the English had to refer every point to London, taking ten days for that purpose between each meeting. Gambier was merely a high naval officer with some of the less agreeable social qualities that sometimes belong to that character. Dr. Adams was an undistinguished author whose experience of good society appears to have been limited. Goulburn was a very young man, who shared with his colleague Dr. Adams, a "prejudice of disliking everything that is not English, and of taking no pains to conceal their taste."

It must be remembered that the American war was, for England, mainly an extremely annoying side issue in the colossal struggle of the Napoleonic wars, and that the United States was far as yet from being able to claim rank as one of the great powers. Nor can it be said, even by their best friends, that the English of 1814 were much given to being conciliatory or even gracious in manner in dealing with foreign nations. The fact that the English commissioners were second-rate men, and, as at once became evident, that they were not trusted by their government as the Americans were by theirs, could be pretty

definitely counted upon to make their manners rather more
aggressively overbearing than would have been those of first-
class diplomatists entrusted with full responsibility. What
they lacked in ability, and even authority, they would be only
too likely to try to make up in aggressiveness. Nor, until
almost the last moment, was the British government itself sure
as to whether it cared whether peace were made or not. The
war was a draw and neither England nor the States had won,
nor had either much cause for pride in its conduct. England
was not exhausted and, with freer hands in Europe, it might
well be that it could make a better peace by stringing the negotiations along. Nor, among the Americans, was Clay himself
opposed to a continuance of the struggle.

Difficulties between the two sets of plenipotentiaries began at
the very start. The British commissioners suggested that the
meetings be held at their lodgings, which the Americans, properly, considered "an offensive pretension to superiority."
Adams cited international law to show that such was the
accepted usage from ambassadors to ministers of an inferior
order. This point having been got over by the British agreeing to the American proposal to meet first at the Hôtel des
Pays-Bas and after that alternately at the lodgings of the two
Commissions, it next appeared that the British demands put
forward for consideration were preposterous, including the erection of a sort of Indian barrier state between the possessions of
England and the United States in America, and a pledge on the
part of the United States to maintain no armed vessels or forts
on its northern boundary, while reserving such rights of defense
to the British. Cession of territory was also demanded, and a
reiteration of the clause in the Treaty of 1783 giving the English
right of navigation on the Mississippi, without a confirming of
the American rights to the fisheries on the Newfoundland coasts.

The American commissioners were dumfounded, and Adams
thought the conference must surely break up in a fortnight, and
he even planned his route back to St. Petersburg. The terms,
of course, did not afford even a basis for the commencement of
negotiations. Adams expressed himself lucidly and emphati-

cally to the British on the subject of the Indians, showing the utter impracticability of the proposal with respect to them. It was incompatible with both the moral and the physical nature of things. It was impossible to "condemn vast regions of territory to perpetual barrenness and solitude" when a nation of eight million people were pressing against them for the means of subsistence. Any such conclusion to the present war could be only the reopening of another. In the written reply which he drafted, but which his colleagues altered, he asked pointedly, if the Indians were not independent nations, on what basis of international right did England claim to have anything to say as to those in the United States, and, if they were independent, where were the British credentials for authority to treat for them? The English, of course, had in time to recede from this point, and the negotiations dragged along, with the invariable ten days' delay after almost every conference for the British negotiators to report back to London.

It is not necessary to follow the discussions in detail. In October came the news of the destruction of Washington by the British, but that piece of vandalism, which had little military significance, rather lowered than raised England's prestige on the Continent, and stiffened the backs of the Americans. News of the Hartford Convention and the talk of secession in the New England states, which had been markedly disloyal to the Union throughout the war, was, on the other hand, damaging to them. Adams was justly enraged against the Federalists, who thus strengthened the hands of the enemy in the midst of negotiations for peace.

Occasionally the meetings were enlivened by unexpected points scored in sharp give and take. The British had captured and held Moose Island in Passamaquoddy Bay, and the Americans demanded that they return it pending arbitration of title. "Mr. Goulburn and Dr. Adams," wrote John Quincy, "immediately took fire, and Goulburn lost all control of his temper. He has always in such cases a sort of convulsive agitation about him, and the tone in which he speaks is more insulting than the language he uses." Bayard coolly referred to the precedent of the Falkland Islands. Transported with rage, Goulburn replied that in that case the English had sent a fleet "and driven the fellows off," and that that was what they would do in this case. John Quincy, from the remarkable stores of his vast and desultory reading, was able to rejoin that the British commissioner was misinformed, as in the case cited it had been the Spanish who had driven the English off, and Lord Gambier rescued his colleague by quickly changing the topic of discussion.

Two of the most important points were those of the fisheries and the navigation of the Mississippi, and in the closing weeks of the conference these caused several sharp clashes between Adams and Clay. Clay, as a Westerner, was rabidly insistent on refusing the English the right of navigation on what had now, by the acquisition of the Louisiana territory some years before, become an interior stream in the United States; and cared nothing about insisting upon the fishing right, which he claimed would benefit only the New England states, which had taken a treasonable stand during the war. Adams made up his mind that whatever the others might do he would refuse to place his name on a treaty which would sacrifice the fisheries, and, on the other hand, Clay had reached the point where he preferred a continuance of the war. On December 11, Adams noted in his *Diary* that Clay "was for a war three years longer. He had no doubt but three years more of war would make us a warlike people, and that then we should come out of the war with honor. Whereas at present, even upon the best terms we could possibly obtain, we shall have only a half-formed army, and half retrieve our military operation. He was for playing *brag* with the British Plenipotentiaries; they had been playing *brag* with us throughout the whole negotiation; he thought it was time for us to begin to play *brag* with them. He asked me if I knew how to play *brag*. I had forgotten how. He said the art of it was to beat your adversary by holding your hand, with a solemn and confident phiz, and outbragging him. He appealed to Mr. Bayard if it was not. 'Ay,' said Bayard, 'but you may lose your game by bragging until the adversary sees the weakness of your hand.'   And Bayard added to me, 'Mr. Clay is for bragging a million against a cent.'"

Clay, indeed, for some months past had been more than willing to see the conference a failure.   As the passing weeks brought, for the most part, only new disasters to the American arms, and it became evident that at best a peace could be merely a wriggling out of an uncomfortable situation, with nothing said in a treaty about the rights for which America had ostensibly entered the conflict, Clay's position became more and more displeasing to himself.   He, more than any other man, had made the war.   He had almost goaded his countrymen and the administration into waging it, and had predicted great victories, the easy conquest of Canada, a peace dictated at Quebec, an acknowledgment by a defeated England of all the rights claimed for our commerce and seamen.   To make peace now would be to stultify all his prophecies and perhaps blast his career.   If peace could be delayed, possibly the fortune of war would turn.   Adams, however, was anxious for peace, provided it could be made without losing any of the rights which his country possessed before it entered the unfortunate struggle. These he would not sacrifice, and stubbornly he held to his position month after month.

Suddenly and unexpectedly, the end came.   The British commissioners sent a note offering to omit all reference to the Mississippi and the fisheries, and the way was clear for signing a treaty.   Nothing that the United States had gone to war for was gained or even mentioned, but no right previously acknowledged was infringed.   Clay asked Adams to refuse to sign and to break off the negotiations, but Adams properly declined.   He had declined to sign any treaty giving up American rights, especially the fisheries, but he would not prolong the war on the "million against a cent" game of brag in order to save Clay's face.   On December 24, all eight commissioners affixed their names to the document, and initiated a peace between the two nations that has already subsisted unbroken for a hundred and fifteen years.   The sudden change of front on the part of the British was mainly due to conditions in

Europe. Lord Liverpool had been anxious for peace from the beginning, but had been opposed by Castlereagh. During the negotiations, Castlereagh had been on a diplomatic mission to Vienna and had there embroiled himself with the Czar of Russia and the King of Prussia. As a result, he had sent a dispatch to the British government that in view of the new clouds in the sky they had best disentangle themselves from the distracting side-issue of the American war. The Duke of Wellington had also advised Liverpool that, as there was no strategical point in the sprawling United States to capture and keep, there was no way of ending the war promptly by a military blow. Moreover the British were complaining of the weight of the property tax, and if more European complications might be encountered it was best to cut off the expense of American operations. This fortunate combination of circumstances should not detract from the diplomatic success, for such it must be considered, of the American negotiators. Less than a week before the end came, they could have had peace had they given up the fisheries, to which Adams clung. In the House of Lords, the Marquis of Wellesley declared that the Americans "had shown a most astonishing superiority over the British during the whole of the negotiations," and it must be recalled that the Americans had been dealing not with the British negotiators but through them with the British government itself. Adams, as head of the American Commission, could certainly take great satisfaction in the result.

He had, for some time, had intimations from home that if peace were declared he might be appointed to the post of Minister to England, and at once wrote to his wife that whether or not the treaty should be ratified in America, and whether or not he should be made Minister, he would not remain in Russia, and asking her to close their house there as soon as possible and proceed with her son, Charles, across Europe to join him in Paris. Evidently, in spite of the fears of Mrs. John Adams, her daughter-in-law had developed qualities that made her no unfit companion for John Quincy. It was no light task that he so casually thrust upon her — to wind up a diplomatic household in Russia and make her way with a seven-year-old child and only one servant for weeks across a war-torn Europe in mid-winter by carriage. Adams himself set to work to clear up the affairs of the Commission. Clay, who was going back to Washington, demanded to carry the papers of the Commission with him, although, by all precedent, they should have remained in Adams's hands, and this entailed a very sharp interchange between the two men which did much to enliven the week following the peace. One by one the commissioners left, and Adams alone remained. His last task was to sell the furniture of the mission. The sale lasted a week, he wrote his wife, adding that "the good people of the place consider the Congress of Ghent as an epoch of so much importance in the history of their city, that they have given extravagant prices for some of our relics. I am told an old inkstand, which was used at the conference, was sold for thirty francs, though it was not worth as many sous. Even the furniture from the British hotel was sold at our house, for the sake of putting it in favor. The worst part of the joke was that they put off quantities of bad wine, as if it had been ours. We did not leave a bottle for sale."

Adams finally got away from Ghent on January 26, and reached Paris, after a thirty years' absence from that city, on February 4. There he settled down to rest and enjoy himself while awaiting his wife and news from home. On the eighth he was appointed Minister to England, although it was some weeks before word of that event could reach him. Lafayette came in from the country to see him, and he renewed many of his old acquaintances. Count de Tracy and Count Marbois had both become peers of France and held office. Madame de Staël had returned since the fall of Napoleon, and Adams called upon her and many others. He was presented to the King and the Royal Family. There was the opera, and he went over and over to the Museum of the Louvre, which had been opened since his last visit to the city. Everything was going happily until suddenly came the news that Napoleon had landed on the French coast, having escaped from Elba, and was rapidly

marching on Paris. As word came of the swarming to him of
recruits, the society in which Adams was moving suddenly dissolved. The Royal Family fled. Adams still made calls on the
Apollo, the Venus de Medici, and the Laocoön, but when
Napoleon entered Paris the doors of the Louvre were closed,
and Adams wrote, "The Museum is now no more." He once
caught a glimpse of the face of the conqueror looking out of a
window in the Tuileries, but Paris had become no place for
tourists. "Communications," he wrote to his mother, "with
the rest of Europe were immediately cut off. The prospects of
the country were from day to day growing darker and more
threatening. The combination of all Europe against them, as
it became continually more apparent, kindled afresh all the
flames of their civil discord; a fearful forboding of the fate that
awaited them took possession of the public mind and, before
we left France, I was strongly impressed with the expectation of
the issue which so shortly ensued."

Mrs. Adams and her child had left St. Petersburg on the
twelfth of February, and by the twentieth of March Adams had
heard only of her having passed through Berlin in the carriage.
On that date he wrote that "the King left the Palace of the
Tuileries at one o'clock this morning, taking a direction to the
northward. Napoleon is expected to enter Paris this day or
tomorrow." It was the day Mrs. Adams was due, but she did
not arrive. Adams wrote his father of his anxiety. "Since the
approach of Napoleon towards Paris vast numbers of foreigners,
and many others, have left the city and taken flight in all
directions," he wrote. "They have employed all the post
horses on the road, so that I am apprehensive my wife may have
been detained for want of them." He feared difficulty at the
frontier. But three days later Mrs. Adams and her little boy
arrived at his hotel, after a forty-day trip, having covered,
behind the fastest horses available, what must have been nearly
two thousand miles of midwinter roads. Considering the
anxiety and what to us would seem the physical rigor and hardship of such a wintry excursion, it is evident that if Mrs. Adams
could not stand Boston she could yet stand much. Her hus-

band noted laconically that the journey "has been of essential service to her and Charles' health."

The party lingered in Paris until May 16, one of the vivid recollections of Charles's later life remaining a glimpse of Napoleon as he stood on a balcony of the Tuileries acknowledging the shouts of the crowds. By May 25 they were in London, again house-hunting for a suitable place for an American Minister. For reasons of economy, they chose one at Ealing, then a village well out in the country about eight miles from Hyde Park Corner. When it had become definitely known that Adams would be accredited to England, the two elder boys had been sent for, and after a separation of nearly six years the family was once more united, although the two younger boys were sent to a boarding school in the near neighborhood, where, Adams wrote his father, "George is studying Greek to your heart's content." During the years that they had remained in America, they had lived with their grandparents, Mr. and Mrs. John Adams, and we may pause here a moment to learn what had been going on in the older generation of the family while John Quincy was in Russia and Holland.

John Adams, since his retirement from the Presidency, had been living quietly, surrounded by children and grandchildren, on his farm at Quincy. In 1812 he wrote to Thomas McKean that the last eleven years had been the most comfortable of his seventy-seven and that he had "never enjoyed so much in any equal period." As age increased he felt to some extent its infirmities, especially annoying being the increase in the tremulousness of his right hand, an affliction that has appeared with odd frequency in the family. But he retained great vitality and an enormous zest for life. On New Year's Day 1812, following a suggestion from their mutual friend, Dr. Benjamin Rush, Adams wrote a letter to Jefferson and renewed their old friendship. From then until their deaths on the same day in 1826 the new relations were cordially maintained, to the delight of each, Adams giving rein to his affection without restraint. Such expressions as "You and I ought not to die until" they had fully explored each other's minds, or "When writing to you I never know when to subscribe," or, in 1823, "Write me as often as possible for nothing revives my spirits so much as your letters except the son of my son and his family," all show how much the old man enjoyed the correspondence with the many-sided friend of a half-century earlier. Adams's letters were frequent and voluminous. He once wrote six in a little over a fortnight, and one of them was over four thousand words. The intellectual interests of both the men were probably wider than those of any others of similar age then in America, and their discussions ranged over almost every topic. Adams, however, carried on a large correspondence with many others besides Jefferson, and the avidity with which his mind seized on a topic and explored it was remarkable, even when he crossed his ninetieth year. He continued to read voluminously, and ploughed his way gayly through such works as Dupuis's *Origine des tous les Cultes* in twelve volumes and Grimm's *Memoirs* in fifteen, and John Quincy in London constantly picked up new works to send him. His interest in politics, past and present, continued keen, and he wrote, not infrequently with a caustic pen, about both.

"No man has ever prospered in the world without the consent and cooperation of his wife," wrote Mrs. John Adams to Mrs. Shaw in 1809. Abigail Adams in her old age had the love and veneration of all who knew her. She brought up her grandchildren, George and John, before they rejoined their father, as she had her own, and the depth of their feeling for her was one of the early recollections of Charles Francis, who never forgot seeing his two big brothers, after they all returned from the English mission, break down and cry because they had done something to offend their grandmother. Certainly few, if any, Boston women of that day had had wider social experience than the wife of the Peace Commissioner in Paris, the Minister to the Court of St. James's, and the President of the United States, and, still more certainly, none had as wide an acquaintance with books or as cultured a mind, but Mrs. Adams had no doubt as to a woman's function in life. "It is very certain," she wrote to Judge Vanderkemp in 1814, "that a well-informed woman, conscious of her nature and dignity, is more capable of performing the relative duties of life, and of engaging and retaining the affections of a man of understanding, than one whose intellectual endowments rise not above the common level." But in the same letter, speaking of Madame de Staël and of the domestic unhappiness that resulted from her too ostentatious display of learning, she quoted with approval the incident of Napoleon. "Upon some occasion," she wrote, "she [Madame de Staël] had solicited an interview with him, and recommended to him some measure for him to pursue. He heard her, but made no other reply than this; 'Madame, who educates your children?'"

No one could ever ask that question of Abigail Adams. Although she had a mind of such quality and cultivation as to provide intellectual companionship for her President husband and President son, and in her unconsidered letters made a contribution to American literature that may well outlast most of those made by our feminist intellectuals of to-day, she maintained her views of the multifarious duties of a woman to the end. "It behoves us," she wrote to a woman friend, "who are parents or grandparents, to give our daughters and granddaughters, when their education devolves upon us, such an education as shall qualify them for the useful and domestic duties of life, that they should learn the proper use and improvement of time, since 'time was given for use, not waste.' The finer accomplishments, such as music, dancing, and painting, serve to set off and embellish the picture; but the groundwork must be formed of more durable colors. I consider it as an indispensable requisite, that every American wife should herself know how to order and regulate her family; how to govern her domestics, and train up her children. For this purpose, the all-wise Creator made woman an help-meet for man, and she who fails in these duties does not answer the end of her creation.

"Life's cares are comforts; such by Heaven designed;
They that have none must make them, or be wretched.
Cares are employments, and, without employ,
The soul is on a rack, the rack of rest.

"I have frequently said to my friends, when they have thought me too overburdened with care, that I would rather have too much than too little. Life stagnates without action." It was to such a mother and such a woman that John Quincy at Ghent wrote the first of his letters to say that peace had been signed. Letters to his father and wife followed. It was to Abigail Adams that everyone who knew her turned first.

The two years of John Quincy's stay in England as Minister were uneventful. Poverty had been disagreeable enough at St. Petersburg, where at least society, from the Czar downwards, had been friendly. England in 1815 was not friendly. Adams, as Minister, naturally had no actual rebuffs to resent. He was not a man easily to be snubbed, and in any case English society knew what was due to diplomatic usage. If Adams could write of Lord Castlereagh that "his manner was cold, but not absolutely repulsive," there were others who were more friendly, but the general atmosphere could hardly have been expected to be cordial. Adams, like his father before him, and, oddly enough, his son after him, was destined to be Minister to England at one of the three precise moments when the opinion of English society was most bitter in opposition to America. John Adams had been presented to Court as a successful ex-rebel. John Quincy represented a country which, with equal grievances against France and England, had chosen to attack the mother country when she was engaged in a world struggle to rescue Europe from Napoleon. On the whole, Adams was well off in the suburban retreat of "Boston House" at Ealing. On the other hand, if he was bored by heavy dinners and post-prandial oratory, he well knew both the pleasure and the advantage of society. "I know very well," he wrote to his mother, "the benefit to a public minister of associating with the people of rank and consequence in the country where he is accredited; but I *feel* that he ought rather to shun than to seek such society, when he can appear in it only as a retainer, receiving unrequited favors, and not as an equal, sharing and dispensing by turns the interchange of social good offices. If I cannot join in the chorus of the convivial song 'and let *him* spread the table tomorrow,' I would fain not be listening to it at the table of another." In answer to an inquiry as to salaries from the Secretary of State, Adams pointed out that the salary of the American Minister to England, which had been fixed at an extremely inadequate figure after the Revolution, had remained unchanged ever since, though the cost of living had doubled, and that then "no man can confine his expenses to it without positive degradation in the eyes of the people of this nation and of his own countrymen." He pointed out that the salary must be largely increased or else only rich men should be sent to represent America. The richest country in the world still prefers the latter alternative, punctuating its regular course by the occasional humiliation of an indispensable man who does not happen also to be a millionaire.

It is not necessary to recount any of the fairly important but rather routine business which Adams was called upon to handle during his English stay. His letters, however, give us frequent glimpses of how his mind was working on American affairs. Always inclined to think in terms of the nation rather than his state, his stay abroad had cleared the last traces of provincialism. Writing to his father in 1816 when it was rumored that Maine was to be split off from Massachusetts, he said, "If I were merely a Massachusetts man I should deeply lament this dismemberment of my native state. But the longer I live the stronger I find my national feelings grow upon me, and the less my affections are compassed by partial localities. My system of politics more and more inclines to strengthen the union and its government." Adams was now a Democrat, but the passage just quoted shows how difficult for him any real party allegiance would be. The quality of the man is shown in another portion of the same letter. America has never had a more valiant and vigilant defender of its rights and honor than he, but commenting upon the toast recently offered by Admiral Decatur, "Our country, right or wrong," he said, "I disclaim all patriotism incompatible with the principles of eternal justice."

If Adams's stay in England was not marked by any international crisis or business of the first importance, it was nevertheless of conspicuous value to him in the next post which he was to hold, and of even greater, perhaps, to his small son, Charles Francis. The fortuitous combination of circumstances which made French almost his mother tongue was preparing, a half-century and more in advance, to give him a great advantage when he should be sent to Geneva to represent his country on the Alabama Claims Commission. The rough and tumble scramble of life in an English boys' boarding school at Ealing was also giving him an insight into the English nature that was to stand him in excellent stead when occupying the difficult position of American Minister during the Civil War. Consideration for the feelings of others is scarcely a schoolboy characteristic in any land, and schoolboy patriotism is of a raw and undigested sort. To throw two small American boys into an English boarding school within a few months of the ending of the war between the two countries was much like throwing Christian martyrs to the lions in the Roman arena. If the impression of English brutality was thus to be rather too deeply impressed upon the third generation of the new Adamses, its youthful members were well able to take care of themselves. If the battle of New Orleans was in its day much exaggerated by Americans for its importance, it nevertheless was quite as good a victory — which was saying little — as was the British one at Washington. The master of the school, a Dr. Nicholas, was therefore not a little amused when in answer to a question, intended as a sly dig, from one of the English boys to young John Adams as to whether he "had ever been in Washington" young Adams at once replied with spirit if not with truth, "No, but I have been in New Orleans." The Adams boys picked up as much historical information as they could at home, and even from such visitors as General Scott, to use in the war of words with their young English tormentors, and the battles must often have been amusing. They amused John Quincy, who reported some of them in his letters to his mother, who continued to take a keen interest in the progress of the boys. At any rate, no better training could have been devised for a future diplomat who was to be pitted against English statesmen for many critical years than squabbling with them in school and learning unconsciously their weak and strong points of mind and character. In the long holidays, spent at "Boston House," the boys also saw something of English society from a less belligerent standpoint, and their father now and then took them all to the theatre.

Adams himself, of course, met almost everybody, as the saying is, at innumerable functions, official and social. Presentation to the Court was naturally one of the first incidents of his stay, both for him and his wife, but he much preferred such dinners as Lord Holland gave to a half-political, half-literary set in his magnificent seventeenth-century house to those of a more official sort. London society immediately after the Napoleonic wars was hardly at its best, and Adams, after two years, was more than ready to go home. Rumors had reached him that he might be appointed Secretary of State by the incoming President, Monroe, and on April 16, 1817, he received a letter before breakfast notifying him of his appointment and requesting his return to Washington with the least possible delay. By the fifteenth of June he and his family were on board the *Washington* at Cowes. An uneventful voyage of fifty days ended August 6 in the Harbor of New York, Adams up before daylight to get the first glimpse of his native land after an absence of eight years. "The new Sandy Hook lighthouse" sent out a welcoming beam of light, the pilot was taken aboard, and with "a fair and light breeze" the ship made dock by one o'clock. John Quincy was home for good.

IV

SECRETARY OF STATE

THE time of Adams's return coincided with one of the most marked changes of direction in thought in the history of his country. Up to 1815 the currents of American life had been deflected this way and that by the political events of Europe. America had awaited with deep anxiety every mail from the Old World. Now, with startling suddenness, she was to turn away completely from that world and concentrate all her thought and energies upon herself. Her population was advancing by leaps and bounds. "We are," as Calhoun said in 1817, "greatly and rapidly — I was about to say fearfully — growing." The tide of immigration was rising rapidly and in that year twenty thousand Irish and Germans sought our shores. More significant was the westward drift of the fast-multiplying native population. By 1820 the number west of the Alleghanies, about two and a half million, was as great as the entire population of the colonies at the time of the Revolution. New states were being admitted to the Union, adding to the weight of Western sentiment in Congress — Louisiana 1812, Indiana 1815, Mississippi 1817, Illinois 1818, Alabama 1819, Missouri 1820. In 1818, whereas Massachusetts exported only $5,700,000 worth of produce, Louisiana exported nearly $12,250,000 worth.

Manufacturing had developed so enormously, particularly in the Middle and New England states, that Madison, in his message of 1815, predicted that with moderate protection Americans could not only hold the home market for themselves but would produce a surplus for export. Even Jefferson was led to say, though he later recanted, that the manufacturer must at last be placed beside the agriculturist. A vision began to take form of a partially closed circle by which America would produce its own raw materials, manufacture its own products, sell in its own expanding markets, and export surpluses. For this, great improvements in the means of communication were called for — roads, canals, improved river transport. Horses and boats were still the elements out of which transportation must be developed, as it seemed, but the successful steaming down the Ohio River from Pittsburgh of the *Orleans*, as well as experiments in the East, were beginning to open fantastic possibilities for the future. Better communications, more manufactures, a home market, — in a word "the American System," as Clay, with his flair for popular catchwords, termed it, — became the main political preoccupations of the day. The first protective tariff was enacted in 1816. On March 6, 1819, Chief Justice John Marshall, the last-minute appointee of John Adams in 1801, read his decision in the case of M'Culloch *vs*. Maryland, among the greatest judicial utterances of all times, establishing the doctrine of implied powers in the Constitution. In the succession of epoch-making decisions rendered during these years by him, the Constitution, as Bryce has said, "seemed not so much to rise under his hands to full stature, as to be gradually unveiled by him till it stood revealed in the harmonious perfection of the form which its framers had designed." It may be questioned whether all of its framers had, indeed, so designed it, but there is no doubt that, as Bryce added, "that admirable flexibility and capacity for growth which characterize it beyond all other rigid or supreme constitutions is largely due to him." John Adams, through his appointee, was moulding the destinies of a nation far greater, more complex, and more powerful than had been dreamed of by most of its founders.

In the decade of Adams's return, Prescott, Palfrey, Bancroft, and Emerson were students at Harvard. Bryant and Irving were beginning to write, and the *North American Review* issued its first number in 1815, but these were not the driving forces of the new American life, of "the American System." Those forces were implicit in the dream of irresistible and illimitable economic expansion. That expansion, especially westward, was to bring political results in its train that were to be as powerful in their way, but were by-products, not aims directly sought or even desired by the new economic leaders. The day was not far off when aristocratic leadership in politics was to give way before the release of new social forces. The older system was already cracking in New York, and when Adams, a few days after his arrival, was invited to a public dinner of Tammany Hall, at which Governor De Witt Clinton was present, the first named on the Committee of Arrangements to call upon Adams at his hotel and tender the invitation was "Mr. Astor." It was, in a way, a portent of the new America to which Adams had returned — an America much less new and strange than Henry would find his after a similar absence when he should return in 1868, but still an America in which there were signs of the breakdown of the old order.

At the threshold of a new era we cannot, perhaps, do better than take Mr. Astor as a symbol and a guide. As we watch this man, one of the most powerful and, in his field, wide-visioned of the leaders of the new day, we are struck by many facts. As contrasted with the men who have occupied the leading rôles heretofore, the Jeffersons, Adamses, Washingtons, Jays, Livingstons, Hamiltons, Madisons, Monroes, he is indeed a new type. He is neither of the old colonial nor the English stock. He is a German, an immigrant of 1784, who never lived under English rule. He is neither planter nor merchant of the old sort. His education in books is of the scantiest, and he writes a scrawl, defying the rules of grammar. But he will leave the greatest fortune America has known. The largest hitherto has probably been about one million dollars. Mr. Astor will bequeath twenty. In extending his business operations in the fur trade he thought in empires. He founded Astoria, in Oregon, in 1811, to collect furs where they were cheapest and most plentiful. A fleet of ships carried them to the richest market, China, where, in turn, they loaded with Chinese goods and sailed to New York, and thence with supplies for his trading colony back to Oregon. When New England disloyalty threatened the financial life of the government in 1814, Astor joined with Girard and Parish of Philadelphia to save it, making incidentally a colossal profit. Congress passed laws at his behest. He almost ruled the country from St. Louis to Alaska. His influence at Washington, his enormous wealth, his vast organization, enabled his agents to defy those of the Federal government. This was indeed different from being a shipping merchant in Boston or a planter of Mount Vernon or Monticello. And so Mr. Astor in New York invited John Quincy Adams to be a guest of honor of Tammany Hall, and beyond the Alleghanies there were two and a half million settlers, scrabbling for a living and dreaming of an empire, clamoring for roads, canals, more and more boats on the rivers, more and more outlet of any sort, at anybody's expense, to carry to market the products of boundless energy and expansion.

The great houses of the New England merchants and the Southern planters were charming. We have never equaled them and still do our best to copy them. They were symbols of the refined and cultured lives of their still eighteenth-century owners, men and women of gracious manners, of intellectual interests, representatives of an established and polished social order. All the high posts of government were filled from their ranks. But Mr. Astor with his twenty millions was ruling a business empire, encircling the globe, from his house at the corner of Broadway and Vesey Street, and beyond the mountains were two and a half million men and women who snapped their fingers at learning, at drawing-room manners, at refinement, at social standards, and dreamed of fortunes at the end of the trail. Thus, with only a stroke or two of the brush, may we try to picture the America to which the second-generation Adams was coming home from Europe to find his place in it. The country was evidently to be in, before long, for some sort of big change. John Adams had fitted his environment in 1765 like a glove. Could the family shift and alter to meet the changing conditions? Could they in an altered world go on being popular leaders, statesmen, and, perhaps, Presidents? Time would tell, and meanwhile John Quincy was due at Washington to take his place as the leading member of Mr. Monroe's cabinet. There, after a brief and happy visit with his father and mother at Quincy, he found himself at four in the afternoon of September 20, 1817, having left the Indian Queen Tavern in Baltimore by stagecoach at six that morning.

He had been chosen in part for sectional reasons. The long dynasty of Virginia Presidents and Secretaries of State had been broken only by Adams's own father. Monroe, as he had written to Jefferson, wished to choose a man from the East, and Adams, there, was unquestionably the best choice. In fact, apart from any geographical consideration, no man in the country was better qualified than he for the post, and a century later the verdict seems assured that he was, if not the greatest, at least one of the two or three outstandingly great men who have thus served their country. The work was new to him. Except for the months at Ghent he had, as yet, to a great extent played a lone hand, without partners, and, as he wrote, "These Cabinet Councils open upon me a new scene and new views of the political world. Here is a play of passions, opinions, and characters different in many respects from those in which I have been accustomed heretofore to move. There is a slowness, want of decision, and a spirit of procrastination in the President, which perhaps arises more from his situation than his personal character." During his term, however, Adams came greatly to appreciate his chief, and never for an instant failed in complete loyalty to him, whatever he might at moments confide to his diary.

In the few pages which we can devote to this period in the life of one member of the family, it is evident that we can give no adequate — indeed, scarcely even an understandable — account of the many problems with which he had to deal, so wide were the complexities and ramifications of even the more important ones, and so lengthy were the negotiations concerning them. Every Secretary of State inherits problems not of his choosing, even though he may create or have new ones thrust upon him. The most pressing, for Adams, of the inherited sort was the question of Florida. It had formed one, for successive secretaries, since the beginning of the century.

Adams — and he himself considered it one of his greatest achievements — solved it.

The Florida question, interwoven with that of the western boundary of Louisiana, with Spain's inability to suppress the freebooters of Amelia Island and Galveston, with spoliation claims, and with the problem of neutrality in the contests between Spain and her revolting colonies in South America, was so complex and pressing that even the European powers threatened to intervene, and England offered her services as mediator, which Adams and the rest of the administration promptly rejected. Hyde de Neuville, the French Minister at Washington, who was to prove helpful to Adams on many occasions and with whom the Secretary usually got along most amicably, also tried to intervene. With the Spanish Minister, Onis, matters went no more smoothly at first. Onis sent an extremely long note on the subject of Spanish grievances to Adams, using such phrases as "Truth is of all time," to which, in the true Adams style, John Quincy replied that "the observation that truth is of all time, and that reason and justice are founded upon immutable principles, has never been contested by the United States. But neither truth, reason nor justice consists in stubbornness of assertion, nor in the multiplied repetitions of error." A few days later, March 12, Adams wrote again, setting forth the American view with great ability and plausibility.

In St. Petersburg, Ghent, and London, Adams had been far removed from politics. He could play his part as statesman, looking only to his own conscience, unhampered by the play of passions about him. Washington, he soon found, was another world. The week of the Onis note we find the entry in his *Diary:* "Lee came to give me a hint on a very ridiculous affair, but which shows how I am situated. My office of Secretary of State makes it for the interest of all the partisans of the candidates for the next Presidency (to say no more) to decry me as much as possible in the public opinion. The most conspicuous of these candidates are Crawford, the Secretary of the Treasury, Clay, the Speaker of the House of Representatives, and De Witt Clinton, Governor of New York. Clay expected himself to have been Secretary of State, and he and all his creatures were disappointed by my appointment. He is therefore coming out as head of a new opposition in Congress to Mr. Monroe's administration, and he makes no scruples of giving the tone to all his party in running me down. On the publication of the concluding part of my late letter to Onis, he went about the House of Representatives showing and sneering at a passage where it said that the United States, after waiting thirteen years for justice from Spain, could, without much effort, wait somewhat longer."

In his earlier days in Washington, in the Senate, Adams had taken what came and had gone his way. But from now on, continually goaded, and not seldom thwarted, by the politics of the "era of good feeling," a tone of bitterness and invective is more and more evident in his communings with his diary. At times, however, he had to soothe the feelings of others. Onis, one day, came to Adams to complain loudly about having found a dead chicken tied to his bell rope the night before, "a gross insult to his sovereign and the Spanish monarchy, importing that they were of no more import than a dead old hen." Adams blamed it on mischievous boys and the envoy was comforted.

Onis had really no powers to treat of the Florida question in such way as to bring about a settlement. A messenger had to be dispatched to Madrid and the negotiation lapsed for some months. During this interval, a new phase of the problem was initiated by the wild career of General Jackson in that province. Jackson, sent south to protect our citizens from Indian raids, did no less than to march into Florida and seize it. Not only that, but he captured two Englishmen, presumed, probably correctly, to have been concerned in instigating Indian hostilities, and promptly executed them. He proceeded on his march, and captured Pensacola, pleasantly agreeing with the Spanish authorities to hold it subject to negotiation between the two governments. Having thus debonairly involved us in what well might have been war with two foreign governments at once, the impulsive general sat down at Pensacola to await a letter of commendation from Washington and to let Adams negotiate. The British Parliament was in an uproar over the murder — it was hardly less — of the Englishmen, and later, in conversation with our Minister, Rush, Lord Castlereagh said that had he lifted a finger war would have come. Fortunately, Castlereagh's policy was friendship with America, and war did not come.

Adams had a harder time with Spain, but in six successive cabinet meetings Adams proved not only Jackson's staunchest defender, which should be noted in view of the General's later attitude toward him, but the only advocate of defiance of Spain. At the first meeting, July 15, both the President and the entire cabinet, except Adams, were for disavowing Jackson. Curiously enough, Adams seemed to sense the political atmosphere better than any of his colleagues. Monroe was won over, and in an adroit note the Secretary managed, perhaps with the help of de Neuville, to pacify Onis. Spain, however, was still to be heard from, and when it was Adams had to pen one of the most noted documents — the letter to Onis of November 28 — which he ever wrote. It has been called special pleading of the most flagrant sort, and in it assuredly Adams gave full rein to the nationalism of the period and to his own gift of rhetoric. He no longer cited volumes of international law or precedent. "It is engraved in adamant on the common sense of mankind," he wrote of one principle advocated. He excoriated the two Englishmen. He defended Jackson. He showed the inability of Spain, from weakness, to perform her duties as a civilized nation with colonies. It may not have been good international law, but it was magnificent, and effective. We need not follow the subsequent ups and downs of the negotiations. On February 22, 1819, Adams and Onis signed a treaty ceding Florida to the United States and settling the western boundary of Louisiana. The Senate promptly ratified it, but there were still, as it proved, obstacles to be overcome. In connection with large land grants by the Spanish crown, which would greatly decrease the value of the cession and which Adams had declined to consider valid, he had been misled in the matter of dates.   Moreover, the Spanish government long delayed ratification on its part.   But in the end the treaty went through as Adams negotiated it.

That, however, was not until exactly two years later, and how much Adams had suffered in the meantime is shown clearly enough by the entry in his *Diary*, February 22, 1821, when the final ratifications were exchanged.   After noting the happiness of having, apparently, succeeded in his task in 1819, he continued, "It promised well for my public reputation.   Under the petals of this garland of roses the Scapin, Onis, had hidden a viper.   His mock sickness, his use of De Neuville as a tool to perpetrate a fraud which he did not dare to carry through by himself, his double dealings before and after the signature, his fraudulent declarations to me, and his shuffling equivocations here and in Spain, to acquire the reputation of having duped the President and me, were but materials in the hands of my enemies to dose me with poison, extracted from the laurels of the treaty itself.   An ambiguity of date, which I had suffered to escape my notice at the signature of the treaty, amply guarded against by the phraseology of the article, but leaving room for chicanery from a mere colorable question, was the handle upon which the King of Spain, his rapacious favorites, and American swindling land-jobbers in conjunction with them, withheld their ratification of the treaty, while Clay and his admirers here were snickering at the simplicity with which I had been bamboozled by the crafty Spaniard.   The partisans of Crawford, and Crawford himself, were exulting in the same contemplation of a slur upon my sagacity, and delighting in the supposed failure of the negotiation, because its failure brought unavoidable disgrace upon me.   By the goodness of that inscrutable Providence which entraps dishonest artifice in its own snares, Onis divulged his trick too soon for its success.   Clay was the first to snuff the fragrance of this hopeful blasting vapor and to waft it as his tribute of incense to the President.   The demand of a formal declaration by Spain that the grants in question were by the treaty null and void, completely and unequivocally obtained at last, has thoroughly disappointed all the calculators of my downfall by the Spanish negotiation, and left me with credit rather augmented than impaired by the result."

This passage has been quoted at length because it expresses so well a marked change that came over his nature about the time of the second election of Monroe. It was evident that he had found the life of a cabinet officer irksome, although he had invariably performed his duties at cabinet meetings with ability and restraint. The give and take of teamwork, however, were not suited to him and called for constant self-control. The incessant pressure of his own office was also wearing. It was due less to the legitimate demands of negotiation and State Department work than to the constant intrusions upon his time. "Members of Congress, visitors at the office, occupied again all the hours of business," he records in November 1820. "Every man comes with a story, demand, or solicitation of his own; almost every one comes to ask favors. No sooner has one left the office than another enters. I have often attempted to keep a minute of the names of the persons who come from day to day, but without success. I have not time to write the name of one who retires before another comes in. Eight or ten thus succeed one another without leaving a moment's interval. When they are gone, often while some of them are here, comes in a mail of letters, dispatches, and newspapers. Pressing business of the office, suspended while the visitors are with me, admits of no further delay. The sun goes down upon business uncompleted." Other similar entries denote a man who was being overstrained.

In addition to the regular work of the State Department he had also been asked by Congress to prepare a Report upon Weights and Measures, and he threw himself into what was, for months, the most difficult mathematical task of his life. Working under the most trying conditions, without proper instruments or books of reference, he at length produced a treatise of two hundred and forty-five printed pages which thirteen years later was acknowledged to be more accurate than anything produced in England, and which each successive investigator in the subject to the present day has pronounced a classic. It was completely ignored in America. Apart from its mathematical value it is interesting as an exhibition of the Adams mind, for its author, not content with the immediate subject in hand, traced the whole history of it and discussed philosophically the moral principles involved. There was the same effort to correlate scattered data under law that we shall encounter again in the work of his grandson. The effort, however, amid all the interruptions and against all the odds encountered, added heavily to his daily burden for months.

On October 28, 1818, he had lost his greatest source of comfort and strength. His mother, Abigail Adams, had died. "Had she lived to the age of the Patriarchs," Adams wrote in his diary, "every day of her life would have been filled with clouds of goodness and of love. There is not a virtue that can abide in the female heart but it was an ornament of hers. She had been fifty-four years the delight of my father's heart, the sweetener of all his toils, the comforter of all his sorrows, the sharer and heightener of all his joys. It was but the last time when I saw my father that he told me, with an ejaculation of gratitude to the Giver of every good and perfect gift, that in all the vicissitudes of his fortunes, through all the good report and evil report of the world, in all his struggles and in all his sorrows, the affectionate participation and cheering encouragement of his wife had been his never-failing support, without which he was sure he should never have lived through them." John Quincy's letters bear abundant testimony to the love and veneration which he himself felt for her, and of the influence she exerted over him, of the comfort and solace she gave him. His wife was, indeed, left to him, but with the death of his mother a great and beneficent influence went out of his days.

Always quick to anger, he had also hitherto been quick to recover his poise, and he had borne no lasting malice. He had looked upon the world, even his enemies, with much equanimity, as was evident in his attitude at the time of his dismissal by

Jefferson, and in his judicial summing up of his own and Clay's characters and tempers at Ghent. For a little while, there were to be moments of the old calm. Writing to his wife in August 1821, he said, "I well know that I never was and never shall be what is commonly termed a popular man, being as little qualified by nature, education, or habit, for the arts of a courtier, as I am desirous of being courted by others. Such as I am I envy not the reputation of any other man in the Union. There is not another man in the Union, excepting the Presidents past and present, who receives or continues to receive from the people of this country indications of esteem and confidence more distinguished and flattering than I have. . . . If ever man had reason to be grateful for the portion of public consideration which has been shown him, it is I, and I trust I am grateful for it."

Adams, however, was passionately ambitious. From his earliest youth he had looked forward to the possibility of a notable public career. It was in no sense an ignoble passion, and his ambition had never for a moment swerved him from his principles. Not only was the culmination of any great public career in America the Presidency, but in Adams's case — and here family history began to exert what was to be its more and more potent influence — the fact that his father had held that office would make any career falling short of that end appear less successful than his. When Adams had been appointed Secretary of State he had placed his foot on the rung next to the top of the ladder, as the post of Secretary had come to be considered as not only a necessary but as the inevitable step to the nomination as President. Writing, for example, of Gallatin in 1820, Adams noted that, although he had been twelve years Secretary of the Treasury and seven years Minister at foreign courts, his foreign birth had prevented his appointment as a Secretary of State, which cut off forever his hope of becoming President. Traditions were not ancient in the young republic, but this one had come to seem almost a political axiom. When, therefore, Adams was appointed to the office, his way appeared to be absolutely certain, after eight years of service (granted a probable second term for his chief), to the presidential nomination by his party.

As far as parties were concerned, the era may have been one, as it was called, of "good feeling." So mixed, indeed, was party allegiance that the parties themselves were gradually exchanging positions as to political principles. If for a while, however, the strife of party was lulled, that among the leading politicians was as bitter as at any moment in our history. It had early become clear to Adams that the prize which had seemed so indubitably his, and which his services and the traditions of succession seemed to make so, so far from being inevitably within his grasp, was going to be contended for by a number of politicians who, in his opinion, had no legitimate claim to it.

We have already noted his principle that public office should be accepted but not striven for. To this, throughout his life, he clung. In 1820, answering a Massachusetts Congressman who spoke to him of the probable contest for the Presidency in 1824, saying he hoped Adams would not think of not fighting, Adams replied as noted in his *Diary*. "I told him," he wrote, "the principle of my life had been never to ask the suffrage of my country, and never to shrink from its call. If life, and health, and private circumstances admitting of it, and a belief of competency to the station, not inferior to others who may be competitors for it, should be mine after the vicissitudes of the next four years, I shall adhere to the principle upon which I have always acted." He was fully conscious of the difficulty of such an attitude. "I know the disadvantages on which I now stand," he added, "and am conscious of my inability to make interest by caballing, bargaining, place-giving, or tampering with members of Congress." A few months later, noting a conversation with another man, he wrote down that he told him: "To one thing, however, I had made up my mind: I would take no one step to advance or promote pretensions to the Presidency. If that office was to be the prize of cabal and intrigue, of purchasing newspapers, bribing by appointments, or bargaining for foreign missions, I had no ticket in that lottery.

Whether I had the qualifications necessary for a President of the United States, was, to say the least, very doubtful to myself. But that I had no talents for obtaining the office by such means was perfectly clear. I had neither talent nor inclination for intrigue."

Adams's stand, so far from being appreciated, became the nightmare of his own political followers, practical men, and gave enormous advantages to his competitors for the nomination, who knew no such scruples as he did. Adams stuck to his principles, but, as he watched the orgy of wire-pulling and political manipulation by those seeking to obtain what he felt was justly his of right, bitterness entered into his soul. It has been shown over and over in our history what strange changes the ambition for the Presidency, once it has taken possession of a man, will work in his mental or moral character. With Adams it served to screw up to an even higher tension the stoicism of his stern Puritanical code of ethics, but as he kept his will clenched and watched others using every resource of political office and power to outdistance him in the race he became soured and embittered. He seemed to himself to stand alone with God against a degenerate people. His opponents ceased to be merely opponents and became endowed in his mind with every trait of evil men. His father's health was rapidly failing, and Adams got little solace from that quarter. He had always turned to his mother rather than to his wife. When, for example, he had been elated at signing the treaty at Ghent, he wrote a long letter to his mother a few minutes later. That to his wife waited for three days. Now his mother was gone. The intense struggle in the soul of the rigid moralist who held his gnawing ambition at arm's length and would not advance a hair's breadth to attain it at the expense of his principles, who would break his life but would not close his eye an instant to wrong, wrought strange changes in him. It distilled a poison in his mind, and when he poured himself out to his diary he touched his pen with its venom.

He continued to perform with extraordinary ability, if somewhat increased asperity, the duties of his office. On one occasion, although Adams was quite in the right, he so incensed the French Minister that that official, forgetting all etiquette, flung himself out of the room in a frantic rage and rushed from the house without a thought of his overcoat, with which a servant pursued the fleeing diplomat.

During his service in Monroe's second term, unquestionably the most lasting impression which he made on our national history and policy was in connection with the formulation of the Monroe Doctrine and the events leading up to it. Those events, which occurred over a period of several years and in widely separated parts of the Western Hemisphere, can only be touched upon. European nations were nibbling here and there at the American pie, and, as the Secretary of State watched them or warned them off, a general policy was formed in his mind, which in the main was adopted by the administration but for which the chief credit must be given to him, though the President shared in giving it the precise form in which it has come down to us.

Astor's settlement at the mouth of the Columbia River had not survived the War of 1812, and by an agreement with England in 1818 the whole question of title to the northwest country was left open for another ten years, during which both nations were to have fullest access to the section for trade. In January 1821, from some remarks made in Congress, the British Minister, Stratford Canning, gained the impression that the Americans were considering a further settlement there. He promptly called upon Adams for explanations, and the famous conversations, reported verbally in Adams's *Diary*, ensued. His previous relations with the Minister had been conciliatory and friendly, so he was much surprised both at Canning's question and at his tone. He replied, however, that with the prevailing disposition of the country he considered it not improbable that the settlement at the mouth of the Columbia "would at no remote period be increased." Canning, with a change in manner and "a tone," wrote Adams, "more peremptory than I was disposed to endure," asked him if this were "the determination of the American government" to which

Adams replied that it was merely his personal opinion. The Englishman then said that he would consider it a violation of the Convention of 1818. Adams rose from his seat, took a copy of the Convention from the bookshelf, and after reading the section on boundaries aloud, said, "Now, sir, if you have any charge to make against the American Government for a violation of this article, you will please to make the communication in writing." "Do you suppose, sir," asked Canning then, with great vehemence, "that I am to be dictated to in the manner in which I am to communicate with the American Government?" To this Adams replied no, that he knew the privileges of foreign ministers, but that the government was free to determine what communications they would choose to receive and how, and that "we are as little disposed to submit to dictation as to exercise it."

The following day, Canning returned to the attack, and after some preliminary countering Adams pointed out the impropriety of Canning's asking the government for explanations of a speech of a Congressman. He asked what the British Prime Minister would think if the American Minister, after hearing a speech in Parliament which suggested sending troops to the Shetland Islands or a colony to New South Wales, should ask for an explanation. Canning asked if Adams considered the cases as parallel with that of the Columbia River. The rest can be given in Adams's report of the conversation. "'So far as any question of right is concerned,' said I, 'perfectly parallel.' 'Have you,' said Mr. Canning, 'any claim to the Shetland Islands or New South Wales?' 'Have you any claim,' said I, 'to the mouth of the Columbia River?' 'Why, do you not know,' replied he, 'that we have a claim?' 'I do not know,' said I, 'what you claim nor what you do not claim. You claim India; you claim Africa; you claim —' 'Perhaps,' said he, 'a piece of the moon.' 'No,' said I; 'I have not heard that you claim exclusively any part of the moon; but there is not a spot on this habitable globe that I could affirm you do not claim; and there is none which you may not claim with as much color of right as you can have to Columbia

River or its mouth.' 'And how far would you consider,' said he, 'this exclusion of right to extend?' 'To all the shores of the South Sea,' said I. 'We know of no right that you have there.' 'Suppose,' said he, 'Great Britain should undertake to make a settlement there, would you object to it?' 'I have no doubt we should,' said I."

These conversations, which had no immediate result at the moment, and of which only a small portion, by no means the most heated or dramatic, has been quoted above, undoubtedly gave the Secretary food for thought. For some years past, his mind had also had to turn frequently in a quite different direction. For long, the colonies of Spain in South America had been carrying on protracted revolts against their mother country. There had been some sympathy with them in certain quarters in the United States, and Clay, particularly, in Congress, had urged their recognition as independent nations, mainly, Adams rather unjustly thought, to hamper the administration. Adams had laid down the principle, which has in the main been the one always followed by us since, and which has found a place in international law, that recognition should await fair proof that the cause of the mother country had become desperate. His insistence upon absolute neutrality extended to the sale of arms, and was the cause of a notable entry in the *Diary*. After vehemently opposing a proposal to sell arms to Colombia, he noted that "a remark that I have occasion frequently to make is, that moral considerations seldom appear to have much weight in the minds of our statesmen, unless connected with popular feelings. The dishonorable feature of giving secret aid to the revolutionists, while openly professing neutrality, was barely not denied [in the Cabinet]. The President admits it. No one else seems to think that it ought to stand in the way of measures otherwise expedient, especially if supported by popular prejudice. My own deliberate opinion is, that the more of pure moral principles is carried into the policy and conduct of a Government the wiser and more profound that policy will be."

In Europe, the Holy Alliance, so misnamed, was in favor of

coming to the aid of Spain and assisting her to subdue her revolting colonists. Adams sagely believed that they would not advance to the point of actual armed intervention, but when England, which was drifting away from the policies of the Alliance, suggested that she and the United States should join in a declaration recognizing the new nations and passing a self-denying ordinance as to any acquisitions of their own, new questions were opened. Adams had no wish to follow in the wake of England, although he also had no desire to have the United States make any immediate acquisitions either in the West Indies or South America. He would not, however, tie the hands of the United States in future contingencies.

Meanwhile there had also been trouble with Russia over the question of the Pacific coast of America, and Adams assured the Russian Minister, Tuyl, that the United States "would contest the right of Russia to any territorial establishment on the American continent, and they would distinctly assume the principle that the American continents were no longer subjects for any new European colonial establishments." Adams at first may have been influenced largely by the question of trade, being the earliest American statesman to assert the principle of the "open door," but the doctrine in time was to assume greater importance as a political one. He gained the adherence of the President, and in Monroe's Message of 1823, largely influenced by Adams, America was made to declare not only that it was against colonization by European countries in the Western Hemisphere, but, further, that it would look upon "any attempt on their part to extend their system to any portion of this hemisphere" as dangerous to our peace and safety. The doctrine, which has been of enormous influence upon American thought and policy, naturally took the name of the President who enunciated it, but the credit for it, if not wholly, at least in the main, must be given to Adams.

In bringing the negotiations with Russia to a successful conclusion, he had succeeded in delimiting the claims of that power to the Northwest, a section of our country of which at that time Adams alone among our statesmen understood the value.

In the controversies leading up to the recognition of the South American republics in 1822 he had laid down abiding principles of international law. In winning Florida he had performed a service of the first magnitude, and in his share of the formulation of the Monroe Doctrine he had contributed to American foreign policy a principle that has become as firmly embedded in the American mind as those of Washington's Farewell Address. His whole diplomatic correspondence, covering these and other transactions, based upon deep understanding, wide knowledge, and a lucid logic, was phrased with an almost unequaled force and vigor. Few, if any, American Secretaries of State could have looked back on eight years of greater achievement or service. Had it not been for the ambitions of others, there was every reason why he should have been allowed to receive the approbation of his countrymen and succeed peaceably to Monroe as President in 1824.

As the time for election approached, however, the attacks on him increased in virulence. Not only was his integrity questioned, but the Philadelphia newspapers descended so low as to paint him as an uncouth sloven who would disgrace the White House, a man who wore neither waistcoat nor cravat and went to church with bare feet! Every device of political power and chicanery, as we have noted above, was ruthlessly employed. Except for a pamphlet answering charges brought against him by his former colleague at Ghent, the second-rate Russell, he kept silence, but in May 1824 he wrote in his diary: "To suffer without feeling is not in human nature; and when I consider that to me alone, of all the candidates before the nation, failure of success would be equivalent to a vote of censure by the nation upon my past service, I cannot dissemble to myself that I have more at stake upon the result than any other individual in the Union. Yet a man qualified for the elective Chief Magistracy of ten millions of people should be a man proof alike to prosperous and adverse fortune. If I am able to bear success, I must be tempered to endure defeat."

His three chief opponents were General Jackson, whom
Adams had so stoutly defended, Crawford, and Clay. When
the electoral votes were counted it was found that Jackson had
ninety-nine, Adams eighty-four, Crawford forty-one, and Clay
thirty-seven. Communication was slow and the result was not
known until December, when it was found that there had been
no election by the people and that the decision would thus be
thrown into the House of Representatives. Crawford, who
had had a paralytic stroke and was a physical wreck, was
obviously out of the race, and the problem was whether Clay
would throw his influence toward Jackson or Adams. He had
always been hostile to the former and it was foreseen that in all
probability he would favor Adams. The excitement was
intense, and in the midst of it the Jackson forces played one
of the dirtiest tricks that has ever been played in American
politics. In order to sway Clay or to forever blacken the
reputations of him and of Adams, a story was given to the
papers that Clay would throw his influence to the candidate who
would agree to make him Secretary of State, an office which it
was clear he probably would be called to fill in any case. It was
stated that he had offered to vote for Jackson on those terms
but that Jackson had refused. The inference was that if he
voted for Adams he would only do so as a result of a corrupt
bargain with that candidate. The story, traced to its source,
was shown, as anyone might know, to have no foundation
whatever. Clay and Adams did not like each other, but Clay
disliked Jackson far more, and from his own record in public
life, from his abilities, and from the fact that he was one of the
three leading candidates for President (Crawford aside), it was
natural that he should receive the next highest post in the
government. When, after Adams's election by the House,
Clay became, as the Jackson party had foreseen he would,
Adams's Secretary of State, they pointed to it as evidence of
the slander they had propagated, and, the American public
always taking delight in vilifying their great men, the story
was believed by large numbers of the people. During the
weeks that the election was pending in the House, Washing-

ton swarmed with politicians of all sorts and grades. Anyone familiar with American politics can realize the pressure brought to bear on the candidates and the temptations before them. To the end Adams maintained the same lofty, if impractical, attitude he had always had as a candidate for public office. He became, perhaps, a little more conciliatory in manner, but otherwise would not make a pledge or lift a finger to aid himself.

The election in the House did not take place until February 9, when on the first ballot Adams received thirteen votes, Jackson seven, and Crawford four. John Quincy Adams was declared elected President of the United States.

In his now lonely home at Quincy, the old father and ex-President, John Adams, had heard the news with profound emotion. His son had been to visit him in the preceding September and found him much changed by the infirmities of age. His physical powers were nearly prostrated, his hearing affected, his eyesight so dim that he could neither read nor write, and he was so weak that he could not walk without aid. Yet he bore his condition with fortitude, and his mind was scarcely impaired at all. He was still keenly interested in political movements, and dictated answers to the letters received. His months were now numbered, but he had lived to see his son, so dearly loved by him, raised to the highest office in the nation. As soon as the election had been decided in the House of Representatives, John Quincy had immediately dispatched the news to the old man waiting in the farmhouse which had sheltered the family for so long, whether farmers or Presidents — the old man who from his own experience could so well understand the trials as well as the honors that lay in store for the son treading in his own footsteps. On the twenty-eighth he wrote the following brief reply to the momentous news received : —

"My dear Son, — I have received your letter of the 9th. Never did I feel so much solemnity as upon this occasion. The multitude of my thoughts, and the intensity of my feelings are too much for a mind like mine, in its ninetieth year. May the blessing of God Almighty continue to protect you to the end of your life, as it has heretofore protected you in so remarkable a manner from your cradle! I offer the same prayer for your lady and your family, and am your affectionate father. John Adams."

V

THE PRESIDENCY

OWING to the disputed election, there were scarcely more than three weeks between the decision becoming known and the inauguration of the new President. On the fourth of March, 1825, Adams wrote in his diary: "After two successive sleepless nights, I entered upon this day with a supplication to Heaven, first, for my country; secondly, for myself and for those connected with my good name and fortunes, that the last results of its events may be auspicious and blessed." At half-past eleven in the morning he proceeded to the Capitol escorted by the militia, was sworn into office by his father's appointee, Chief Justice John Marshall, and exchanged salutations with Ex-President Monroe, upon whom he also called in the afternoon. In the evening there was a grand ball at "Carusi's Hall," from which Adams withdrew early, and at home he "closed the day as it had begun," with thanksgiving to God and a prayer for continued help. A four years' martyrdom had commenced.

As we have seen, Adams had for years consistently befriended and defended General Jackson. On the day of election he noted in his diary that when attending the reception at the White House that evening "General Jackson was there, and we shook hands. He was altogether placid and courteous." It was the last time that they met as friends. It was evident that the defeated General was a strong candidate for the Presidency in 1828, and the fight for office began almost before Adams had moved into the White House in 1825. The chapter on Adams's administration in the *Life of Jackson* by his ablest biographer, John Spencer Bassett, is all too truly named "The Campaign against John Quincy Adams." The story of those four years is that of a man at bay, not of a President carrying out his policies with the support of his party.

Indeed, as we have already pointed out, there scarcely were parties in 1824. The old Federalist Party was dead and all five candidates in the election were recognized Republicans. That party, however, was chaotic. After 1815 it had ceased to stand for the principles of Jefferson, and had developed no new ones that secured the adherence of all its members. It had established a National Bank five years after it had been declared unconstitutional; it had adopted Hamilton's theory of a high protective tariff; it had come out for internal improvements on a grand scale. It was made up of a heterogeneous mass of voters, who constituted a majority but of whom perhaps half were opposed in theory to the policies advocated. It was the only party by adherence to which one could reach elective office, but it was torn by the internal personal strife of its own leaders. In the course of some years, after Jackson's election, men became so clearly divided for and against the Jacksonian principles that new parties again arose, but during Adams's administration the situation can best be described as a free-for-all fight, with no sense of party allegiance to the man in the White House. That man was the only one who, in spite of a natural ambition, was guided in his conduct solely by the thought of his country. The others all had their eyes on 1828 and, in a period of almost unparalleled political passion, were jockeying for position, building up their own personal followings. In such a condition of public affairs, not only, from his own character and views, was the ultimate fate of Adams certain, but it soon became apparent that his administration was bound to be a failure. His own following among politicians was small and he would stoop to nothing to increase it. His opponents had everything to gain and nothing to lose by hampering him at every turn. As attack after attack was launched against him from every side, Adams could only stand and fight back, confiding all his bitterness to his diary, which more and more took on the character of that "treasury of damnations" which it has been called, although, owing to the pressure of business, the entries are less full for this than for any other period in his life.

As yet, the "spoils system" of bestowing public office on political supporters had not become established. That was a legacy to be bequeathed to America by Adams's successor, Jackson, but its possible usefulness to political aspirants was already beginning to be envisaged. As the nation had grown and the number of federal employees increased, the patronage in the gift of the President had also increased. Adams at once set his face against any qualification for office other than that of fitness. He refused point-blank to use any office as a reward for political support or to build up a political machine. "I determined," he said, "to renominate every person against whom there was no complaint which would have warranted his removal." "Efforts," he also wrote in the diary, "had been made by some of the Senators to obtain different nominations, and to introduce a principle of change or rotation in office at the expiration of these commissions; which would make the government a perpetual and unremitting scramble for office. A more pernicious expedient could scarcely have been devised." He even refused to remove men known to be hostile to him, and it at once became evident that, if there was nothing to be gained in the way of perquisites by working for Adams, neither was there to be anything lost by working against him. So little did he have in him of the politician that he even considered making Jackson Secretary of War, and refused to get rid of McLean, Postmaster-General in his cabinet, when he was known to be working for Jackson against his chief, Adams. Yet all this did not prevent Jackson and his followers from proclaiming loudly after the election that Adams had bought his office with the bribe of the Secretaryship of State to Clay, working on the ignorance of the masses so as to build up a legend among them of Adams's venality. The tide of democracy was rising and it was not a critical or an intelligent audience to which the politicians had to address their arguments as the scope of the franchise was steadily widened. The day had not yet come when in the legislature of the greatest state of the Union a legislator could stand up, when asked for his vote on a measure, and blurt out openly that all he wanted to know was "what there is in it for Mrs.

Murphy and the children," but that day was coming, and already the high morality of Adams's stand counted heavily against him as opposed to the promise of a postmastership or a clerkship by his opponents.

Adams's fundamental beliefs also ran counter to the changing political ideas of his time in another respect, and when he voiced his own point of view in his Inaugural Address his political friends must have felt that he had himself driven another nail in his political coffin. We have already noted the change which democracy invariably brings about in the function of its elected representatives. Gladstone once said, after the effects of the Reform Bill had had full opportunity to show themselves, that "he felt strongly that the statesman was becoming every day more and more the delegate, and less the leader of the people," and this is to be observed universally. No Adams could consent to be a mere delegate, a rubber stamp to record the will of the voters. Democracy was not yet in the saddle in America. It was to leap there with the election of 1828, but Adams's closing sentence in his Inaugural was the flaunting of a standard to which few would gather. Every politician and public man had read the writing on the wall. After outlining a vast plan of public undertakings in education and science as well as commerce, Adams added: "While foreign nations, less blessed with that freedom which is power than ourselves, are advancing with gigantic strides in the career of public improvement, are we to slumber in indolence or fold up our arms and proclaim to the world that we are *palsied by the will of our constituents?*" This doctrine that the man at the top of the scale was a better judge of what was worth doing than the man at the bottom was completely opposed to the doctrines of democracy, especially the raw democracy of the America of the 1820's. Adams had been President just twenty-four hours when it became evident that the family was not to change with the times. The forces which had moved John Adams in 1776 had coincided with the major social forces of that time. Growing industrialism, the expansion of the West, a constantly widening electorate, the rise of democracy, had all powerfully deflected the social forces of John Quincy's time. It was clear that the forces which moved Adams and the forces which moved society, so far from coinciding, were rapidly diverging, and that Adams, moving straight along the family line, was already far from the social and political opinions which spelled power in 1825 and were more and more to do so.

In his speech he had advocated, as we have said, a vast scheme of public improvements. It was characteristic of the man that he did not limit these to roads and canals, although he also proposed them. The object of government, he stated, was to improve the condition of the people. Economic improvement was, of course, essential, "but," he added, "moral, political, and intellectual improvement are duties assigned by the Author of our Existence to social, no less than to individual man." He suggested that the government should maintain a university, explore the coasts and interior country, and erect astronomical observatories. He pointed out that the United States did not possess a single one of these latter, which in an unfortunate phrase he termed "lighthouses of the skies," whereas Europe had one hundred and thirty.

At once the attack opened on the address. The country, as has been said, "rang with jeers and denunciations," not simply against the "lighthouses of the skies," but at Adams's whole policy. He had received practically his entire vote in the popular election from New England and New York, getting only seven electoral votes from the remainder of the Union. Adams's views of broad construction of the powers of government under the Constitution were, of course, far removed from those of Jefferson, but, as we have pointed out, the Republican Party was composed of men of the most diverse views. The strict constructionists, however, were numerous and powerful in the North, and they at once took alarm from the President's address. Clay, whose influence was almost wholly in the West, added, as it happened, nothing to Adams's strength there, as Clay had much weakened his own position by giving his support to Adams instead of Jackson, the hero of that section. Most of the influential men in the party whose constitutional views coincided with those now expressed by Adams were already committed to the Calhoun wing of the party, and as it became evident that the Crawford-Calhoun-Jackson forces would become more closely allied a complete combination of West and South was aligned against the President. The South, always with the fear of legislation against slavery, was bound to be strict constructionist, and the Virginian John Randolph of Roanoke went so far in his denunciation of Adams in Congress as to speak of "the coalition of Blifil and Black George — the combination, unheard of till then, of the Puritan and Blackleg." Clay promptly challenged Randolph to a duel, and the two men exchanged shots, although neither was wounded.

The immediate cause of Randolph's vituperation was the suggestion by Adams that commissioners be sent to attend a proposed conference of South American republics to be held at Panama. The cause of South America had always been popular in the United States, and Clay had been one of its champions. On the other hand, during his eight years as Secretary of State Adams had always been wary of any entangling alliances or hasty action in that quarter. He had no intention of being drawn into any such now, but, while some of his own friends feared a change on his part, his enemies feared that if he and Clay should become sponsors for a popular policy the cry of fraud and corruption between them, of which the most was being made, might lose some of its potency. They determined to fight the proposal and make it unpopular. For immediate results, the easiest appeal in a democracy is always to passion, and in this case, in the South, that passion could be quickly aroused. Two of the questions to be considered at the conference were the recognition of the Negro republic of Hayti and the abolition of the slave trade. In Congress Hayne's rhetorical appeals to Southern susceptibilities brought that section at once to a high pitch of feeling against the administration. Calhoun, who, as Vice-President, might have been considered a part of it, ranged himself openly against it and refused, as presiding officer of the Senate, to rule out of order attacks on the President. The debate was carried on until

April 1826, when, although the appointment of the commissioners was ratified, it was too late for them to do anything.

Meanwhile, another line of attack had been opened up, and in view of all the circumstances perhaps nothing could show more clearly the character of political life at that time. We have already spoken at length of Adams's attitude toward the use of patronage and appointments, and of how he was greatly damaging his own political prospects by the high-minded if somewhat Quixotic stand he had taken on that question. His enemies, however, now raised the cry that the abuse of patronage was a danger to the life of the Republic. Lurid pictures were drawn of what might happen, and, with innuendoes utterly unworthy of public men, the leaders of the opposition endeavored to make the people believe that they were happening under Adams. In view of what both men knew of Adams and of what Jackson was to do in the way of abusing the use of the appointing power when he became President in 1828, one can scarcely repress a feeling of nausea when we find Calhoun writing Jackson that "it must be determined in the next three years whether the real governing principle in our system is to be the power and patronage of the Executive, or the voice of the people. For it is scarcely to be doubted that a scheme has been formed to perpetuate power in the present hands, in spite of the free and unbiassed sentiment of the country; and, to express it more correctly, those now in power act on a scheme resting on the supposition, that such is the force of the Executive influence, that they who wield it, can mould the public voice at pleasure, by an artful management of patronage." [1] As a commentary on this we need only add, to show how completely Adams carried out his ideal, that with all the vast federal patronage at his disposal he removed only twelve office-holders in four years, an average of three men a year, and all for cause.

The charge of the corrupt bargain with Clay was kept alive and in the spring of 1827 the legislature of Jackson's state,

[1] J. S. Bassett, *Andrew Jackson*, New York, 1925, p. 389. Quoted from Jackson MSS.

Tennessee, passed a resolution on the subject the preamble of which read: "Mr. Adams desired the office of President; he went into the combination without it, and came out with it. Mr. Clay desired that of Secretary of State; he went into the combination without it, and came out with it." Fortunately for the politicians who devised this choice bit of logic, the electorate to whom it was served had votes if not intellectual discrimination. Owing to the publication of a certain letter, Clay at last secured the opportunity of having a thorough investigation made of the affair. Of the principals who brought the charges against him and Adams, one wrote a letter of retraction, another denied all he had been asked by Clay's opponents to prove, and a third later sent Clay a letter of deep regret. Jackson, however, continued to reiterate the charges that his own witnesses had, when brought to the point, to deny. The suspicion had been sufficiently planted in the minds of the people. They merely argued, after having had the syllogism planted in their minds by men who should have been thoroughly ashamed of their work, that Adams could not be elected without Clay; Clay wanted to be Secretary; Adams was elected and Clay became Secretary. In their own small, dirty minds the proof was perfect, and it is not a pleasant commentary on the moral state of the American public that it has always gladly believed the worst rather than the best of its own elected leaders.

As far as the questions of national policies were concerned there was no great difference between those advocated by Adams and those by Jackson, who more and more was becoming the acknowledged candidate for the Presidency in the next election. In one respect there was, indeed, a wide difference. Adams looked solely to the good of the nation as he saw it, and regulated his private conduct by the most rigid code of Puritan morals. Jackson was bent on securing office and regulated his conduct by the code peculiar to the politician. While hungry office-seekers knew that they could expect no loaves and fishes from Adams, they knew quite well what they could expect should Jackson be elected — an expectation in which they were not disappointed. Nor were the American people at that time, as they have never been since, seriously opposed to bribery and corruption in political life. In the mad scramble to acquire riches quickly, which has been an American characteristic from the days of earliest Western exploitation, men have lightly brushed aside laws which stood in their way. Knowing that they themselves were doing so, they have looked with lenient eyes at others who did the same, and from village boss to cabinet officers, as recent examples show clearly enough, the tone of public life has all too frequently been extremely low. The code of the politician, and of the citizen as a voter, has been far removed from that of the moralist and the gentleman. The open acknowledgment of this was to be made when Jackson assumed office, but the public was already prepared for it, and in a contest which was one of personalities Jackson's political practice was far more popular than Adams's moral ideals. Had there been, other than this, any great division on political questions, men might have separated into new parties, but there was not, and there was no doubt that the swaggering hero of a Western general, the conqueror of New Orleans, was far more to the taste of the public than was the stern Puritan in the White House. Moreover, it must be confessed that Adams was not conciliatory even in manner. He would make as little concession in his ways of doing things as in the things themselves.

As we have seen, Adams had regarded his election as not merely accession to the high office of President, but as the judgment to be passed on his previous conduct by the people. Holding as he had the lower position which had hitherto led inevitably to that office, a rejection of him would have been peculiarly bitter. The same test would be applied in the case of his running for a second term. So far in the history of the country all the Presidents — Washington, Jefferson, Madison, Monroe — had been thus reëlected, with one exception. That exception was Adams's own father, and as it became probable that he himself would also be rejected Adams's bitterness became extreme. Had there been any great division of the public mind on questions of principle or policy, he might have found solace, but it was all too clear that it was a mere matter of personality. Moreover, he felt, justly, that he was being attacked by methods despicably unfair, methods to which he would not himself stoop in retaliation. Many of the slanders spread about him, such as the charges of bribery and corruption and the bargain with Clay, were of a sort that would wound him most keenly as sullying his morality and personal honor. Although he kept a firm hold upon himself in his personal and public relations with others, he gave his pent-up emotions full play in the *Diary*, which becomes fairly vitriolic in its comments upon his antagonists. He described Randolph, Ingham, and their group as "skunks of party slander who had been squirting round the House of Representatives thence to issue and perfume the atmosphere of the Union." Again he spoke of the "besotted violence" of Randolph, and described Calhoun as "stimulated to frenzy by success, flattery, and premature advancement," "showering favors with lavish hands to make partisans, without discernment in the choice of his instruments, and the dupe and tool of every knave cunning enough to drop the oil of fools in his ear." One of the charges he brought against Calhoun was that, as presiding officer of the Senate, he allowed Randolph, drunk with porter, "in raving balderdash of the meridian of Wapping to revile the absent and the present, the living and the dead," and more particularly the President and his Secretary of State.

Adams's relations with the members of his cabinet were pleasant and without friction, except in the case of McLean, who proved a traitor to him and was aiding Jackson, not unknown to Adams. The latter, however, declined to remove him, and the Postmaster-General filled out his term under the man he betrayed, and on the accession of Jackson was promptly rewarded with a judgeship. In the old days at Ghent and also while serving as Secretary of State himself, Adams had often come into conflict with Clay, but Clay proved loyal and something like affection sprang up between the two men. Toward the end of the term, Clay's health partially gave way and there was some question as to whether he should not run for Vice-

President rather than remain as Secretary of State should Adams be reëlected. In an interview on the subject Adams advised him if possible to retain the far more important, though more arduous, post of Secretary, saying that, without any intent idly to flatter him, he, the President, would find it very difficult to find anyone else as competent. Clay rejoined that, also without any desire to flatter, he had found every facility offered him under Adams to transact business and if his health permitted would be very happy to continue in the same relation. When, after the catastrophe of 1828, the time came for Clay to take leave of his chief, he appears to have shown genuine emotion. That, under the long strain of those terrible four years, the man in the White House could get along with his entire cabinet, including Clay, a defeated opponent and a man with as high a temper as himself, shows that, difficult as he might be, he was by no means an impossible man to work with.

The history of his administration is in the main the story of the machinations of his political enemies. It was a time of profound peace and neither in domestic nor foreign relations is there anything of importance to record. In the mid-term election of 1827, for the first time in the history of the country, a majority opposed to the administration was returned to both Houses of Congress. With this solid adverse majority, with the Vice-President presiding in the Senate, and the Speaker of the House opposed to him, there was small chance of a President carrying through any policy of his own. There was little for Adams to do except to suffer and endure.

He had his family with him, and we may here note that his son Charles Francis spent the four years with his father in the White House. When the latter had returned from the English mission, the boy had at once been placed in the Boston Latin School, and had entered Harvard in 1821, only a few weeks after reaching his fifteenth year. Graduating in 1825, he was thus free to take a sort of post-graduate course in men, manners, and measures, history in the making, by the simple process of living at home with his President father. On the fourth of July, 1826, came the death of the old ex-President,

John Adams, at Quincy. Advised of the approaching end, John Quincy made a hurried journey from Washington, but arrived too late. From the attending physician, Adams received an account of his father's last hours, and we cannot do better than quote the entry from the *Diary*. "He had in the morning," his son wrote, "been removed from one bed to another, and then back. Mrs. Clark [his daughter-in-law] said to him that it was the 4th of July, the fiftieth anniversary of independence. He answered, 'It is a great day. It is a good day.' About one in the afternoon he said, 'Thomas Jefferson survives,' but the last word was indistinctly and imperfectly uttered. He spoke no more." The old man had nearly completed his ninety-first year, and the end, which came about five in the afternoon, was merely the cessation of the functions of a body worn out by age. Unknown to him, and by the strangest of coincidences, almost at the instant when he murmured, "Thomas Jefferson survives," Jefferson was breathing his last in far-off Virginia. On the fiftieth anniversary of the famous Declaration, its last surviving drafters and signers passed from the scene of their labors forever and together. Throughout the country great preparations were made to celebrate the anniversary fittingly. Four days before his death John Adams had been asked to give the toast for the celebration at Quincy. The orator of the day was permitted to see him for a moment and made the request. "I will give you," said the old man, "'Independence Forever.'" Asked if he would not add anything to that, he answered shortly, "Not a word." On the afternoon of the Fourth, as Adams was struggling for his breath, the only pain he suffered, the assembled crowd greeted his toast with prolonged applause. A few moments later, it was informed that John Adams was dead.

John Quincy lingered through the summer in his old home. It had been left to him by his father, subject to a payment of ten thousand dollars, and Adams could not bear to let it pass to other hands, thinking also that it would prove a safe place of retirement at the end of his public life. On the nineteenth of October he returned to Washington and the next morning noted that he "rose to the cares and trials, anxieties and dangers, which surround the station assigned me, and from which I have been for about a hundred days partially released. As my day shall be, so may be my strength for action in the performance of duty, and for submission to the will of Heaven."

In his *Diary* he gives us many descriptions from which we can readily picture his daily life. On one occasion he records: "I rise about five; read two chapters of Scott's Bible and Commentary, and the corresponding Commentary of Hewlett; then the morning newspapers, and public papers from the several departments; write seldom, and not enough; breakfast an hour, from nine to ten; then have a succession of visitors, upon business, in search of place, solicitors for donations, or from mere curiosity, from eleven till between four and five o'clock. The heads of departments of course occupy much of this time. Between four and six I take a walk of three or four miles. Dine from about half past five to seven, and from dark till about eleven I generally pass the evening in my chamber, signing land-grants or blank patents." By the end of his term he was rising each morning at a quarter past four. In the summer, with his servant Antoine, who had remained with him from the days of Ghent, he went swimming in the Potomac, sometimes fighting the current for an hour and a quarter without touching ground, and on more than one occasion having a close escape from being drowned. One day, when they had started across the river in an unseaworthy canoe with the idea of swimming back, the canoe sank under them, and although Antoine, who was wholly naked, reached the shore easily, Adams, who was partly clothed, was so much impeded by the loose sleeves of his shirt that, as he said, "while struggling for life and gasping for breath, [I] had ample leisure to reflect upon my own indiscretion." Finally gaining the opposite shore, he sat there, stripped in the sunshine, while Antoine, clothed in what few garments the President had worn, went to fetch the presidential carriage to drive him back to the White House, half dressed. A week later, going back to his usual swimming place, he found a crowd dragging the bottom for the body of a drowned man. The swimming escapades of the President caused his friends much anxiety, but he himself felt that he could not carry the strain of his life without them.

By the end of 1827 it was clear that Adams could be sure of nothing but the New England states in the next election. New York was the scene of conflict between the contending groups adhering to Van Buren and Clinton, but Clinton's sudden death in February 1828 and Van Buren's astute capturing of the allegiance of the Clintonians spelled ruin for Adams in that quarter. It became evident that the popular enthusiasm for Jackson would prove overwhelming. In January it was arranged to have a great celebration at New Orleans commemorating the battle, at which, of course, the military candidate could figure prominently. Politicians flocked from all over the country, and the newspapers were filled with accounts of the occasion and the speech made by the General, written for him by someone else.

Long before autumn there was little doubt of the final result of the election. The campaign, however, was waged with a ferocious disregard of decency that has never been equaled in our political history. The administration press heaped every possible obloquy on Jackson. As he had killed his man in a particularly cold-blooded duel, the charge of murder was easy, but in addition he was described as drunken, illiterate, a loose-liver — every possible epithet that might be made to blacken his character with the mob. Not content with attacking him, the press stooped so low as to attack the good name of his wife. Mrs. Jackson, who in her girlhood had made a most unhappy marriage with a man who turned out to be a wretched creature, had understood that a divorce had been secured when she married Jackson. Unfortunately the divorce proceedings had not been legally consummated. As soon as the error could be rectified, another marriage ceremony had been gone through, and the lifelong union with the General was a devoted and happy one. The dragging of her name into the campaign in order to defeat her husband was a lasting disgrace to American political life, which has all too often been equally unsavory.

Adams, of course, had nothing to do with this filthy libel. Whether, as Jackson claimed, he could have kept it out of the papers by the use of his influence it is impossible to say. The countenancing of such an attack would be wholly out of character with Adams's entire life, and at this time he would have had only that modicum of influence over editors which a completely defeated candidate would have. The battle was lost, and the partisan editors knew that it had in part, at least, been lost because of what they regarded as Adams's Puritanical squeamishness in practical politics, and when passions were unleashed, as they have never been in any campaign before or since, they may well have declined to listen to any more of Adams's scruples.

On the other side, the Jackson press was equally unscrupulous in attack. Adams was accused of having dissipated habits. It was claimed that he had stolen enormous sums of public money, that he had made the fraudulent bargain with Clay, and, even, that when Minister at St. Petersburg he had played the pander and ruined the life of a beautiful American girl by procuring her for the lust of a Russian nobleman.

It is needless to dwell longer on the campaign in which democracy came into its own and secured control of the government. The result of the election was a foregone conclusion. When the votes were counted, Jackson had one hundred and seventy-eight, and Adams only eighty-three. The President had the added bitterness of having been defeated by a man whose own career might have been broken long since had Adams not been his staunchest defender. Jackson had many admirable traits and developed an ability as President that could not have been foreseen, but we may adopt Professor Channing's verdict that "on the whole, possibly, it was more honorable to have been defeated in 1828 than to have been elected."

Defeated Adams was, and soundly. On February 11 Jackson arrived in Washington, and, the electoral votes being counted that day, his hotel at once became the centre of Washington. It swarmed with office-seekers and all who had, or hoped to show they had, some claim upon him for service rendered in the campaign. In the White House, Adams, his hands now empty of gifts and power, lived almost deserted. On the twenty-eighth he wrote in his diary: "Three days more, and I shall be restored to private life and left to an old age of retirement, though certainly not of repose. I go into it with a combination of parties and of public men against my character and reputation such as I believe never before was exhibited against any man since the Union existed. Posterity will scarcely believe it, but so it is, that this combination against me has been formed, and is now exulting in triumph over me, for the devotion of my life and of all the faculties of my soul to the Union, and to the improvement, physical, moral, and intellectual, of my country. The North assails me for my fidelity to the Union; the South, for my ardent aspirations of improvement. Yet 'bate I not a jot of heart and hope.' Passion, prejudice, envy, and jealousy will pass. The cause of Union and of improvement will remain, and I have duties to it and to my country yet to discharge." Words more prophetic than the saddened man could possibly then have foreseen!

The bitterness of the campaign had been too great to allow of personal intercourse between the candidates. Adams sent a courteous message to Jackson, who had not communicated with the President in any way since his arrival, to say that he and his family would move out of the White House before the fourth of March so that Jackson might receive his congratulations there after the Inauguration, but Jackson merely returned thanks for the offer and told Adams not to hurry. Adams wrote that Jackson's avoidance of the usual courtesies toward himself had been noticed by the newspapers and that the reason assigned was that he had been concerned in the attack on Jackson's wife in the *National Journal;* to which Adams added in the diary: "This is not true. I have not been privy to any publication in any newspaper against either himself or his wife." He consulted the members of his cabinet as to whether it would be proper for him to attend the Inauguration, and, with the exception of Rush, they were unanimous against it. About nine in the evening of March 3 he left the White House with two of his sons and rode out to join the rest of his family, who had already moved out to Meridian Hill. The Republic as envisaged by the framers of the Constitution in 1787 had passed away. Democracy was in the saddle. The old order had gone, never to return. When Adams passed from the door of the White House into the dark of that March night perhaps even he did not realize that it was not the mere passing of a President and the close of an administration, but the end of an era.

VI

PAUSE

FOR some weeks Adams lingered at Meridian Hill, before returning to the old home at Quincy. He was sixty-two years old, but as yet in full vigor, and his father had lived for nearly thirty years longer than the age at which he now found himself without occupation. "I can scarcely yet realize my situation," he wrote a few days after leaving office. "Hitherto I have prayed for direction from above in concerns of my country and mankind. I need it not less, and pray for it with equal fervor, now, for those of myself, my family, and all whose dependence is upon me. From indolence and despondency and indiscretion may I be specially preserved!" Few persons came to call upon the man who was no longer the fount of power and possible gifts. Jackson in earlier days had declared that he would never forget the services Adams had rendered him. All the members of his administration had at one time and another been on friendly terms with Adams and had accepted his hospitality. With the exception of Van Buren, however, none now paid him the civility of even calling to pay the usual visit of ceremony. "After fourteen years of incessant and unremitted employment, I have passed to a life of total leisure," he wrote, "and from living in a constant crowd, to a life of almost total solitude."

The problem of how to employ his time was a serious one, mentally and financially. Some months earlier he had noted his situation in the latter regard. From the very day that his father had entered public service, that service, owing to the necessary expenses incurred in it as compared with the miserly salaries allowed for it, had been a constant drain on the meagre resources of the family rather than a source of gain. All of John Quincy's real estate in Boston and Quincy was mortgaged for the payment of his debts, including the $10,000 liability with which the family home had been bequeathed to him. His whole private income was less than $6000 a year, of which $2000 had to be allocated for interest on the mortgages. As we shall note later, a large proportion of the wealthy and influential element in Boston business and social life was bitterly hostile to him. A commercial career was obviously out of the question, and equally so was any attempt to re-study law and begin again to build up a practice after a lapse of nearly a generation. At first, to break the fall into complete leisure he turned to his books — Cicero, Plutarch, Shakespeare, even Bulwer-Lytton's novel of *Pelham*, then just off the press. Returning to Quincy early in the summer, he set to work to gather materials and to write the life of his father.

The return was not a happy one. The old home held sad memories for the son of Abigail and John. His own career seemed not only at an end, but had been broken in a way to leave rankling thoughts of bitterness. In addition, the most prominent and influential men in Boston and Eastern Massachusetts all turned the cold shoulder to the returned ex-President. In the course of the presidential campaign, William B. Giles of Virginia, a man of exceedingly low repute, had published a story that Adams had been convinced about 1808 that some of the Federalist leaders in Massachusetts were planning secession from the Union and that he had mentioned these fears to Jefferson and other Republicans. Some years earlier Giles had obtained a letter from Jefferson giving his hazy recollection of the affair, which, with the intent of bringing the name of the great Revolutionary patriot into the campaign against Adams, Giles published in the autumn of 1828.

Adams could well have afforded to ignore Giles, but thirteen of the leading Federalists of Massachusetts, including such men as Harrison Gray Otis, Henry Cabot, John Lowell, William Prescott, and T. H. Perkins, called on Adams publicly in print to name the men who he had asserted had been plotting treason in 1808 and to give the whole of the evidence he had for his assertion. Adams replied immediately. Jefferson had said in his letter that his memory was nearly a blank and that it was afflicting to him to be asked to recall, with the infirmities of eighty-three years, the details of an interview long years past. Adams had no difficulty in showing the error of Jefferson's version of the interview, gave his own, and in other respects offered a straightforward answer to the Federalist leaders. They refused to be satisfied and published a long document displaying the keenest resentment. Adams prepared a long reply, buttressed by documents and affording a complete vindication of himself. Most fortunately for his opponents, however, he decided with rare restraint not to publish it, and the reply, a volume of over four hundred pages, never saw the light until published by Adams's grandson, Henry, in 1877. Those opponents, bitterly reviling Adams, little dreamed that there reposed in the ex-President's desk a weapon by which their reputations could be blasted had their victim chosen to raise his finger. They were, however, the financially and socially elect of Boston, and Adams's return to live among them must have been greatly embittered by the knowledge of the injustice that they were wantonly inflicting upon his reputation. The grandson of one of them, a historian of ability and unbiased mind, wrote two generations later that a study of all the evidence had utterly convinced him, however reluctantly, that Adams had been "unquestionably and completely right," and that there was no escape from saying so. Happy were the thirteen, he added, in going down to their graves thinking they had had the last word of the controversy, and they must "have writhed beneath their moss-grown headstones on the day when *his* last word at length found public utterance." Adams had always been a fair fighter, but in this withholding of damning evidence against the men of high repute who were hounding him with unjust accusations he displayed a magnanimity that was far above the conception of any other public man of his day. With deep bitterness of spirit, but with a strong courage, he turned to his library and his farm for employment and consolation. A pleasant ray of sunshine among the dark clouds was his unexpected election to the Board of Overseers of his old college, Harvard.   But a much greater occasion of service was in store.

In September 1830, he was unexpectedly asked to allow his name to be voted on as a candidate for the House of Representatives from the farming district of Plymouth in which his home at Quincy was situated.   He replied that, if the people wished him to, he would serve them, but "I shall not ask their votes. I wish them to act their pleasure."   Of the 2565 votes in twenty-two towns, 1817 were cast for Adams and the rest scattered among several candidates.   On taking his seat, Adams announced to his constituents that he would hold himself accountable to no party and to no section, and it was on these terms, honorable alike to him and to them, that they returned him year after year until his death in the very hall of Congress itself.

For a man who had been Minister to several foreign countries, Secretary of State, and President, to begin again, as Clay said, like a boy, and go to Washington as a simple Congressman was an ordeal that few would have had the courage to face.   Adams himself was well aware of what he was undertaking, but, as he said to Clay in answer to his question, "labor I shall not refuse so long as my hands, my eyes, and my brain, do not desert me." The plunge into the new life, considered beneath his dignity by most of his friends, was made even more difficult by strong opposition within his own household, his son Charles Francis in particular being so opposed to his father's embarking upon this new and dangerous venture as seriously to impair, for a time, the happy relations between the two.   In 1828, soon after his defeat, he had lost his eldest son, George, by sudden death, and the second son was to be lost to him in 1833.   The business ventures of this last had also heavily involved the small fortune of Adams himself.   Charles Francis alone was prospering.   In November 1828 he had entered the law office of Daniel Webster and six months later had been admitted to the bar.   Some months after that, September 5, 1829, he had married Abigail Brown, a daughter of the wealthy merchant Peter Chardon Brooks, thus gaining for himself as father-in-law one of the richest men in Boston and a remarkable trio of brothers-in-law in Nathaniel L. Frothingham, William Emerson, and Edward Everett. Possibly the young man's new position in life added somewhat to his distaste for seeing his father enter once more the bloody arena of American political life instead of indulging in the dignity of retirement.

The old man, however, was right and the son was wrong. Not only were the greatest years of service still ahead, but those years were to win for the father the respect of the entire nation, even of his enemies. His feelings when the result of the election was known were set down at length in that diary to which as the years passed he came to turn, lonely and self-repressed, as one turns to a loved and trusted confidant. "No one knows," he wrote on November 7, "and few conceive, the agony of mind that I have suffered from the time that I was made by circumstances, and not by my volition, a candidate for the Presidency till I was dismissed from that station by the failure of my re-election. They were feelings to be suppressed; and they were suppressed. No human being has ever heard me complain. Domestic calamity, far heavier than political disappointment or disaster can possibly be, overtook me immediately after my fall from power, and the moment of my distress was seized by an old antagonist to indulge a hatred overflowing with the concentrated rancor of forty years, and who could not resist the pleasure of giving me what he thought the finishing blow at the moment when he saw me down. . . . In the French opera of Richard Cœur-de-Lion, the minstrel, Blondel, sings under the walls of his prison a song, beginning: —

> O, Richard! O, mon Roi!
> L'univers t'abandonne.

When I first heard this song, forty-five years ago, at one of the first representations of that delightful play, it made an indelible impression upon my memory, without imagining that I should ever feel its force so much closer home. In the year 1829 scarce a day passed that did not bring it to my thoughts. In the course of last winter a vacancy occurred in the Board of

Overseers of Harvard University. Absent, I was very unexpectedly elected to fill that vacancy. I attributed this to the
personal friendship and influence of President Quincy. But
this call upon me by the people of the district in which I reside,
to represent them in Congress, has been spontaneous and,
although counteracted by a double opposition, federalist and
Jacksonite, I have received nearly three votes in four throughout the district. My election as President of the United
States was not half so gratifying to my inmost soul. No
election or appointment conferred upon me ever gave me so
much pleasure. I say this to record my sentiments; but no
stranger intermeddleth with my joys, and the dearest of my
friends have no sympathy with my sensations."

VII

THE GREAT YEARS

JOHN QUINCY ADAMS believed profoundly in God.   For him God was not a rarefied philosophical abstraction, a mere name for the Unknown, but a Being who ruled the universe.   If His rule were not a beneficent one, all meaning would drop out of human existence and of human morality.   To deny that there was meaning to existence, and reality to moral belief and conduct, would be to commit intellectual and spiritual suicide. For Adams no amount of material comfort and well-being, either for the individual or the nation, could compensate for the void created by the denial of a God, and consequently of meaning in a moral universe.   Adams also believed that man had been given mind, and its product, science, for the purpose of improving the condition of the race.   He had also profoundly believed in his country.   It was blessed with unexampled riches of virgin soil and hidden wealth, with a form of government that appeared the most susceptible of any in the world of being utilized for the good of all the people, and the problem of governing for him had been that of so conserving the resources and administering the powers of government as steadily to raise the material, intellectual, and moral conditions of the entire nation.   With unquenchable faith and perhaps the most unflinching will of any American, he had set himself to the task. He had believed that the people would desire that which was good if they could see it.   He had believed that a government should be administered by trained men who should not be disturbed at their work so long as they did it well and with a single eye to the public welfare.   He had believed that the resources of the nation should be used wisely, not for private speculation, but as the source from which the nation could draw the means to promote its advancement of all sorts.   The government should be responsible to the people, but only to the best interests of that people, not to its low or sordid desires. In his own life he had exemplified this high ideal. If severe in his judgments on others, he was always even more so on himself. He had fought with iron will to make himself conform in every point to what he believed the moral pattern of the universe. He had fought with his whole strength to put his theory of government into practice when at the head of it. He had done his best to build up a trained public service uncontaminated by political corruption or fears. He had tried to develop a wise policy of conservation of the national resources. He had tried to foster education among the people, and to have them use their corporate power and wealth to advance science, which, as he believed, would inevitably improve both their material and spiritual condition.

All this must be taken into consideration when we encounter the bitterness of his comments on public life and public men in his latter years. Had he gone down to utter defeat on some such debatable question as to whether or not a tariff was good for fostering manufactures; or had he been a mere self-seeking politician striving for office by the usual means; or had he been a man who did not believe that anything, perhaps least of all moral issues, really mattered much — then the defeat, bitter as it might have been from the standpoint of his personal pride and ambition, would not have meant to him what the accession of Jackson and his party did mean. But when Adams saw the whole nation treat his belief in science with laughter and scorn; when he saw the civil service which he believed should be made up of experts ruined to make places for the lowest rabble of political hacks; when he saw a man whom he considered utterly uneducated preferred by an overwhelming majority of the people to himself; when he saw the Western lands, the heritage of the nation, plundered and pillaged to satisfy the greed of individuals; when he realized that all this was what the people really wanted, he could not but feel that evil had triumphed over good and that all the best elements of the nation had deserted their moral standards.

As he looked at the storm-clouds gathering above the problem of slavery he rightfully foresaw the terrific struggle that was to come, in which he believed the Union would be dissolved. He did not, nevertheless, for an instant lose his faith in God and in the fundamental morality of the universe. It was possible that his dream of a free people wisely governing themselves, and advancing, generation by generation, in comfort and intellectual and spiritual welfare, might have been shattered for the country to which he and his father had devoted the whole of their energies and lives, but it made him fight only the harder against all the forces and the individual leaders who were arrayed against the genuine good of the nation. It was to be a single-handed fight. He felt himself, and was, deserted by parties, by all the political leaders of the nation, by those in highest social standing in his native state, and by the press. Sustained only by the farmers of Plymouth, who returned him year after year to wage his bitter warfare against his opponents in Congress, the old man was to lay about him with his sword, slashing at everyone, right and left, with no fear of striking a friend, for he had none, until at the end he stood on a higher pinnacle of public esteem than any of his family before or since. He had traveled a long and flinty road since, a young lawyer in Boston, looking forward to the possibility of a career of service to the country he loved, he had never had a bitter word for any enemy. He cared nothing now for a career. He had reached the summit of any career America could offer and had been hurled from it. He saw his country given over to every force of greed and hate and ignorance. He was the servant of God, fighting God's enemies and his own, with his back against the wall. His fight was for human freedom — freedom from shackles in the South, freedom for the right to petition in Congress, freedom of the human mind in knowledge and science.

We cannot follow his long Congressional career in detail and can touch only on some of his more famous contests. On his way to Washington in November 1831 to take his seat, we may note a characteristic act. Passing through Philadelphia, he called upon Nicholas Biddle at the United States Bank and handed him a certificate of stock with the request that it be sold immediately, because, although the investment was a profitable one and Adams believed in the Bank, he felt that possibly he would be called upon to vote on some measure connected with it and therefore ought to have no personal interest in it.

Congress convened on the fifth of December and on the twelfth Adams presented fifteen petitions from Pennsylvania for the abolition of slavery and the slave trade in the District of Columbia. "It is so long since I was in the habit of speaking to a popular assembly," he noted in his diary, "and I am so little qualified by nature for an extemporaneous orator, that I was at this time not a little agitated by the sound of my own voice." Adams had always been opposed to slavery, and, although his real connection with the antislavery movement did not begin until about 1835, he had felt from the beginning that compromise was fatal. When South Carolina threatened nullification in 1832 he was for strong measures and was disgusted with the inconclusive handling of the situation by Jackson and Clay. He was for fighting it out and settling once for all the question of states' rights and secession.

That his usual opposition to Jacksonian policies was based on reason and not on mere dislike of the man was shown in 1835, when Adams, more than any other man in the House, stood by Jackson at a most critical moment and secured a unanimous vote for his action against France. By the treaty of 1831 France had agreed to pay the United States the sum of five million dollars in settlement of the spoliation claims, but after ratifying a solemn treaty had declined to pay. After waiting four years the patience of Jackson was properly exhausted; he recalled the American Minister from Paris and sent a message to Congress recommending that if France did not promptly comply with her agreement the United States should issue letters of marque against her commerce — that is, declare war. A signed treaty and national honor having both proved insufficient motives for France to fulfill her obligation, it was evident that force was the only alternative left, but a great many timid Americans opposed its use, and Adams almost alone, in a vigorous and patriotic speech, upheld his nation's rights. That in doing so he rescued the administration of his enemy Jackson did not for a moment weigh against what he felt to be his duty. Needless to say, occasional support rendered solely from a sense of duty called for no gratitude from Jackson, and, in spite of one abortive effort made to reconcile the two men, they continued on terms of the deepest hostility. In 1844, when, owing to his being in Boston, Harvard bestowed on the President the degree of Doctor of Laws, Adams refused to attend, writing to President Quincy that "as an affectionate child of our Alma Mater, I would not be present to witness her disgrace in conferring her highest literary honors upon a barbarian who could not write a sentence of grammar and hardly could spell his own name."

By 1835 there was, as Adams noted, "a great fermentation" of the subject of slavery throughout the Union. He himself had had no connection with any of the abolitionists or movements outside Congress, and declined to have any throughout his career, deeming, rightly, that his best service to the cause could be rendered by keeping strictly to his duties in that body. In the following years, as passions steadily mounted, his course brought down on him in ever-increasing force the wrath of the wealthy, conservative, and socially prominent people of the North, especially Boston, who wished nothing to be done to disturb the peace of the country and the profitable business which they carried on with the South. The almost constant feud which had existed between the Adamses and "State Street" had merely entered upon a new phase.

Meanwhile, he had continued to present petitions on the subject of slavery in the House. It had been the custom of that body, on receiving the petitions, to order them laid on the table, and when, on January 4, 1836, Adams presented a new one he stated that it was his intention to move to lay it on the table as usual. In the heat of the growing passion of the time on the slavery question, the pro-slavery men had been becoming more and more irritated by the constant stream of petitions, and on this day Adams was instantly interrupted in making his motion by John M. Patten, who asked the Speaker whether the petition had been received. The Speaker replied it had not, when Thomas Glascock, from Georgia, immediately moved that it should not be. Points of order were raised and the debate adjourned. On the eighteenth, the day to which the debate had been postponed, Adams presented several more petitions, when a New York Democrat, Gideon Lee, attempted to prevent the reception of them by the device of moving that the motion not to receive be laid on the table. This scheme was finally referred to a special committee, of which H. L. Pinckney was chairman. The report, made three months later, declared that Congress had no power to interfere with slavery in any state; that it ought not to interfere with it in the District of Columbia; and, since discussion of the topic was disquieting, all petitions regarding it should in future be laid on the table without being printed or referred and without any further action being taken on them. When the first resolution was read, Adams rose and pledged himself to prove it false, but he was forced to take his seat again amid wild cries of "Order!" and it was passed by a vote of 182 to 9. When the last of the three resolutions was also read, Adams again leaped from his chair and amid frantic cries from all over the House managed to finish a declaration that he considered the resolve "to be a direct violation of the Constitution of the United States, the rules of this House, and the rights of my constituents." Passed by an overwhelming majority, this "gag," as it was called, became a standing rule, abridging the constitutional right of the citizen to petition his government. The pro-slavery men had overreached themselves, and Adams was henceforth to receive support outside the House, not merely from the antislavery petitioners, but from a growing number of citizens whose sense of decency was outraged by the denial of constitutional guarantees.

Adams himself had now entered upon the great contest of his life, a struggle that was not limited by slavery, but that was waged for the maintenance of the constitutional rights of each and every citizen. Had the subject matter of the petitions been other than it was, Adams would have waged the same fight. He refused to be silenced by the "gag." At the opening of every session of Congress he moved to have it rescinded, only to be voted down year by year. In May 1836, opposing the annexation of Texas, he made what he considered the greatest speech of his career to that point, and noted in his diary that opposition to the extension of slavery "is a cause upon which I am entering at the last stage of life, and with the certainty that I cannot advance in it far; my career must close, leaving the cause at its threshold. To open the way for others is all that I can do. The cause is good and great."

In spite of the "gag," he continued to offer petitions to the House, and as his stand in the single-handed fight became known throughout the country these flowed in on him from all quarters. In February 1837, he asked the Speaker if the "gag" rule would apply to a petition from twenty-two persons who stated that they were slaves. Immediately the House was in a wild uproar, and motions to censure and even to expel Adams were hurled at the Speaker from all sides. When Adams was finally allowed to speak, he said that the wording of the resolutions condemning him were wrong, that he had not presented a petition, but had merely inquired whether a certain petition would be received under the rules of the House; and also that the petition was not, as his opponents had hastily concluded, an antislavery one, but one from slaves asking that slavery should *not* be abolished. As to the allegation that he had introduced frequent petitions for the abolition of slavery in the District of Columbia, Adams said that it was well known that he was opposed to the prayer contained in such petitions, but that what he stood for was the right of petition. When it was said by a member from Virginia that the Negroes named in the one that Adams held in his hand were of a low sort, Adams replied, "I adhere to the right of petition. . . . Petition is supplication — it is entreaty — it is prayer! And where is the degree of vice or immorality which shall deprive the citizen of the right to supplicate for a boon, or to pray for mercy? Where is such a law to be found? It does not belong to the most abject despotism. There is no absolute monarch on earth who is not compelled, by the constitution of his country, to receive the petitions of his people, whosoever they may be. The Sultan of Constantinople cannot walk the streets and refuse to receive petitions from the meanest and the vilest in the land. . . . The right of petition belongs to all; and so far from refusing to present a petition because it might come from those low in the estimation of the world, it would be an additional incentive, if such an incentive were wanting."

Thompson of South Carolina said that Adams ought to be hauled before the Grand Jury and that he would be if he were in South Carolina, to which Adams replied: "Thank God I am not a citizen of South Carolina! . . . Are we from the Northern States to be indicted as felons and incendiaries, for presenting petitions not exactly agreeable to some members from the South, by a jury of twelve men appointed by a marshall, his office at the pleasure of the President! If the gentleman from South Carolina, by bringing forward this resolution of censure, thinks to frighten me from my purpose, he has mistaken his man. I am not to be intimidated by him, nor by all the Grand Juries of the universe."

The petition proved probably to be a hoax, but that had nothing to do with Adams's position, save that he would not present it except to have its author convicted of forgery, but for four days the terrific debate on censuring him continued. In the course of the debate, which was of almost unparalleled violence and passion, Adams, although seventy years old, showed himself capable of holding all his antagonists at bay. In the end only about twenty voted for even the mildest and most indirect censure.

In April he wrote in his diary that "at this time the most dangerous of all the subjects for public contention is the slavery question. In the South, it is a perpetual agony of conscious guilt and terror attempting to disguise itself under sophistical argumentation and braggart menaces. In the North, the people favor the whites and fear the blacks of the South. The politicians court the South because they want their votes. The abolitionists are gathering themselves into societies, increasing their numbers, and in zeal they kindle the opposition against themselves into a flame; and the passions of the populace are all engaged against them." In September he noted that "the abolitionists generally are constantly urging me to indiscreet movements, which would ruin me and weaken and not strengthen their cause. My own family, on the other hand — that is, my wife and son and Mary — exercise all the influence they possess to restrain and divert me from all connection with the abolitionists and their cause. Between these adverse impulses my mind is agitated almost to distraction. The public mind in my own district and State is convulsed between the slavery and abolition questions, and I walk on the edge of a precipice every step I take."

He continued to present the petitions. On September 28, for example, he presented petitions for the abolition of slavery in the Territories; for refusing to admit any new slave states into the Union; and for the prohibition of the inter-state slave trade. With the last he asked leave to bring in a resolution calling on the Secretary of the Treasury for figures of the imports and exports of slaves at our ports in the coasting trade, but, he says, "there was what Napoleon would have called a superb 'No!' returned to my request from the servile side of the House." The next day he presented fifty-one petitions and remonstrances against the "gag" rule, making in all about two hundred of these last since the rule had been passed. In November came the Alton riot and the murder of Lovejoy.

On December 21, after a wild scene on the preceding day, a resolution was again introduced to prevent the reading of a petition relating to slavery or the slave trade, and any action being taken on such petitions. When it came Adams's turn to declare his vote, "amidst" as he said, "a perfect war-whoop of 'Order!'" he succeeded in declaring it a violation of the Constitution, and of his right to freedom of speech as a member of the House.

The new year began, Adams noted, "with one of the most beautiful days that the course of the seasons ever brought round," but the year brought no cessation of fighting to him. On January 28 he received in the mail thirty-one petitions, which "consumed the whole evening in assorting, filing, endorsing, and entering them on my list." In the House on February 14 he presented three hundred and fifty. There was one, he wrote, "praying that Congress would take measures to protect citizens of the North going to the South from danger to their lives. When the motion to lay that on the table was made, I said that 'in another part of the Capitol it had been threatened that if a Northern abolitionist should go to North Carolina and utter a principle of the Declaration of Independence —'. Here a loud cry of 'Order! Order!' burst forth, in which the Speaker yelled among the loudest. I waited till it subsided, and then resumed, 'that if they could catch him they would hang him.' I said this so as to be distinctly heard throughout the hall; the renewed deafening shout of 'Order! Order!' notwithstanding. The Speaker then said, 'The gentleman from Massachusetts will take his seat;' which I did, and immediately rose again, and presented another petition."

The year ended as it had begun. On December 14, when called upon for a vote in connection with another aspect of the "gag" rule, Adams declined to answer merely "Aye" or "No." The Speaker insisted. "With a reinforced voice," Adams tells us, he said, "'I refuse to answer because I consider all the proceedings of the House as unconstitutional.' While in a firm and swelling voice I pronounced distinctly these words, the Speaker and about two-thirds of the House cried 'Order! Order!' till it became a perfect yell. I paused a moment for it to cease, and then said, 'A direct violation of the Constitution of the United States.' While speaking these words with loud, distinct, and slow articulation, the bawl of 'Order! Order!' resounded again from two-thirds of the House. The Speaker, with agonizing lungs, screamed, 'I call upon the House to support me in the execution of my duty!'. I then coolly resumed my seat."

The struggle, which must have told heavily on a man of Adams's age, was to continue for some years, but 1839 was notable for another episode which clearly brought out his character in another way. When Congress convened on December 2 of that year, the clerk began to call the roll of members as usual preliminary to the election of a Speaker and the organization of the House. When he reached New Jersey, he stated that there had been a contested election in that state and that he would pass over the names of the five contested seats, as he did not feel qualified to decide on their claims. It was, of course, his duty to read the names of those who presented the usual credentials from the state authorities, whatever might be the dispute at home. Moreover, the House was so nearly divided that these five might swing the balance one way or another. This assumption of power by the clerk raised a storm, and a violent debate ensued. Resolutions were offered, but the clerk ruled that he could put no question until the House had organized itself. The ruse was evident — that the House should organize itself and elect a Speaker without the deciding votes of the five New Jersey members. Day after day the futile debate went on. The deadlock seemed as desperate as it was ridiculous. Throughout Adams had maintained a complete silence, but nothing had escaped him. On the fourth day, when the clerk had once more come to New Jersey in the roll, suddenly Adams rose in his seat, grasping the edge of his desk, as was his custom, to help him rise. "I rise," he said, "to interrupt the Clerk." The House sensed at last that a leader had risen, and there were cries throughout the confused hall of "Silence! Silence! Hear what he has to say! Hear John Quincy Adams!" Utter silence fell upon the entire assembly. Adams, with a withering look at the clerk, said in a quiet voice that it had not been his intention to take part in these extraordinary proceedings. He had hoped that the House would organize itself. But the clerk, the mere clerk, whom the House employed, had usurped the throne to himself. If he refused to do his duty and if the House could not organize itself in any other way, then let it imitate the example of the

Virginia House of Burgesses, which, "when the colonial Governor Dinwiddie ordered it to disperse, refused to obey the imperious and insulting mandate, and, like men —" At this point the old man was interrupted by deafening cheers that, as a newspaper said next day, "seemed to shake the Capitol to its center." Adams then made a motion requiring the clerk to call the roll. But, as the clerk had for four days refused to put the question so that a motion could be acted on, Adams was greeted by cries of "But how shall the question be put?" "Who will put the question?" Then suddenly the force of character showed itself. Above the tumult, the voice of Adams was heard: "*I* intend to put the question *myself!*" For four days the House had been, as Mr. Wise of Virginia said, a mob. Now at last character had triumphed over chaos. A man had taken the lead because he had dared to say *I*. The wildest enthusiasm broke loose. Rhett, of South Carolina, jumped on a chair and moved that Adams take the Speaker's chair until the House could organize. "One universal, deafening, thundering AY responded to the nomination," and the man so hated by the South was led to the chair by Rhett of South Carolina and Williams of North Carolina. Wise of Virginia, turning to Adams, said, "Sir, I regard it as the proudest hour of your life; and if, when you shall be gathered to your fathers, I were asked to select the words which, in my judgment, are best calculated to give at once the character of the man, I would inscribe upon your tomb this sentence: 'I will put the question myself.'"

It was, indeed, a proud moment, and Wise was right in that it exemplified the essential character of the old fighter. John Adams had said, "I will take the responsibility," in the negotiations in Paris when a pusillanimous Congress at home wished to betray the country. Now John Quincy rescued its successor by again using that simplest but rarest of formulas in public life, "*I* will." The triumph, however, was short-lived. The passions of political life in that era were too intense to give more than momentary show of courtesy to an enemy. When Adams returned to his weary task of fighting for civil liberty under the Constitution, the whole pack were on his trail once more, and none were more insulting than Wise. Adams occupied the chair for eleven days, when Hunter of Virginia was duly elected Speaker. There was some talk of moving a vote of thanks to Adams, but he declined to allow it to be put, noting in his diary that "in the rancorous and bitter temper of the Administration party, exasperated by their disappointment in losing their Speaker, the resolution of thanks would have been lost if it had been offered."

Adams's health was failing, but he worked and fought unremittingly. He passed sleepless nights, and on one occasion when attending a session in the House he went twenty-eight hours without food. His voice at times was feeble, and his eyesight troubled him greatly. Every calumny was heaped upon him, the rumor even being sent around that he was insane. In 1842 a terrific attack was launched against him in the House in an endeavor to have him tried for perjury or treason. For ten days he fought his enemies, Rufus Choate being one of the few men who came to offer their assistance. The strain was terrible. One evening he notes in his diary: "My dear wife, in her kind and affectionate assiduity and in her anxious and faithful solicitude for me, overplied the energies of her nature, so that she suffered this day a fainting fit; but it was transient, and she soon recovered, and was up again when I returned this evening from the House." In the midst of the combat an anonymous letter threatened him with assassination. The administration journal, the *National Intelligencer*, refused to print his speech of self-defense. Finally, when the vote was taken and Adams won, he wrote, "I came home scarcely able to crawl up to my chamber, but with the sound of 'Io triumphe' ringing in my ear." He was then seventy-five years old.

Year by year he continued to present the rejected petitions and move for the rescinding of the "gag" rule. The hostile majorities slowly declined in size. Ultimate victory seemed to be coming if his life held out. Finally, on December 3, 1845, when the old man was seventy-eight, the vote on rescinding the "gag" showed 108 votes in favor against 80 opposed. Adams had won. "Blessed, forever blessed, be the name of God" were the words with which he closed his diary for that day. There had been barely time. Within a year, on November 19, 1846, he was struck by paralysis, and although he recovered from this first stroke he could not have continued the fight, although he remained in Congress. When he returned to that body from Boston, where the seizure had occurred, every member rose in homage and stood while the feeble old warrior who had fought them all was led to his chair by two of the members.

In following his career in Congress we have neglected innumerable matters, for want of space, in which he took active part. In them he displayed the same independence of judgment and indomitable courage as in the great struggle which we have briefly described. One matter, however, we may mention as being closely connected with one of the abiding passions of his life — the love of science and the desire for its diffusion in his country. In 1835, an Englishman, James Smithson, bequeathed his estate, valued at over a half-million dollars, to the United States to establish an institution "for the increase and diffusion of knowledge among men." Adams was made chairman, first of a committee to decide whether the bequest could legally be accepted, and, after that point had been decided, of another committee to consider how to apply the fund. The money was received, but Congress evinced no interest in the matter, beyond making a political job of investing it in bonds that defaulted on their interest and seemed all too likely to do so on their principal. For eight years Adams labored to have proper use made of the bequest. When the money was lost, he pointed out that the United States had pledged itself to carry out the purposes of the donor when it accepted the legacy and that its honor was involved. Finally, he had the pleasure of seeing, solely as a result of his own determined efforts, the fund safely invested and the Smithsonian Institution established, although he was balked in his greatest desire, that of applying part of the money to the erection of an astronomical observatory, a project that he had labored for publicly since his first Message as President. Congress did at last appropriate the money for one, but did it in such a way as to disconnect Adams's name from the matter.

Adams's love of science was pure and disinterested, but it was closely connected, as we have seen, in his mind with the problem of government. An ignorant people, of low mental and moral grade, could be governed, but such a people could not govern itself. If democracy were to succeed it would have to be by bringing up the general level to such a point as to make the people intellectually and morally capable of doing so. In a democracy, therefore, the spread of enlightenment was an essential part of the problem of government. The continued refusal of Congress to take the slightest interest in the spread of education or the advancement of science was thus of the deepest concern to Adams, and as he watched the democracy itself almost wholly concentrated on a competitive struggle to gain merely material wealth his hopes for its future steadily declined. In 1843, however, he was informed that the first observatory in America was to be built at Cincinnati, and he was asked to deliver the address at the laying of the cornerstone in November. He was then seventy-six years old and far from well. A western journey by the means of transport then available was a long and extremely wearying one, and, taken in winter, the danger to his health, and even life, was great. A trip earlier in the year through the state of New York had demonstrated that his popularity had greatly increased among the people, and what had been intended as a health excursion for his daughter-in-law had turned out to be a continual ovation for himself. He determined, regardless of the result to himself, to make the journey to Cincinnati and to throw the weight of whatever influence and popularity he might possess into increasing the interest of the people in science and calling attention, in a marked way, to this building of the first observatory. Everywhere along the route he was received with what to him was unaccustomed applause. Without any consideration for his age and condition, he was called upon over and over again to make speeches and public appearances. The physical hardships of the trip, utterly unknown to our generation, proved greater than he had anticipated. He performed the duty he had set out to do, but finally reached the East again almost a physical wreck, and never entirely recovered from the immense strain.

His activity during the last dozen years of his life was almost incredible. In addition to the struggle which we have outlined for the right of petition, he took active part in the debates on such matters as the tariff, the annexation of Texas, and others in which controversy ran high. He made many long addresses, mostly on historical topics, before the New York Historical Society and other bodies and audiences throughout the North-eastern states. He continued to read widely in history, government, and the classics, and solaced himself with that translating of poetry that had been a hobby from his youth.

Meanwhile, he was watching with much interest the career of his son Charles Francis. Possessed of ample means through his marriage, he could afford to turn to more interesting ways of spending his time than building up a law practice. If the father watched over the son with paternal pride, the son also looked after the father with filial duty. John Quincy, though exceedingly economical, had never been a good business manager, and after his losses his independent income, with the modest addition of $1500 to $2000 a year as member of Congress, could not have left him free to continue his career had not his son taken complete charge of the old man's finances and made a reasonable degree of comfort and peace of mind possible to him.

The younger man, like all the family since its change of phase, had strong literary tastes and a desire to write, and from 1829 to 1843 had been contributing regularly to the *North American Review*, writing in all seventeen articles, mostly on historical topics. In 1835 he had written articles on the Patronage Bill, then discussed in Congress, which were published in pamphlet form some months later, and which, under the title of *An Appeal from the New to the Old Whigs*, brought the young man his first genuine fame apart from that reflected by his family connections, although its authorship was by some attributed to the father. Almost until his father's death, indeed, the son was not unnaturally overshadowed by him in the public eye, although the younger man continued an active contributor on public topics to various newspapers and magazines. In 1840 he published the letters of his grandmother, Abigail Adams, which met with instant success from the public, but which, of course, added nothing to his own literary reputation, save for a long Introduction prefixed to the volume.

In 1840 the younger Adams was elected to the state legislature as one of the forty-odd representatives of the city of Boston, and, much to his surprise, received the highest number of votes on the list. Writing to him on this occasion, his father pointed out that he feared the son was too sensitive for the battles of public life, its "opposition and defeats and slanders and treacheries, and above all fickleness of popular favor," but added: "Let me entreat you, whatever may happen to you of that kind, never to be discouraged or soured. Your father and grandfather have fought their way through the world against hosts of adversaries, open and close, disguised and masked; with many lukewarm and more than one or two perfidious friends. The world is and will continue to be prolific of such characters. Live in peace with them; never upbraid, never trust them. But — 'don't give up the ship!' Fortify your mind against disappointments — *aequam memento rebus in arduis servare mentem* — keep up your courage, and go ahead!" Young Adams remained in the legislature five years, three in the Lower House and two in the Senate, and acquitted himself with success. On the last day before his voluntary retirement, he wrote: "My resolutions placing the Whig party and the State on the basis of resistance to slavery in the general government, passed the House by a vote of five to one, and constitute, as it seems to me, a fair termination of all my labors." Of the work in which he was engaged at the time of his father's death, not long after, we shall speak later, and must now return to the older generation.

After his stroke, the elder Adams, though constant in his attendance in the House of Representatives, never but once more rose to speak in that body. On February 21, 1848, he was at his seat as usual, when he was seen partially to rise. The Speaker was putting a question when suddenly there were cries of "Stop! Stop! Mr. Adams!" The old man had fallen insensible. He was carried to the Speaker's room and the House hastily adjourned. Doctors were summoned, but they could do nothing. The end was near. It was decided not to move him, and he lay there until the evening of the twenty-third. He recovered speech and consciousness only once, when he murmured, "Thank the officers of the House," and then, clearly, "This is the last of earth! I am content!"

THE THIRD GENERATION
CHARLES FRANCIS ADAMS

CHARLES FRANCIS ADAMS

I

BOSTON AND QUINCY

PETER CHARDON BROOKS died January 1, 1849. He left what was then estimated as the largest fortune in Boston, about two million dollars. To each of his sons-in-law — of whom, of course, Charles Francis Adams was one — he bequeathed seventy-five thousand dollars, dividing the rest of his estate equally among his seven children. Mr. and Mrs. Adams must thus have inherited about three hundred thousand dollars, a handsome fortune in the middle of the last century. For the first time, an Adams was also a rich man. The deaths of his father and father-in-law within a few months of each other had given Charles Francis, in a double sense, independence. He was then but forty-two years of age, and the fame and fiery character of his father had made it difficult for the son to be known independently of his relation to the old man who was so continuously — we may say obstreperously — in the public eye. With the passing of that indomitable figure, the way was opened for Charles Francis to be himself. With the death of Brooks, the way was opened to him also, financially, to any career he might choose. At this crucial point in his life we must look, therefore, both at the man and at his environment.

His son, Henry, wrote that long after his father's death he and his brothers used to discuss the quality of his mind and temper, and he and his brother, the younger Charles Francis, have left their impressions of both. The Adamses had never been companionable. "The Adamses," James Russell Lowell once wrote in a letter (and his editor, Charles Eliot Norton, was not a little embarrassed to have one of them confirm the truth of the statement), "have a genius for saying even a gracious thing in an ungracious way." We may recall Sir John Temple's comment on John Adams in Paris in 1782 as "the most ungracious man he ever saw." Charles Francis, in the opinion of at least one of his sons, was even less companionable than old John Quincy in his latter years. He had the Puritan traits, the New England conscience of his ancestors, without their firm belief in the Puritan theology. On the other hand, he had, in Henry's opinion, the most perfectly balanced, in fact the only perfectly balanced, mind in the whole family line. The mind was not bold like John's, or restless like John Quincy's, but "worked with singular perfection, admirable self-restraint, and instinctive mastery of form." His Puritan nature, like that of all the Adamses, was restrained, inhibited, touchy, and reserved. Henry says that he never showed a shade of vanity, self-conceit, or snobbishness, and that he was utterly indifferent to social distinction. On the other hand, he appears to have been sensitive to social dislike. In his earlier days, at least, he was morbid and introspective, as all his race had been. He felt keenly the antagonism of Boston, politically and socially. The unhappy days of the past weighed on him, and even when he was serving in the legislature, with Bostonians evidently feeling kindly toward him and interested in him, he could not become kindly and sympathetic in return. His marriage had of necessity brought him into close social contact with that portion of Boston which had been bitterly opposed to his father and grandfather.

He may have had, as Henry claimed, the most perfect judgment of all the family, but certainly in his deep opposition to his father's entering upon a Congressional career he was wrong and his father was right. In his opposition to that course, in his inability to share his father's feelings as to slavery, in the very perfection of his mental poise, one finds a something lacking at this point in the family line that had constituted a driving force hitherto. In other respects it was to remain as before. It would insist as always upon absolute independence of judgment and action. It would be ready to assume responsibility

F. P. Vinton

Wm. M. Hunt

Mr. and Mrs. Charles Francis Adams

(By permission of Mrs. F. R. Nourse)

and stand alone, however unpopular and however solitary. It
was as keen as ever to have its hand on the lever of power. I
am not sure but that Henry has given us a clue in his description
of the "mental calm of the Unitarian clergy."   Of all the conditions of his youth, he wrote as an old man, nothing puzzled
him more than the complete disappearance of religion. "The
children reached manhood without knowing religion, and with
the certainty that dogma, metaphysics, and abstract philosophy
were not worth knowing."   The high priests of Boston had
become Theodore Parker, Octavius Frothingham, and Waldo
Emerson.   After one has lived with John Quincy through the
pages of his *Diary*, heard his agonized prayers and his impreca-
tions on his and God's enemies, one realizes as never before that,
however more justifiable intellectually a mild deism may be,
it is no substitute as a driving force, in a solitary man fighting a
nation on what he believed to be a moral principle, for the
stronger religious feeling of the earlier generation.   Since the
change of phase in the Adams family, they had fought the world
on the side of the Puritan God.   That world, politically, had
been becoming more and more impossible for an Adams, but
somehow John Quincy, after a fourteen-year struggle, had
brought it round to do his bidding.   The Puritan God might
or might not have possessed Reality, but John Quincy would
never have deflected the political world — already so wide of
the orbit in which the Adamses had traveled, and always would
travel — unless he had believed with all his soul in that Reality.
Around 1850 the Puritan God evaporated, leaving only the
New England conscience.   The Adamses were, so to say, left
alone in the cosmos to recapture a political world that was
whirling into space far off from the line of their own family
orbit, intellectually and morally.   The fanaticism, if we are
forced so to designate it, of John Quincy had been succeeded
in the family line by a perfectly balanced mind.   But the
world in which that mind had to act was not perfectly balanced.
It was a wild welter of base passions.   There was, perhaps, no
decrease in the family ability in Charles Francis Adams.   He
was to prove himself for several critical years the ablest diplo-

mat in the family line and the match for the strongest of his country's enemies. That line, however, was moving straight onward without deflection, whereas the line that American public life was following was describing a wide curve that was carrying it far from the common starting point of both in the eighteenth century. The mass of the nation was infinitely greater than the mass of the Adams family. It was evident that the Adamses could no longer deflect the nation, and, contrary to physical laws, it was impossible for the nation to deflect the Adamses. They stood firm on their own beliefs and standards.

The American scene that Adams contemplated when the death of John Quincy left him head of the family was a very different one from that of a generation earlier. The population had mounted to twenty-three millions, and the chief city, New York, with its seven hundred thousand inhabitants, had become one of the great cities of the world. Ten million Americans were living in the Mississippi Valley and around the Gulf. In spite of John Quincy's violent opposition, Texas had been added to the Union, and at the end of the war with Mexico in 1848 the great cession of the Southwest and California had also been added to the national domain. It was the era of "Manifest Destiny," and the raw democracy of the West, backed or exploited by the capitalists of the East, had entered upon an orgy of material utilization of the national resources. In 1830 there had been scarcely a mile of railroad in the country. By 1850 nine thousand miles were in operation. The telegraph had begun to link distant communities into instantaneous communication. The needed capital was suddenly discovered. A few weeks after annexation, gold was found in California, and in 1848 five million dollars was sent East, forty millions in 1849, fifty millions in 1850.

The political world also presented a new aspect. If population had doubled between 1830 and 1850, the electorate had tripled, indicating a large extension downward in the scale. In the same period illiteracy had increased from 3.77 per cent to 5.03 per cent. A permanent wage-earning class had come into existence.   Everywhere, except in the South, aristocracy in the old American sense had been driven from political power.   The presidential campaign of 1840, almost more than the campaign of 1828, showed how the political centre of gravity had shifted, and for the first time brought out the full voting strength of the people.   It is indicative of the change that although the Whig candidate was a man of wealth, living as a country gentleman in a large house on an extensive estate, it was considered necessary to picture him as living in a log cabin, drinking hard cider and swinging an axe with a coonskin cap on his head. The mob had come into power and it was henceforth for them to call "thumbs up" or "thumbs down" over the contestants in the political arena.   Emotion would henceforth count for more than mind.   The new ruling dynasty was the crowd, in whose reign we still live, and the crowd exhibits the same qualities in all countries and all ages.   On the very morning on which I write these lines, far from America, in what is perhaps still the most stable country in the world, with the least emotional people, I read in the morning paper, regarding an exhibition of crowd emotion yesterday at an inquest, that "it is a sad reflection on democracy that those who could not restrain their feelings or exercise their brains during the Reading inquest are a part of that vast engine of the electorate that controls the destinies of a great nation. . . . Examples are constantly occurring in which the crazy adulation of the crowd is showered impartially on the just and the unjust, on the famous and the notorious, with a total lack of discrimination.   To-day it may be a film star, to-morrow a Minister of State, the day after a criminal or a prize fighter. . . .   He who is applauded one day may the next day be reviled."   The transfer of power to the crowd came first in America, and it came most markedly during the youth of Charles Francis.   His father was right when he warned him of what would have to be expected in public life.

Entrance into such a life had also come to be controlled in a new way.   The convention system of nominating candidates for office was inaugurated in 1831 and by 1840, in spite of the opposition of such men as Webster and Calhoun, had become firmly established, with the rule in the Democratic party that a candidate must receive a two-thirds vote of all the delegates. Moreover, in the 1840's the dual party system had become firmly entrenched. Practically all of the electorate "were tagged, and proud of their tag." The only entrance to public life on the national stage came to be as a party man through the favor of the political machine. If one had to be a party man in order to arrive, it was also becoming evident that one would have to remain a strict party man in order to remain. The case of Tyler, who became President by accident on the death of Harrison, brought squarely before the public the moral issue of whether he should remain true to his own views or vote on party lines. His decision to do the former ended his political career and he was never again elected or given a public office. In the next administration more conclusive evidence was added. In that case, Dallas, the Vice-President, was placed in a similar situation, not through the death of the President, but by the political manœuvres of his enemies. He cast his vote in the Senate against his own beliefs and in favor of the party, and at the end of his term was appointed Minister to England. The double lesson was clear enough to anyone who dreamed of holding public office, even if he could get it, and of retaining his intellectual and moral integrity. An Adams might be sent to Congress by his neighbors in the Plymouth district, but presumably he would never be sent to the White House by a major party convention.

From the time when Adams had returned from his Ealing school with his father at the end of the Ministry to England in 1817, he had never returned to Europe, but had spent his whole time between Boston and Quincy. At first he lived in the house on what was then Hancock Avenue, a street running from Beacon Street to Mount Vernon Street, almost skirting the State House grounds. There, preceded by the birth of a daughter, Louisa, afterwards Mrs. Charles Kuhn of Philadelphia, his three older sons were born — John Quincy, September 22, 1833, Charles Francis, Jr., May 27, 1835, and

Henry Brooks, who was to drop his middle name in later life, on February 16, 1838. In 1842 Mr. Brooks presented his daughter with a house at 57 Mount Vernon Street, and the family continued to reside there until after Adams's death, and there the fourth of the four children with whom we shall be concerned in later chapters was born and named Brooks, June 24, 1848. There was also another son, Arthur, who died when only five years old, and another daughter, who became the wife of Dr. H. P. Quincy of Dedham.

At Quincy, which was then rural, and not reached by a railroad until 1846, the family had a house similar in type to that of the old one in which John Quincy lived and not far removed from it. There they spent the summers, and Henry has given us a vivid description of the impression left on him as a child of the alternate seasons between town and country life. When the children first went there, the old President grandfather, John Quincy, was still living, and appears to have impressed them all. The boy Charles, late in life, recorded his memory of him: "An old man, absorbed in work and public life. He seemed to be always writing — as, indeed, he was . . . a very old-looking gentleman, with a bald head and white fringe of hair — writing, writing — with a perpetual ink-stain on the fore-finger and thumb of the right hand." Both Charles and Henry agree that the old man was always kind to the children and liked to have them in his library, but "his was not a holiday temperament. Always unaccompanied, he used to wander about the ragged, unkempt old place — with its pear and cherry trees, and old-time orchard — hatchet and saw in hand, pruning and watching his seedlings." Henry also recalls his grandmother, the storm-tossed wife of the old man, even less fitted than her husband "to impress on a boy's mind the standards of the coming century," so singularly peaceful she seemed, "a vision of silver gray, presiding over her old President and her Queen Anne mahogany; an exotic like her Sèvres china; an object of deference to everyone, and of great affection to her son Charles" — hardly more Bostonian, however, than fifty years before.

The children, although they did not know it, were watching the passing of one era and the coming of a new. In driving back and forth between Boston and Quincy, indeed, they were constantly passing between the one era and the other, so close were they to each other and so timed was the childhood of the youngest generation. At Quincy, until he died, the old ex-President lit his own fire each morning with flint and steel. Heat came only from the hearths, light from candles; of bathroom and conveniences there were none. On the other hand, the magnificence of the grandfather Brooks's house in Boston belonged to the era of Californian gold and extending railroads, of plumbing and furnace and gas. The grandfather in Quincy presented each grandchild at birth with a Bible; the grandfather in Boston, a silver mug. Yet the children, for the most part, clung symbolically to Quincy.

Their father, as we have seen, had retired from the state legislature, after five years' service, in 1845. He had done his duty, and the path seemed to lead no further. The legislature was good enough for a while as a legislative school, but the topics to be dealt with were for the most part small and local, and Adams felt that to remain too long had a tendency to narrow the mind by confining it within too close a range. With characteristic Adams bent, he had concerned himself as far as possible in his service with the larger issues, such as the Latimer slave case, Texan annexation, and others as they came up, in each case, again characteristically, dwelling elaborately on the law and principles involved.

II

ANTISLAVERY

ORIGINALLY a Democrat, Charles Francis Adams had changed to the Whig side some years before entering the legislature, mainly on account of his growing interest in the slavery question. Little by little, his father's stubborn fight in Congress had enlisted his sympathy and affected his ideas. A great impetus to his feeling had come as result of what he witnessed at the Faneuil Hall meeting of 1837 in connection with the Lovejoy murder at Alton. A few days before, he noted that he had had "a warm argument" in his father-in-law's house with three of his wife's relatives regarding abolition and mobbing. "They are always of the conservative order, and I cannot often be," he added. His balanced mind, however, prevented his going whole-heartedly with either side. "I wish I could be an entire abolitionist," he wrote a fortnight later after his cousin, Edmund Quincy, had thrown himself on that side with a public speech. "But it is impossible," he noted. "My mind will not come down to that point." From 1830 to 1850, the United States, and notably Massachusetts, abounded in "isms" of all sorts. Cranks, fanatics, idealists, spread over the land like locusts, none of them appealing to "a perfectly balanced mind." If, however, Adams could not give rein to his emotions rather than his intellect and become an abolitionist and a follower of Garrison and Phillips, he had, by 1844, become a determined antislavery man, and by about that year abolitionism had spent its force. Adams, and those who thought as he did, did not realize that the slavery problem, in little more than a dozen years, was to plunge the nation into war and drench it with blood. They did, however, see great danger if the situation as it was in 1846 continued unchecked, and wished to bring the discussion within constitutional limits. The Whig Party by that time had split into two parts, the "Conscience" and the "Cotton" Whigs, and Adams naturally was a prominent member of the first-named faction.

Adams's closest friends, who met frequently in his large library in the Mount Vernon Street house, were Charles Sumner, Richard H. Dana, and John G. Palfrey, the historian. In May 1846, this small group, with a few additional members, decided to organize what the Conscience Whigs in Massachusetts needed to get their views before the public, a daily paper, Adams supplying two fifths of the total capital required, and becoming the editor. Abolitionism had called for the dissolution of the Union as the only way to get rid of slavery. The Conscience Whigs, of whom Adams now became the mouthpiece, demanded that the Union be saved at all costs, and stated that the obvious first cost must be the total, and constitutional, abolition of slavery. Wealthy social Boston was thoroughly averse to disturbing the South in any way, and, hating the abolitionists, believed Adams was playing into their hands. Adams, on the other hand, was now thoroughly aroused and earnest and laid about him valiantly in his editorials. The Abbotts, Lawrences, and other leaders of Boston finance felt the lash. Within six months, the two factions in the Whig Party were irreconcilable. One or the other must conquer.

The test came at the famous state Whig Convention in Faneuil Hall, September 23, when, the Conscience Whigs having all but captured the organization, Abbott Lawrence left the meeting, presently to return with Daniel Webster on his arm. The statesman, regarded by many as a renegade to the cause of freedom, made a brief speech, and the convention closed after the Cotton Whigs had won. In the November elections, the Conscience Whigs were completely routed, though Palfrey managed to get to Congress a few weeks later by an extremely narrow margin in a special election. The National Convention of the party was held at Philadelphia in June 1848, and after four ballots, in which both Clay and Webster were defeated, nominated Zachary Taylor for President. The Conscience Whigs could not vote for a Southerner and a slave owner, and a few days before the vote was taken had consulted at Adams's office in Boston on bolting the party if such a condition arose. It was decided to hold a separate convention at Buffalo in August and organize and put a third party in the field, the Democrats having already met and nominated Cass.

Adams was elected a delegate from his father's old Congressional district, and at the convention was elected chairman. We need not here enter upon the difficult political position which confronted the new "Free Soil" party, which at best could only hope to succeed so far as to defeat Taylor, though its other wing, the "Barnburners," wished to defeat Cass for his treatment of Van Buren. Suffice it to say that the convention nominated Van Buren for President and Adams for Vice-President. In thus noting Adams linked with Van Buren on a national ticket we cannot but recall the election of 1828, when Van Buren was as much responsible as anyone for the defeat of John Quincy. The combination brings out the singular independence of the several generations. John Adams, in his old age, became reconciled to Jefferson and friendly with him, whereas John Quincy grew more and more bitter against his memory as he grew older. John Adams was hostile to Washington and John Quincy named his eldest son George Washington. In the last session of Congress the old man attended, 1848, he voted for Winthrop as Speaker of the House while Charles Francis was doing all he could to defeat him. And now Van Buren!

In the election in November the new party polled close to three hundred thousand votes, over 25 per cent of the total cast by all parties in the New England states and New York, and Adams emerged from the campaign a nationally known figure with a reputation, for the first time, wholly independent of his father and grandfather. In the campaign the rallying cry of the new party had been "Van Buren and Free Soil; Adams and Liberty," and the contest had at least disproved Rufus Choate's sneering reference in the campaign to John

Quincy as "the last of the Adamses." The new party, however, was not destined to remain a political force. The choice of Van Buren had been a mistaken and illogical one. Moreover, the death of Taylor and the accession of Fillmore to the Presidency altered the situation.

Adams's newspaper, the *Boston Whig*, had been far from profitable, and he had found the editorial and other supervision becoming more and more mere drudgery. In February 1848, he had severed his connection with it entirely. Both as editor of the *Whig* and as a leader of the Free Soil Party, Adams had taken an independent and courageous line in the antislavery conflict. The star of his friend Charles Sumner was now fast rising, and the leadership in Massachusetts naturally fell to him. Adams retired to his library and a task he had long had in his mind and close to his heart. He had often urged on his father the writing of a life of John Adams and the editing of his papers and correspondence, a task which John Quincy completely, and wisely, declined to assume. Adams now took it upon himself and in the years from 1850 to 1856 devoted himself almost wholly to it, the ten volumes of the *Works of John Adams* being the result. It is in this generation that we find the accumulated weight of the family's past beginning to make itself markedly felt. John Quincy and his career had, of course, been influenced by his father's fame, but the elder man, by his crushing defeat in 1800, had been wholly eliminated from the political field when the younger was yet but thirty-three years of age, by which time he had also acquired an independent reputation of his own by service on foreign missions while his father was in the centre of the stage at home. Moreover, there was but one generation between the son and the yeoman ancestry of the family in its first phase. Under the conditions of public life at the time he entered it, the achievements of his father did not constitute a crushing weight. For Charles Francis the situation was rather different. There were now two Presidents and two lives of public service of the premier order to be lived up to and by which defeat or success must be measured. Moreover, as we have pointed out, the changed conditions of public life had made success, for an Adams, much more difficult, if not impossible, to attain in elective office, and anything short of the highest success of all was beginning to spell failure. The weight of the past may also be noted in another particular. For John Adams there was no family past to be concerned with. His mind played wholly with ideas entirely disconnected with any thought of his family. For him the world was fresh. John Quincy resolutely declined to busy his mind with the achievements of the one generation before himself, and kept his mind open to the world about him. Charles Francis, it is true, had written much occasional material on current questions, but it is to be noted as significant that the two most important works that he had published up to his fifty-second year were lives of his own grandparents and editions of their letters and papers.

While the third generation was thus for some years busying itself with the first, the fourth was receiving its youthful education, which in its formal phase took the usual form of small private schools, then the Boston Latin School, followed in due course by graduation from Harvard — John Quincy in 1853, Charles in 1856, Henry in 1858, and the much younger Brooks in 1870. All agreed in later life as to the utter uselessness of their schooling, although they disagreed as to the value of Harvard. Charles also gave voice to what he considered a serious defect in the lack of any boyhood comradeship in outdoor life and sport. His father had evidently failed to profit by John Quincy's reiterated wishes that his children should be inured to an outdoor life and made to take an interest in it. John Quincy could leave his loved library and books to tramp for miles or to cast off his clothes on the bank of the Potomac and swim for an hour against the current. Charles Francis never tramped, in fact he scarcely knew what the country was like around his own house at Quincy, and never fished, swam, or sailed with his boys. He read aloud to them in his Boston library, and at his dinner table and in gatherings of his friends they heard as good talk as was to be heard anywhere, but the education so derived, although of the first quality, was almost solely political and literary. The small Henry, still a school-boy, corrected the proof of his father's life of *his* grandfather, and the weight of the past began to settle even more heavily on the fourth generation. The passion for writing, which had appeared so suddenly in the line with the first John, was growing steadily, and all the boys wrote for the college paper. Charles and Henry were both excessively sensitive and shy, making friends but slowly. Charles later noted in his *Autobiography* that he had not been popular in college or ever since, that with all the desire in the world to make friends he did not know how. Young John Quincy, on the other hand, seems to have escaped the family inheritance. He was what is called a "good fellow," with much social aptitude and charming manners and presence, popular with everyone.

The boys' father, having completed in 1856 his long toil on his grandfather's *Works*, was left without occupation and without any apparent opening in a public career. He had a high and deserved reputation throughout the nation, but the party with which he had been identified had disintegrated. He had been frequently mentioned for public office as one who would adorn it, but the current of practical politics swept along swiftly, leaving him on the bank. It was the period of the "Know-Nothing" party, which had carried all before it even in Massachusetts, and John Quincy's old district was represented in Congress by an otherwise utterly unheard-of man who had not had even a common-school education. A reaction followed, however, and in 1858, largely through the influence of Charles Sumner, Adams received the nomination for his father's Congressional seat and was elected by a handsome majority, a strong candidate, George R. Russell, having generously withdrawn in his favor.

Congress met in December 1859, but there was comparatively little for Adams to do. The House itself was largely impotent from the division of parties, and Adams's own party, the Republican, had almost no support in the executive branch of the government. It was also the year before the national election and, as usual, the main thought of Congress was on President-making. One of his best political friends had advised him to allow "no delicacy or scruples to stand in the way" of pushing himself forward for office or place, but this was obviously out of his character, and he found himself, when it came to naming committees, to have been shoved out of the way by men, including one of his own Massachusetts colleagues, who had not, perhaps, received the same advice, but who obviously did not need it.

Adams was an avowed supporter of Seward for the nominee as President, and the only speech which he made in the session was one strongly advocating the necessity of electing a Republican candidate as the only way of disentangling the country from its difficulties. Although clearly intended as a campaign document, and thus printed and distributed, it showed singular moderation and clear thinking at a time of passionate denunciation, and added considerably to Adams's reputation. When the Republican National Convention in May 1860 nominated Lincoln instead of Seward, Adams was disappointed, believing that although Lincoln was "honest and tolerably capable" he had had no experience. Nevertheless, he took an active part in the campaign, accompanying Seward on a speaking tour through the Northwest as far as St. Paul, although he had none of the qualifications of a campaign orator. In his own district he was reëlected without opposition, and he returned to Washington with the satisfaction of seeing the anti-slavery forces at last in charge of the government. When he closed his house at Quincy, the old house of his father into which he had moved after the latter's death, thinking that he was doing so only for the summer as usual, he little dreamed that he would not see it again for the seven most eventful years of his life.

Of his three sons who had already graduated from Harvard, John had been admitted to practice at the Bar; Charles had also become a lawyer, but had already realized that success for him would not lie in that profession; and Henry had gone off to Europe to study in Germany. Charles had accompanied his father to the Buffalo Convention as far back as 1848 and also on his speaking trip through the West in the campaign now just ended. In 1860 and again in 1861 he made long visits to his father in Washington, and by these means had formed a large acquaintance among public men, to complete the political education which he had daily received in his father's house. The fruits were beginning to show in his literary work, and he was greatly encouraged to have an article on "The Reign of King Cotton" accepted by Lowell for the *Atlantic Monthly*. During these years, like his forbears, he was keeping a diary which, unfortunately, he destroyed in later life and of which only a few extracts have come down to us. Among these, besides reports of significant conversations, are many excellent sketches of the men of the day. We see Seward, "small, rusty in aspect, dressed in a coat and trousers made apparently twenty years ago and by a bad tailor at that, lolling against the partition as he talked with my father or those about him, with a face and head in no way striking," and, again, the same states-man then looming so large in the public eye, "the same small, thin, sallow man, with the pale, wrinkled, strongly marked face — plain and imperturbable — the thick, guttural voice and the everlasting cigar." The boy meets Andrew Johnson in the House and notes that he has "a deep, black eye, and, with his somewhat neat black clothes and clean-shaven face" that he "looks, physically and intellectually, like a strong man." He hunts the Tennesseean up in his poor lodgings and finds him "stived up in one miserable room, littered with folded speeches and copies of public documents, and otherwise containing a bed and some scanty chamber furniture." There were talks with Seward and Sumner, all remarkable for a young man to record and making us deplore the destruction of the rest.

On returning to Washington, his father found the Republican Party divided on the policy to be followed, and looking to Seward for leadership. Almost immediately on organizing, both Houses of Congress appointed committees on the state of the Union, and Adams at once took the lead on his committee in the House as Seward did on his in the Senate. The period was an extremely dangerous one. The new administration would not come into power for nearly three months — not until the inauguration of Lincoln in March. Meanwhile the government was in the hands of the enemy, and no one knew what each day might bring. The South looked upon the election of the Republicans as a hostile move. What move might they make in turn before the new government was established and while they still possessed control of the machinery in Washington? Had the slave states at this most critical juncture been wholly united, they might have seized Washington and wrecked the nation before Lincoln became President. Fortunately they were not. The Southern tier was wholly so, but the border slave states, notably Virginia and Maryland, were still wavering. Clearly the part which the Unionists must play was above all else to work for time and to delay any overt act until the new government was established at the Capitol. On January 31, 1861, Adams made his only speech, a conciliatory and statesmanlike one. The hot-heads, however, could not see the need of the times, and Adams's speech lost him the friendship of Sumner.

It is true that Adams did not fully appreciate the inevitability of what must come, but the course he pursued is now generally recognized as the wise one. Working not by public speeches but on his committee and behind the scenes, he took the position that the Southerners on the committee must declare what they wanted, and managed to spin the months out in discussion and threshing out plans and proposals. Before the end came the Southerners had one and all resigned from the committee, but time, which was the one essential, had been gained. Lincoln was peacefully inaugurated on the fourth of March. A few weeks later Adams, defending his course in a letter, wrote, with the spirit of the true diplomat, that "our only course in the defenceless position in which we found ourselves was to gain time, and bridge over the chasm made by Mr. Buchanan's weakness."

With the inauguration of Lincoln, Seward passed from the Senate to the post of Secretary of State. Adams was mentioned for cabinet rank, but Lincoln wished to have only one

New England man among his advisers, and turned the choice, for Secretary of the Treasury, over to Senator Hamlin of Maine, who, for political reasons, decided on Gideon Welles of Connecticut. Without consulting Seward, a distinct breach of courtesy against the new Secretary of State, Lincoln had pitched on William L. Dayton as Minister to England and John C. Frémont as Minister to France. Seward naturally and properly objected to giving such a post to Frémont, and it was his own wish that Adams should go to the Court of St. James's. Lincoln, however, was convinced with much difficulty, though he finally agreed that Dayton should go to Paris and Adams to London. John Adams had negotiated peace between England and his country in 1783 and then, when feeling was most bitter against him and his people, had represented the new nation at the Court of the King. John Quincy also had made peace after the War of 1812, and then, at a similarly disagreeable time, had represented his country at the same Court. Now, in the third generation and, as it was to prove, at a time of even more hostile feeling and greater crisis, their son and grandson was called upon to hold the same post.

The appointment had been discussed in Washington, but Adams had returned to Boston with his family, thinking that nothing would come of it. The news, in the form of a telegram on the breakfast table, came, the son recorded in his diary, like a thunderclap. "My mother," he wrote, "at once fell into tears and deep agitation; foreseeing all sorts of evil consequences, and absolutely refusing to be comforted; while my father looked dismayed. The younger members of the household were astonished and confounded." The family, Charles wrote in later years, all too often with a pen dipped in gall in speaking of both his father and his mother, had got into a rut. His father, he claimed, had lived too long in Boston and felt that the great opportunity of his life was in reality a great sacrifice, while his mother "took a constitutional and sincere pleasure in the forecast of evil."

Adams, deeply impressed, and cognizant of the difficulties and responsibilities of the work which lay ahead, returned to

Washington and went to the White House with Seward to pay his official call upon the President and receive any communication which the latter might make as to policy. As he entered the White House, where, thirty years earlier, he had lived for three years and more, watching his own father perform the duties of President, he was little prepared for the reception he was about to meet. In the room which he knew so well, as he often described the scene later, a door opened, and a tall, uncouth, shabbily dressed man in worn slippers entered. It was Mr. Lincoln. The Secretary of State introduced the new Minister, who made the usual brief and dignified speech of appreciation of the confidence bestowed upon him. Lincoln, while they seated themselves, listened in abstracted silence, and then replied carelessly that he had not made the appointment and that Adams should thank "Governor Seward"; then, lying back in his chair, stretching out his long legs and folding his hands behind his head, he remarked, "Well, Governor, I 've this morning decided that Chicago post-office appointment." That was all. Not only was the Minister dismissed, but also every thought of a foreign policy. Lincoln had no idea that anything further was expected from him. Adams never wholly recovered from the shock, and the sudden dismay at what seemed the revelation of complete unfitness for his office on the part of the President remained with him for years. Sumter fired on, the nation in civil war, the relations with foreign nations, particularly England, of the utmost importance, and a country bumpkin at the head of the government dismissing the Minister to discuss post-office appointments. Adams assuredly had plenty to think about when, on May 1, 1861, he boarded the steamer which was to carry him away from the country his family had helped to build, now in the flames of fratricidal war, to deal with a government and a society which would be all too anxious to see the structure of his own perish in the conflagration.

Nominated on the eighteenth of March and at once confirmed by the Senate, Adams had delayed his sailing on account of the approaching marriage of his eldest son, John Quincy, to

Fanny C. Crowninshield, of a wealthy Boston family, the date having been set for April 29. In his *Autobiography*, the younger Charles blames his father severely for not having proceeded to his post at once, and it is somewhat difficult to understand why he did not do so. He had, it is true, Seward's permission to linger, but he should not have asked it, nor should Seward have permitted it. Three years later, Seward remarked to the son in a casual way that "the greatest misfortune that ever happened to the United States was that the marriage of your brother occurred on the 29th of April, 1861." Neither Seward nor Adams foresaw the immediate opening of hostilities, but even the firing on Sumter, April 12, did not change the date of the wedding or the departure of the Minister. In spite of Seward's later comment, the delay would seem to have been fortunate, as we shall see, but it is none the less inexplicable, and assuredly Seward had no right to complain, for he was the chief on whom the responsibility of the decision rested. The fact was that neither he nor Adams realized how swiftly events were now to move, and Seward did not send Adams his instructions until April 27, four days before he sailed.

Adams's attitude toward Europe was peculiar and marks an odd sort of "dead point" midway in the new phase of the family. The grandfather, though springing from the Quincy farm, had not only enjoyed much that Europe had to give him, but appreciated the educational advantages of a stay there. John Quincy, Charles's father, never had the slightest doubt on this latter point. On one occasion, when urging Gallatin to go abroad, he had said that he believed a knowledge of Europe to be indispensable to an American statesman. For Charles's children, at least Henry and the younger Charles, Europe was to be as familiar as it was indispensable. The Minister Charles, however, had a curious dislike and mistrust of it. Keenly interested in history, if not art, and preferring a foreign tongue to his own, he had never had the slightest wish to return to Europe since his boyhood, and had not approved of his own children going thither, though with the characteristic Adams parental attitude he had interposed no strong objection

JOHN QUINCY ADAMS II AS AN UNDERGRADUATE, 1853

(By permission of Mrs. Robert Homans)

when Henry had done so. Europe, indeed, both as the origin of forces and as a field for endeavor, may well be said to have made the Adamses what they were, and without Europe as a lever they might have remained at most mere local celebrities. The Minister's dislike of the country to which he was now accredited may be more easily explained. Opposition to that country had become, as it were, part of the inherited stock in trade of the family. Their experience of England, moreover, had always been at the moment when that country was in the worst possible of tempers with their own. Charles's personal experience in being sent to an English boarding school the year after the War of 1812 must have been unhappy enough, and an English boy who might have been similarly placed at an American school in 1815 would scarcely recall his young companions and "raggers" with affection. In addition, Boston society and finance were exaggeratedly Anglophile, and Adams, reacting constantly against both, would naturally react also against their so marked trait.

He had, however, as we have said, allowed Henry to have a couple of *Wanderjahren*, the motive of which on the young man's part appears to have been a somewhat vague and romantic desire to try European, particularly German, university life at the instigation of James Russell Lowell. The ostensible aim, since New England social conscience insisted upon one, was the study of the Canon Law, though Henry noted, with his usual ironic exaggeration, that neither he nor his parents knew what the Canon Law was or what good he would get by studying it. Leaving America in November 1858, he had landed at Liverpool and made his way to London, the train passing through the "Black Country" of the new industrial era, which Henry in his old age suggests might have taught him something had the boy he then was not run away from it, "as he ran away from everything he disliked." Arrived in Berlin, by way of Antwerp, his first lecture proved his last, he having rather quaintly discovered the obvious fact that he could not understand lectures in a language he did not know. The German university pleased him no better than Harvard, which he considered to have been, in his case, a total failure, but, although he did study the language, it is difficult to see just what he could have gained by a winter spent solely in Berlin, that city being then, as he truly said, "a poor, keen-witted, provincial town, simple, dirty, uncivilized, and, in most respects, disgusting." Some notion of the power of music over his unemotional nature did indeed come to him here, suddenly one afternoon in a *Bierstube*, but on the whole one can only marvel at the ineptitude of wasting one's first year in Europe in the Prussian capital of 1859. There was not even any social life to supplement the meagre training that the boy-and-girl affair of provincial Boston had afforded. His grandfather had once been the American Minister in this very city, but oddly enough the grandson and great-grandson of men who had known half the social and diplomatic people of their day appears to have been sent abroad with not a single letter of introduction to anyone and left to pick up acquaint-ances as best he might. In the two years he spent in Germany, for he stayed a second winter in Dresden, the only women he mentions as having met were a landlady or two and the "usual plain daughters" of a government clerk. A chance encounter with Charles Sumner, pompous as ever, and intercourse with Harvard acquaintances as much adrift as himself, made up his social experience. It is all a bit difficult to understand, for obviously his father could have provided him with a line or two that would have made his entry easy into a decent social milieu in any capital he visited. In the summer of 1859 he went to Italy to meet his sister, Mrs. Kuhn, and turned over the reins to her.

The following spring found him again in Italy, writing travel letters which were printed in the *Boston Courier*, and absorbing impressions of infinitely greater value than anything Prussia had to give him. At Naples, by fortunate chance and the kindness of the American Consul, he was given a chance to meet Garibaldi by being made a dispatch bearer to an American naval officer at Palermo, and the picturesque leader of the Red Shirts was the only celebrity with whom he had an interview in his two years abroad. That an Adams should spend two years abroad for his education and achieve his only personal contact with the men and forces then moulding the world through a Garibaldi would seem to have called for some comment from Henry himself, who later appreciated social values keenly enough, but it did not. At any rate, this particular incident was picturesque, and Henry continued his incipient literary career by more letters in the *Courier* narrating it. A few months in Paris, which he then disliked, and the boy was back in Boston. Allowing for exaggeration, there was truth in his comment that "he had made no step toward a profession. He was as ignorant as a schoolboy of society. He was unfit for any career in Europe, and unfitted for any career in America." One cannot but contrast Henry's muddle at twenty-three with John Quincy's clear-cut determination at seventeen, when he of his own volition turned his back on being private secretary to his father, the Minister to England, and returned to Harvard to start a deliberately planned career of his own.

Henry's father refrained from comment, and did not even, we are told, inquire maliciously about the Canon Law. It was not the Adams nature, and he was, at the moment almost of Henry's return, preparing to go to Washington for the winter's session of Congress. Henry repacked his trunk and went along as secretary, writing in the course of the winter a very able article on the cross-currents of politics in that most confusing session. At the end he returned to Boston with his family to study law in the office of Horace Gray, but had been there only a week when the news came of his father's appointment to the English mission. The father decided to take one of his sons as a secretary, though not officially. John had already established himself. Charles, although practice did not come, had been three years at the Bar and presumably had started his career. Brooks, a boy not quite thirteen, would be taken along, but merely to be put to school. Henry was the logical choice, and so once more he packed his trunk and accompanied his father. Oddly enough, his own experience of Europe, slight as it was, was thus the most that any of the party had had. His father had not been over since he was ten years old. His mother and Brooks had never been. Henry went as son, personal secretary, courier, and general handy man. The care of the family property was turned over to Charles, and the family sailed. John was at last married.

III

THE ENGLISH MISSION

AFTER a voyage of just under a fortnight, the Adamses arrived in London late on the evening of May 13; and Adams had scarcely reached his room in the hotel when he received news that made him realize vividly at what cost he had lingered on those six weeks, waiting to see John married at Mrs. Crowninshield's house in Longwood. Exactly one week before, while Adams was in mid-Atlantic, Lord John Russell, the British Foreign Minister, had announced in Parliament that the government intended to recognize the Southern Confederacy as belligerent, and the Proclamation of Neutrality, in which such acknowledgment was made, was dated the day Adams arrived and published in the *Gazette* the following morning, a bitter bit of marmalade for the Minister's first English breakfast. To understand the position in which Adams found himself, it is necessary to run over very briefly the changes in English public opinion in the months immediately preceding his arrival.[1]

Throughout the nineteenth century, England's position with regard to slavery had been an honorable one. It was immensely fortunate for Africa, just at the beginning of its exploitation by European powers, and on the eve of the enormous demand for cheap labor due to the industrial revolution, that the conscience of England, under the lead of men like Wilberforce and his associates, had put an end to the slave trade in

[1] As all the quotations in this book have been from printed and well-known sources, I have not thought it necessary to trouble with references the reader of a book which is essentially popular. In the present section, however, as I have availed myself of many extracts quoted from the sources by Professor E. D. Adams in his *Great Britain and the American Civil War* (Longmans, Green & Co., 1925), I wish here to make blanket acknowledgment of my indebtedness.

1807. In 1833 that country had also made an end of slavery in the British Empire and had emancipated all the slaves in the West Indies. The best public opinion in England watched with sincere sympathy the agitation in America for the abolition of slavery there, and up to 1850 not only had been on the side of the North but had been hopeful that America might in some way follow the humane example of the mother country. However, in the States compromise followed compromise, and when the greatest of all was made, that of 1850, and American statesmen of the first rank declared that the question was settled forever on the basis of permanent slavery in the South, England lost hope, though not all interest. In 1852, Mrs. Stowe's *Uncle Tom's Cabin* sold, in one year, one million copies in London as compared with only a hundred and fifty thousand in the United States. Hope was renewed with the election of Lincoln, and the *Times* led the whole English press in applause. It rejoiced that Lincoln had been elected and that "a vast community of our own race has at length given an authoritative expression to sentiments which are entertained by everyone in this country." Herbert Spencer was unquestionably right when he wrote to a friend a year later, when sentiment had changed, that the feeling at first had been "*very decidedly* on the side of the North." When the violence of the Southern reaction to the election was first realized all the papers which were afterward against us, such as the *Times, Saturday Review,* and the *Economist,* expressed their belief that political control and expression there had been seized upon by the ignorant and lawless elements. In April, the *Edinburgh Review* asserted that the whole difficulty was over slavery and that English sympathy would unquestionably be with the antislavery side. When Fort Sumter was fired on, secession announced, and the war actually begun, the *Times* still proclaimed that "there is a right and a wrong in this question, and that right belongs . . . to the States of the North." The sympathy of the common people of England remained with the North throughout the struggle, but this opinion was not reflected in the press, which was owned by and published for the privileged classes. At the beginning, however, this press was almost unanimous in its expressions of adherence to the North on the moral issue, which it believed was the sole issue, of slavery.

Unfortunately even Northern public opinion in America was passionately divided. Lincoln had been elected on a platform repudiating any further extension of slavery, but he had been elected largely by people who would have as clearly repudiated any idea of interfering with slavery in the South. For the sake of this large body of opinion and of the border states, Lincoln talked not of the abolition of slavery but merely of the forcible preservation of the Union. The leading statesmen still sought compromise. Adams himself and Seward had been conciliatory. In Lincoln's Inaugural Address he proclaimed flatly that he had no purpose to interfere with the institution of slavery where it existed. "I believe I have no lawful right to do so, and I have no inclination to do so." It is no wonder that the British public, like all publics never too well informed on the internal affairs of another state, should have suddenly come to believe that they had misjudged Lincoln, the meaning of the election, the entire situation, and that a revulsion of feeling should have occurred.

If slavery were not the issue, then what was the issue? Apparently it could only be the retention by force of the seceded states, with a population of nine million people in a Union no longer desired by them. On constitutional grounds the right to secede was at least justly debatable if not clearly established. When Lincoln washed his hands of slavery, and with the legal aspect of the quarrel a judicially open one, the moral issue had clearly evaporated in the eyes of even fair-minded foreign observers. The war became like any other war — a mere effort to settle debatable political and economic questions by brute force. At first, the South acted more promptly and with much greater spirit than the North. If all the slave states should secede, as seemed likely, they would have a population of ten million against thirteen million in the North, according to the latest census then available. To Europe it seemed impossible as well as immoral that thirteen millions should hold ten millions permanently in subjection against their will. The war thus seemed to have no moral foundation and no prospect of success for the North.

Viewed thus, there was ample reason why a considerable share of European upper-class opinion should be against the Union. In the first place, the astounding economic success and constantly expanding boundaries of the republic across the water had been exerting a profoundly unsettling effect upon the whole fabric of European society. The succession of revolutionary movements which had swept through Europe around 1848 were fresh in the memory. If the United States broke into two parts, or, as seemed not unlikely from the talk of Americans themselves, into several, its deflecting power on European institutions would be greatly lessened. It was, indeed, this very point which was seized upon by the lower and then unprivileged classes and made them the passionate champions of the North. Again, the tremendous expansion of America, following an imperialistic policy based on its boastful doctrine of "manifest destiny," had been watched with no little alarm. Annexation had followed annexation, first by negotiation and purchase, as in the Louisiana Territory and Florida, then by war, as in Texas and California. Such an expansion seemed unwarranted by the needs of the population, and appeared to presage the rise of a powerful and dangerous predatory state. If it were now to divide, the danger would be greatly lessened. We need not look for altruism in *Realpolitik*. Moreover, in England the British merchant, with the whole Lancashire cotton trade mainly dependent upon Southern cotton, began to count the cost of what appeared an unnecessary war. Dallas, the American Minister, had been useless as far as guiding or influencing public opinion was concerned. The appointee of the Buchanan and not the Lincoln administration, he was not wholly trusted by the latter, and was not in their divided counsels. He was merely carrying on routine business pending the arrival of his inevitable successor. It is problematic whether Adams could have availed much had he been on the spot. At any rate, he had not been, and when he arrived it was not only to hear the news that the government had acknowledged the belligerency of the South, but to find the influential press almost a unit against the North and the cause of the Union. Even such a staunch friend, as he was to prove later, as John Bright thought the war was folly. Adams had to face both a hostile press and a hostile upper class in society.

On the other hand, the government had maintained a strict neutrality, although Lord John Russell was convinced of the impossibility of the Northern cause. Neither he, however, nor Lord Lyons, the British Minister in Washington, was opposed to the Union. Adams soon found that England and France had acted together in the question of acknowledging the South as a belligerent, but the motives were different. England was bent on being neutral, whereas Louis Napoleon was already planning his attempted Mexican venture and the setting up there of an empire under Maximilian, an essential element in which would have to be the break-up of the United States.

Very little exception, indeed, could be taken to the action of the British government, save in so far as it might be construed as indicating a somewhat unsympathetic attitude toward the North. Lord John Russell had, indeed, given an interview to the two representatives of the Confederacy, but it had been unofficial and he promptly avowed to Adams that he did not intend to see them again. In his own interview with the Foreign Secretary, Adams, in complaining of the proclamation, laid the main stress upon the haste with which it had been issued, admitting practically that there could be no objection to it if a state of war had been clearly demonstrated to exist.

It was on this point of undue haste that, to the end of the war, American criticism of the English government's action centred. It was said, for one thing, that Russell had given a pledge to Dallas that no action would be taken until the arrival of Adams, and this was widely believed in America. A careful reading of Dallas's own dispatches shows that all that Russell had said was that the sovereignty of the South, not its status as a belligerent, would not be acknowledged. In point of fact Russell was entirely upheld by American practice, though condemned by American opinion.   In the trifling Canadian revolt of 1837, although the status of Canada as a belligerent could not for a moment be held to be as sound as that of the Confederacy in May 1861, the American government had immediately issued its proclamation of neutrality.   The American Minister to England in 1838 had informed the British government of that date that "civil wars are not distinguished from other wars, as to belligerent and neutral rights," that, indeed, they stood upon exactly the same grounds, and that "when a portion of a State seek by force of arms to overthrow the Government, and maintain independence, the contest becomes one *de facto* of war."   Thus had the American government acted and laid down international law to the British, but when that government accepted the principle and acted up to it, her right to do so was not only challenged by the American Secretary of State, but American opinion considered it as a most unfriendly act.   The best opinion now admits that the action taken was the proper one for the British government to have taken, and not simply on the ground of the precedents afforded by the United States itself.

Up to the time of actual hostilities Russell had kept his hands off completely.   His dispatches to the British Minister in Washington show that absolutely.   When, however, armed engagements had taken place, when the South had declared her independence, when Jefferson Davis had authorized privateering and Lincoln had issued proclamations on blockade and piracy, it was clear that if British citizens were not to be involved in unneutral acts a proclamation of neutrality was obviously called for from the British government.   Seward did not see it in that light, which explains his remark about the unfortunate date of John Adams's wedding, and popular opinion never forgave Great Britain.   As a matter of fact that wedding, which played such an unexpected part in world politics, was probably a most fortunate occurrence for the United States — as well as for John.   The North, and Lincoln's administration, had to carry on the war at the beginning under the cloak of a fiction that the Southerners could not throw off their allegiance, that there was no Southern government and no rebelling nation to recognize. To have done so would have vastly involved the problem of how to deal with the rebels in the reunion which the North was convinced would take place. This, however, was a fiction to simplify a domestic situation. It was not a fact, and it could not be recognized by foreign nations. When Adams reached London, England's proclamation was, happily, a fact — a fact that might be objected to, which might astutely be used to put the British government on the defensive, which in the hands of an able diplomat might serve several useful purposes, but which obviously could not result in the recall of a Minister who had had nothing to do with it. Had Adams arrived sooner, had he had to protest as strongly as Seward insisted against the issuance of the proclamation, and had it then been issued in spite of strong protests, Mr. Adams, to put it that way, would in all probability not have spent seven years in London. As it was, he leased a house to serve as the American Legation — for one month.

Adams, indeed, had good reason not to commit himself to a longer term. He had the greatest confidence in Seward's judgment and statesmanship, but at this time Anglo-American relations and the Minister's tenure of office were in far greater danger from the American Secretary of State than they were from the British Foreign Minister. Seward was at the moment at the very crisis of his egomania. As is well known, he believed himself a much greater man than Lincoln, and felt that the responsibility of guiding the country rested upon him and not the President. On April 1, a date that might have warned him not to make a fool of himself, he had handed to Lincoln that extraordinary document in which he not only claimed that the President had no policy, but so amazingly offered to take over the entire direction of the government from him. Patiently and courteously reminded of his proper subordination by the President, and with his own policy of peace and conciliation proved a mistaken one by the rapid course of events, he sought to recover influence and prestige by leading a foreign war party, developing his insane theory that a war against all Europe would bring the two American factions together in face of a common enemy.

On May 21 he penned the famous dispatch of that date to Adams, which assuredly convinced the latter gentleman of the wisdom of a thirty-day lease if of nothing else. And, even so, Adams by no means knew the worst. Seward had for some time been talking flamboyantly against Europe in private conversations, and had told the Minister from the small Republic of Bremen that "if the Lord would only give the United States an excuse for a war with England, France, or Spain" it would be the means of ending the Civil War. In the memorandum handed to Lincoln he had advised creating immediately excuses for going to war with France and Spain, and possibly England and Russia as well. Had it not been for the cool heads of Lincoln and Adams, war with England and the break-up, not the salvation, of the Union would have been inevitable.

According to the American theory that there was no war, only a revolt, Seward and the government, for the time being, held that Southern privateers should be treated as pirates and hung. Seward also held that the British government had no right to hold any communications with the representatives of the Confederacy. These were the two topics treated of in the dispatch of May 21, and it was extremely fortunate that Lincoln was in the habit of reading important dispatches before they were forwarded. With regard to the first point, Seward had written, if the British government should choose to regard the Southern privateers as belligerents and give them shelter, that "the laws of nations afford an adequate and proper remedy, and we shall avail ourselves of it." As soon as such an act should occur, he continued, "from that hour we shall cease to be friends and become once more, as we have twice before been forced to be, enemies of Great Britain." He proceeded to show that this would probably involve a general European war with social convulsions and that "when they shall have ceased it will, we think, be seen, whatever may have been the fortunes of other nations, that it is not the United States that will have come out of them with its precious Constitution altered or its honestly obtained dominion in any degree abridged." Lincoln altered this mad tirade to the statement that "as to the treatment of privateers in the insurgent service, you [Adams] will say that this is a question exclusively our own. We treat them as pirates. They are our own citizens, or persons employed by our own citizens, preying on the commerce of our country. If Great Britain shall choose to recognize them as lawful belligerents and give them shelter from our pursuit and punishment, the law of nations affords an adequate and proper remedy." As to the second point, that of the reception by the British government, either officially or unofficially, of any representatives from the Confederate government, the dispatch instructed Adams that " you will, in any event, desist from all intercourse whatever, unofficial as well as official, with the British government, so long as it shall continue to have intercourse of either kind with the domestic enemies of this country." The whole dispatch was, of course, based on the untenable theory already alluded to that there was no war, a theory that in application to others we would not, and which Europe could not, accept.

Adams naturally knew nothing of Seward's original draft, but even in the form in which he received the dispatch, toned down in several particulars by Lincoln, it was startling enough. The original draft had been a direct challenge to war. Even in its amended form everything would depend on how Adams could present it to Russell and how it would be received. Fortunately Lincoln had added a saving clause. "The paper itself," he wrote, "is not to be read or shown to the British Secretary of State [sic], nor any of its positions to be prematurely, unnecessarily, or indiscreetly made known. But its spirit will be your guide." Lincoln realized the value of Seward, who proved a statesman in spite of this temporary lapse from sanity. Lincoln skillfully extracted as much poison as he could from the dispatch and then rested the whole fate of Anglo-American relations upon the discretion of Adams. Of all this, Adams was totally ignorant. His only interview with Lincoln had, as we have seen, made a most unfavorable impression upon him. For Seward he had had thus far the deepest respect, and regarded him as the main reliance of the government. On first reading the dispatch, he noted in his diary, June 10, that "the [American] Government seems almost ready to declare war with all the powers of Europe, and almost instructs me to withdraw from communication with the Ministers here in a certain contingency. . . . I scarcely know how to understand Mr. Seward. The rest of the Government may be demented for all I know; but he surely is calm and wise. My duty here is in so far as I can do it honestly to prevent the irritation from coming to a downright quarrel. It seems to me like throwing the game into the hands of the enemy." Could Adams have known the whole story of the dispatch as we now know it, he would have been even more perturbed about the possibility of maintaining relations with England. The British government, in fact, knew far more than Adams did of Seward's policy and intentions, and the deep mistrust of him which had thus been engendered was an important diplomatic factor in the early years of Adams's mission.

However Adams might soften Seward's dispatch in communicating its substance to Lord John Russell, he had been given one positive order, which was to break off relations if the British government received the Confederate envoys again. The day following the receipt of the dispatch he had an interview with Russell. Fortunately the two men had already each taken the measure of the other. Adams's school training at Ealing now stood him in good stead in helping him to understand English character, and he was himself very English, not only in manner, but in his unimpassioned intelligence, much as he might rail at Englishmen. After their first interview, Russell had written to Lord Lyons that "Mr. Adams has made a very favorable impression on my mind as a calm and judicious man," and he had again spoken of him as "a reasonable man," both high compliments from Lord John. Utterly distrusting Seward, Russell did trust Adams. At their meeting on June 11, Adams, carrying out his instructions, tempered by his own great discretion, ran over with the Minister the suspicions that had unfortunately been engendered in the American public by the Proclamation of Neutrality, although, he added, he could not convince himself of any unfriendly design on England's part. He then approached the delicate subject of his instructions to break off relations with England if the British government continued to communicate with the Rebel envoys. "It was not to be disguised," Adams said, "that the fact of the continued stay of the pseudo-commissioners in this city, and still more the knowledge that they had been admitted to more or less interviews with his lordship, was calculated to excite uneasiness. Indeed, it had already given great dissatisfaction to my Government. I added, as moderately as I could, that in all frankness any further protraction of this relation could scarcely fail to be viewed by us as hostile in spirit, and to require some corresponding action accordingly." Russell explained that it had long been the custom in England and France, at least, to receive such persons unofficially, as had been done in the cases of Poles, Hungarians, Italians, and others, in order to hear what they had to say, but such reception did not in any case, certainly not in that of the Confederates, imply any recognition of their governments. He added that he had no expectation of seeing them again. Adams had carried out his dangerous instruction. Russell had given no pledge, but a very sharp corner had been successfully turned. With regard to treating privateersmen as pirates, the United States government soon came to see the inadvisability of maintaining such a stand and itself abandoned the claim. To have broken off relations with England on account of an unofficial interview between Russell and the Confederate agents would have been criminal folly.

The incident and its background have been narrated at somewhat undue length in order to give the atmosphere in which Adams began his term of service. The British upper classes socially were, on the whole, on the side of the South. The British government, however, was honestly endeavoring to maintain a strictly neutral stand. On the other hand, it had become, justifiably enough, extremely suspicious of Seward's motives, and, in America, public opinion was exasperated against England on account of the Neutrality Proclamation. A few days after his interview, Adams wrote to his son Charles that "my position here thus far has not been difficult or painful," and on July 2 Henry wrote to his brother saying that "the English are really on our side; of that I have no doubt whatever. But they thought that as a dissolution seemed inevitable and as we seemed to have made up our minds to it, that their Proclamation [of Neutrality] was just the thing to keep them straight with both sides, and when it turned out otherwise they did their best to correct their mistake. America seems to have gone clean daft. She seems to want to quarrel with all the world, and now that England has eaten her humble-pie for what was, I must say, a natural mistake from her point of view, I cannot imagine why we should keep on sarsing her." The situation with regard to public opinion was to become less pleasant later, as we shall note.

By July 18 Adams had dared to engage a house for a year, and wrote to Charles, saying, "I think I have attained a tolerable idea of London society. I have seen most of the men of any reputation, literary or political. The conclusion is not favorable, so far as the comparison with other periods is concerned. Lord Palmerston, Mr. Gladstone, Lord John Russell and Lords Derby and Ellenborough are the orators. Mr. D'Israeli perhaps might be included. Thackeray, Senior, Monckton Milnes, Grote, Lord Stanhope and Mr. Reeve, the editor of the *Edinburgh Review*, constitute pretty much the literature. Perhaps I should include Milman. Gladstone and Cornewall Lewis are the scholar politicians. Intermixed with all these are men of education, if not of eminence, who contribute a share to the common stock of society. But I have not yet been to a single entertainment where there was any conversation that I should care to remember." Considering, however, that he had been there only six weeks, the American Minister was evidently getting on well. He was, nevertheless, beginning to get restive over what should be the declared object of the war at home. Up to now, he wrote his son in the middle of August, "the favorable feature has been union. Maintaining that, we can bear a great deal. But unless we can have a principle to contend for, the money question will infallibly shake us to pieces. I am for this reason anxious to grapple with the slavery question at once." If the American Minister felt the need of some principle in the war, it is not to be wondered at if British society, which had slight knowledge of America, had failed to find any.

Meanwhile, on August 3 had come the news of the Union defeat and rout at Bull Run. The military incapacity of the North appeared to have been clearly demonstrated. The battle was a disgrace, and the full description given in the London *Times* contained nothing worse than was published at home; but, appearing in a foreign journal, the account aroused a storm of anger in the North. In Europe no one took the chances of the Union being preserved as seriously possible. Adams, so his son wrote, expected any week to have to pack up and go home. Henry himself, suddenly seized with war fever, sent a frantic request to his brother Charles to get him a commission in the army, saying that he would return at once. Charles, in Boston, was debating the question with himself also. He loathed the thought of war. Everyone, his father included, believed that it would be short. Charles was looking after his father's business affairs. Was it or was it not his duty to enlist? Month after month the young man debated the question, with, as he thought in later years, no little casuistry. At any rate, he had no doubt that Henry, with his delicate physique and his duties in London, should not be in the army, and he wrote him so very sharply. "If you have any energy," he concluded a long letter, "use it where you are and where it can be of value. If you have n't any keep out of the army." "Don't talk of your connection with the legation to me; cut yourself off if necessary from it and live in London as the avowed *Times* correspondent and force yourself into notice of the London press that way. Wake up and look about you and make yourself useful and don't jog on in this cart horse way.

. . . There I have blown my blast and have done, and you can do as you see fit." Henry was at that time writing letters for the *New York Times*, but unsigned, and without the knowledge even of his father. Whether Charles's advice would have been feasible or not, it was not taken and Henry continued in the Legation at 5 Mansfield Street, where crisis succeeded crisis.

The next of these that we have to record must be described briefly and was of less importance in itself than for the unfortunate psychological atmosphere of mistrust that it created. To understand it, it is necessary to look backward into history for a moment. During the Crimean War in 1854, England and France, the leading maritime nations engaged in that conflict, had agreed, as a very distinct step forward in international law, to respect neutral commerce under either a neutral or an enemy flag. The agreement was accepted by England, France, Austria, Prussia, Russia, Sardinia, and Turkey, and soon all the maritime nations of the world except the United States, which declined, had agreed to it. The four points in the agreement were that privateering was abolished; enemy's goods, except contraband of war, were covered by a neutral flag; neutral goods, with the same exception, were not liable to capture even under an enemy flag; and blockades, to be binding, had to be effective.

The United States refused to accept the really great advance thus made unless with its own doctrine that *all* private property at sea, not contraband, should be declared exempt. On April 21, 1861, however, Seward instructed all the ministers abroad to enter into conventions with the adherents of the Treaty of Paris of 1854 on the basis which had been then proposed to us and which we had formerly declined. Adams promptly communicated this to Russell, who replied that England was prepared to negotiate but preferred to leave the negotiations in the hands of Lord Lyons at Washington, to whom he had already sent authority. A situation existed that was unknown to Adams when he made the proposal to Russell on May 18.

By May 1 the British government was aware that war had been declared in America, that the North had made known its intention to blockade Southern ports, and that the South, on its part, had declared its intention to commission privateers. A serious situation thus confronted neutral commerce. On May 6, Russell suggested to France that each ask the North *and* the South to agree to abide by the second and third articles of the Treaty of Paris, the only two sections on which the belligerents had not made declarations. On the eleventh this was supplemented by a suggestion that adherence be made to all four articles. France did not agree to this, but gladly adopted the first suggestion. She pointed out that very serious international complications might result if the North adhered to the agreement and the South, with her privateers, did not, pointing out also that the best way to approach the Confederate government would be through the English and French Consuls. Agreement being reached, Russell had completed his instructions to Lord Lyons the very day when Adams called and made his totally unexpected proposal that the North offered to adhere to the Convention. The new situation thus suddenly arising evidently required careful consideration. It may be pointed out here that the so-called Treaty of Paris was a convention, and that unless the form of the Confederate government should require it, as in the United States, it did not have to be signed as a mutual treaty, the mere statement that a government adhered to it being sufficient. In approaching the Confederate government indirectly and inducing it to issue its declaration of adherence, France and England would not be acknowledging its sovereignty.

We cannot go into all the details of the negotiation. Russell, it now appears from papers not available some years ago, was sincerely desirous of doing away with privateering all over the world, and welcomed the opportunity of gaining the assent of the United States. Both the British and French Ministers in Washington were suspicious of Seward's motives when it became known he had made his move to adhere to the convention. Russell felt that the South would not dare to hold out if all the rest of the world should agree to the abolition of privateers, but on the other hand England could not agree to the doctrine enunciated by Seward that the South was not a belligerent and that her privateers should be treated as pirates. To have done so would have involved a breach of neutrality as well as possible complications of another sort. Europe had now to consider the South as a belligerent.

Seward refused to do so. His instructions to the American representatives abroad to adhere to the Treaty of Paris had been signed several weeks before the belligerency of the South had been recognized, and had apparently stemmed from the hope of having the privateers treated as pirates or staving off the Proclamations of Neutrality. When he continued to press, through Lyons in Washington, for a hasty signing of the convention, it was with the comment that there was no difference between the condition of the United States and that of a nation at peace, which immediately and naturally aroused the suspicion of the diplomat and made him warn Russell not to sign without a clause that would forestall trouble in view of Seward's theory of there being no state of war and of Southern privateersmen being pirates. As documents have gradually come to light, the theories of Seward's motives have undergone several transformations, but it appears that he did intend to use our adherence to the Treaty as a lever to change the position of the other powers toward the South. Meanwhile, Lyons, as Russell had instructed him, had told Seward that England and France must be able to get into touch with the South for the protection of their interests, and Seward had told him to do so privately, but that the United States would have to protest if notified formally.

Seward now decided to transfer the negotiations to London, and sent more explicit instructions to Adams. Lyons was much relieved at being rid of the matter, and Adams once more called upon Russell. On July 11 he made a formal offer to sign a convention, and on the thirteenth gave Russell a copy. Russell had come to the conclusion to go on if necessary without France and without the South, and on the twelfth had sent word to Lyons to take no further steps to get in touch with the South unless he already had done so. It was decided, however, mainly by Palmerston, the Prime Minister, that it was best that France should sign at the same time. On July 18, Russell advised Adams that England was prepared to sign provided the American Minister in France signed at the same time. This was proper, but involved some delay. On August 19, Russell asked Adams to set a date for signing, and said that to prevent any misconception it was proposed to add a clause to the effect that by signing "Her Majesty does not intend thereby to undertake any engagement which shall have any bearing, direct or indirect, on the internal differences now prevailing in the United States."

Adams pointed out that his instructions did not permit him to go beyond an adherence to the four clauses of the original Treaty, and that the added clause reflected on the motives of the United States. He was perfectly honest in his feeling. Seward, however, could not accept the safeguarding clause without losing the very aim he had been driving at. In the end the negotiation lapsed, but it left Adams with the impression that he could no longer trust Russell, and that "it was difficult to suppress indignation at the miserable shuffling practiced throughout" by the British. On the other hand, Russell saw in the failure of the negotiation proof of what Lyons had been warning him — namely, that Seward had merely been preparing a trap. In this respect the whole affair had been most unfortunate in bringing about a mutual feeling of distrust, and although Russell has usually borne the blame, it would seem more properly to rest upon Seward. It has been said that if Russell had been a farseeing statesman he would have neglected any temporary difficulties in which England might have become involved with respect to Confederate privateers for the sake of the good in the long run of having America a party to the convention. On the other hand, everyone, even Adams, expected the war to be of short duration, and if Seward had been animated only by the wish to have America advance the cause of international law permanently without gaining an undue temporary advantage, there could have been no objection to the English proviso. To claim as he did that there was no difference between a nation engaged in civil war and one at peace with all the world was sufficiently absurd to indicate some ulterior motive. Adams's ignorance of all that had been going on, and his consequent misjudging of the good faith of Russell, naturally colored his later relations with that statesman.

An afterclap of this storm, with which Adams had to concern himself in September, made him even more mistrustful. Papers found on a man who was arrested as he was about to sail from New York showed that the British government had approached the Confederate one with regard to adhering to the Treaty of Paris, and the inference drawn in the American Legation in London was at once that there had been more underhand double-dealing. "By a pure accident it was discovered," Henry wrote his brother in Boston, "that the British Government were *secretly* entering into connections with the insurgents, and they have now been compelled to acknowledge that they have really been acting *behind our backs*. This is no pleasant acknowledgment to make, for evidently secrecy was their object, and the implication is direct against their good faith." This was not the truth, but the Adamses did not know it. As we have seen, Russell had instructed Lyons not to approach the Confederates even indirectly without advising with Seward first, and Lyons had done so. Seward had given his assent, provided the matter was managed unofficially and without making a noise. Unfortunately Bunch, the British Consul at Charleston, who was chosen as the channel of communication in the South, not only did not handle the matter in the manner directed, but made stupid errors, and, when the matter became public by the capture of Mure and his mail bags, Seward had to act as though the British had been wholly in the wrong. The venture was ill-judged and had been entered upon, with the attendant risk of exposure, at the time that Russell deemed it dangerous to have the North adhere to the Paris Treaty without the South. He had changed his mind and tried to stop communicating with the South, but too late. Unwise, however, as the attempt had been, it had not been carried on without the knowledge of Seward, and Russell had not acted behind our backs, as Adams inferred. The American government had to ask for the recall of the muddling Bunch, and Adams had to make the demand on Russell, who naturally stood by the Consul, stating frankly that he had been acting under orders, adding that there had been no intention of recognizing the Confederate government and that even pirates might be asked to subscribe to certain rules of war. Bunch's exequatur was then revoked by the American government and the episode ended, leaving not only the American public but the American Minister with the impression that England had again tried to play a secret game. The French, acting on Seward's consent to go ahead but not get found out, had done just as the English had, but as no incriminating letters were captured from them it was not necessary to ask for the recall of the French Consul, and the public had the impression that England alone was playing tricks.

In London, Adams's position was far from enviable. Officially, of course, he was treated with punctilious correctness, but he was beginning to doubt the honesty of the men he was dealing with, and he had come to realize that England was the front-line trench in the diplomatic front. France had been steadily pressing for a recognition of the South as a sovereign power, but would not move without England, and the other European powers would follow these two. The fate of the United States might almost be said to depend on the British cabinet, and the cabinet depended on Russell and Palmerston. Adams watched them from the gloom of 5 Mansfield Street much as he might have watched in a jungle night two pairs of gleaming eyes, alert to see whether the animals behind them would continue merely to prowl or suddenly spring. They had, at this time, no intention of springing, but the watchful Minister could not tell. And all the summer and autumn the military situation at home seemed to grow worse for the Union.

Socially, Adams, as the saying is, knew everyone, but English society in the 1860's was essentially heavy and dull, and, with most of its members on the side of the South, the Minister found the air of drawing-rooms oppressively unsympathetic and depressing, although there was no overt hostility or discourtesy. A few of the literary men, notably Browning among the first, were on the side of the North. In society Monckton Milnes, afterward Lord Houghton, was a strong support. In politics the Duke of Argyll, Richard Cobden, John Bright, W. E. Forster, and a few other leaders stood by nobly. The working class was pro-Northern, but Adams, although he watched its opinion with close care, did not have social contact with it. The society in which he did move, and for the most part — there were one or two notable exceptions — the newspapers which he read, were all hostile to the American diplomat and his cause.

Young Henry felt the weight of gloom more heavily than did his calmly impassive father. "You complain of the manner in which England has been allowed to wheel round," he wrote in October to Charles, who had complained of English opinion. "Do you know the reason why it is so? How do you suppose we can make a stand here when our own friends fail to support us? Look at the Southerners here. Every man is inspired by the idea of independence and liberty while we are in a false position. They are active, you say. So they are, every man of them. There are no traitors among *them*. They have an object and they act together. *Their* merchants and friends in Liverpool have been warm and vigorous in their support from the beginning. *Ours* have been lukewarm, never uttering a hearty word on our side, and the best of them, such as Peabody and the house of Baring's invariably playing directly into the hands of our opponents. They have allowed the game to go by default. Their talk has been desponding, hesitating, an infernal weight round our necks. How can you suppose that we would gain ground with such allies. But we might nevertheless have carried the day if the news from home had been such as to encourage our party, which was once strong and willing. You know how much encouragement we have had from your side. Every post has taken away on one hand what it brought of good on the other. It has by regular steps sapped the

HENRY ADAMS AS AN UNDERGRADUATE

(*By permission of Miss E. O. Adams*)

foundation of all confidence in us, in our institutions, our rulers and our honor. How do you suppose we can overcome the effects of the New York press? How do you suppose we can conciliate men whom our tariff is ruining? How do you suppose we can shut people's eyes to the incompetence of Lincoln or the disgusting behavior of many of our volunteers and officers? I tell you we are in a false position and I am sick of it. My one hope is now on McClellan and if he fails us, then as I say give it up. Here we are dying by inches. Every day our authority, prestige and influence sink lower in this country, and we have the mournful task of trying to bolster up a failing cause. . . . The English Government is perfectly passive and likely to remain so."

This desponding letter crossed one from Charles to Henry, in which we read, "Six months of this war have gone and we have done much; and by we I mean our rulers. But if we have done much with our means, the rebels have performed miracles with theirs. At the end of six months have we a policy? Are traitors weeded out of our departments? Is our blockade effective? Is the war prosecuted honestly and vigorously? To all these questions there is but one answer. The President is not equal to the occasion; that we cannot now help. The Secretary of War is corrupt and the Secretary of the Navy is incompetent; that we can help and ought to. With the rebels showing us what we can do, we ought to be ashamed not to do more." If the sons of the American Minister could write thus, it is no wonder that European society in general should consider the Northern cause hopeless and without principle or policy. In midsummer, when the shift of sentiment toward the South was strongest, John Lothrop Motley, then American Minister at Vienna, in an effort to stem the tide, wrote a letter to the London *Times*, which did more harm than good. He argued ably and at length against the constitutional right of the South to secede peaceably, denying incidentally that the Federal government had any right to interfere with slavery. The constitutional argument was at once presented just as ably on the other side by others, and the British public had again been told by an American high in station that slavery had nothing to do with the struggle.

Almost from the opening of hostilities, young Charles in Boston had been chafing his mind with the rub of whether or not he should go into the army. In June he had written his father that "it is not as if I were an only son, though many such have gone; but your family is large and it seems to me almost disgraceful that in after years we should have it to say that of them all not one at this day stood in arms for that government with which our family history is so closely connected." It was not the habit of Adams parents to interfere with their children, but, on the other hand, in each generation the children have given great consideration to the opinions, when they have known them, of the parents. Charles knew that his father, believing the war would be short, disapproved of his volunteering, but on September 20 the Minister wrote, saying, "I deeply sympathise with you in your trials about the part you ought to play in the war. Much as I value your assistance during my absence on this side, I should be very reluctant to continue it at the cost of your own convictions of your duty. If you feel that the crisis demands it, I pray that you set aside every other consideration at once. . . . Whichever way you determine, you will know that I appreciate your motives, and that you will have under every circumstance my sympathy and my prayers." A month later Charles replied that he had been promised a commission in the First Massachusetts Cavalry, and on the twenty-eighth of December First Lieutenant Charles Francis Adams left Boston with his regiment en route to Port Royal, South Carolina, whither they had been ordered.

In November, affairs in the London Legation were for the moment drifting in slack water. On the eighth of that month, Henry was resisting the gloom of an even more than commonly gloomy November in town, and his father was in his study calmly pondering the character of statesmen in a letter to the younger Charles. A statesman's first and greatest qualification, he wrote, "in my estimation, is the mastery of the whole theory of morals which makes the foundation of all human society. The great and everlasting question of the right and wrong of every act whether of individual men or of collective bodies. The next is the application of the knowledge thus gained to the events of his time in a continuous and systematic way. It is in this last particular that the greatest number of failures are observed to occur. Many men never acquire sufficient certainty of purpose to be able to guide their steps at all. They then become the mere sport of fortune. Today they shine because they have caught at a good opportunity. Tomorrow, the light goes out, and they are found mired at the bottom of a ditch. These are the men of temporary celebrity — the Charles Townshends, the John Randolphs, the George Grenvilles, the Harrison Gray Otises of their day. Every civilised nation is full of them. Other men, more favored by nature or education, prove their capacity to direct their course, at the expense of their fidelity to their convictions. They sacrifice their consistency for the sake of power, and surrender their future fame in exchange for the applause of their own day. The number of these is Legion. They crowd the records of all governments. The feebleness of perception and the deliberate abandonment of moral principle in action are the two prevailing characteristics of public men. In my opinion no man who has lived in America had so thoroughly constructed a foundation for his public life as your grandfather. His action was always deducible from certain maxims deeply graven on his mind. This it was that made him fail so much as a party-man. No person can be a thorough partisan for a long period without sacrifice of his moral identity. The skill consists in knowing exactly where to draw the line, and it is precisely here that it seems to me appears the remarkable superiority of your grandfather over every man of his time. He derives support from every thing he can seize. But if circumstances force it out of his hands, he is still found standing firm and alone."

The man who was so calmly penning these words little dreamed that on the very day, possibly the very hour, he was writing, a portentous incident was occurring that was to rouse the temporarily peaceful atmosphere of Anglo-American relations into a veritable typhoon of fury. At noon Captain Wilkes, in command of the U. S. sloop-of-war *San Jacinto*, had fired a shot across the bows of the British mail-packet *Trent*, made her lie to, and forcibly taken from her the two Confederate "Special Commissioners," Mason and Slidell.

It had been known that these men had slipped through the blockade at Charleston, that they had reached Havana by way of Nassau, and were proceeding to Europe. The British government had been anxiously considering what the situation might be should the United States attempt to intercept them. An American ship-of-war, the *James Adger*, had been hovering near the English coast off Southampton, and Palmerston was suspicious. He inquired first from the law officers of the Crown what the legal aspect of the question might be and was informed that according to British practice an American might stop a neutral, search her, and, if the Southerners were found on board with their credentials, either take them out or carry the vessel into an American port for trial. On the other hand, although the law officers did not so state, such an action would be in direct violation of those very principles of international maritime law which the United States had been insisting upon from the beginning of its history as a nation. Whatever the law of either nation might be, however, Palmerston properly foresaw that any such act would precipitate an outbreak of international rage that should be avoided at all costs. On November 12, there still being no news of where the Commissioners were or of Wilkes's action, Palmerston asked Adams for an interview, and in the course of it pointed out that although he did not pretend to say what the law was, the risk of very strained relations was certainly not counterbalanced by the mere prevention of the arrival of two more Southerners in Europe. Adams told the Prime Minister that the *Adger* was seeking to intercept a wholly different vessel, the *Nashville*, and that its captain had no orders to capture the Southerners. The interview, at which Russell was present, was an agreeable one, and the British government was clearly trying to avoid what might prove a very difficult situation and to help the American Minister to keep his country clear.   Adams and Russell were now on friendly terms, and in discussing the maritime law Adams remarked that the French had been consistent in maintaining the rights of neutrals, but that he could not pay the British the same compliment.   On the other hand, when certain precedents were cited, Russell remarked that fifty or sixty years ago the English had said and done many things that he would not now undertake to defend.   Adams was himself anxious and ordered the captain of the *Adger* to take himself out of the way, advising him to go straight home, and with that, on November 25, went himself with Mrs. Adams on a visit to Frystone, the Monckton Milnes' place in Nottinghamshire, one of the few country houses which had opened its doors to him.

Suddenly the storm broke.   A steamer from the West Indies arrived in England.   Henry, who had been left in London, wrote nearly a half century later that "one afternoon when he was struggling to resist complete nervous depression in the solitude of Mansfield Street, during the absence of the Minister and Mrs. Adams on a country visit, Reuter's telegram announcing the seizure of Mason and Slidell from a British mail-steamer was brought to the office.   All three secretaries, public and private were there — nervous as wild beasts under the long strain on their endurance — and all three, though they knew it to be not merely their order of departure — not merely diplomatic rupture — but a declaration of war — broke into shouts of delight.   They were glad to face the end.   They saw it and cheered it!   Since England was waiting only for its own moment to strike, they were eager to strike first."   England, as a matter of fact, was not waiting to strike, and a good deal must be allowed to the state of the young men's nerves.

The news was at once telegraphed to Adams at Frystone. With the rest of the house party he was visiting the ruins of Pontefract Castle, and the telegram was handed him as he was examining them.   It suddenly prevented him, he noted, "from thinking much of historical associations."   Presently, however, in a cool voice, he told his friends that he had "stirring news" and showed them the telegram.   At once they offered every facility for an immediate return to London, but Adams replied that he would remain where he was and that London was the precise place where he would prefer not to be for the moment.

The news had been known in America on the fifteenth when Wilkes, with his prisoners, arrived at Fortress Monroe. He had acted absolutely without any orders from the government, and his act stultified completely all that America had claimed to be international law and justice in such cases for nearly a century, but the United States went altogether off its head in a perfect frenzy of rejoicing. Nor was this limited to the mob, the press, and irresponsible persons. The Secretary of the Navy thanked Wilkes for his "great public service." Congress passed a joint resolution praising his deed and requesting the President to give him a gold medal. Only Lincoln and Seward kept silence. America lost her senses more completely, perhaps, than ever before or since over any particular incident. In England, on the other hand, one commentator wrote that "there never was within memory such a burst of feeling. The people are frantic with rage, and were the country polled, I fear 999 men out of a thousand would declare for immediate war. Lord Palmerston cannot resist the impulse if he would"; and another, "I have never seen so intense a feeling of indignation exhibited in all my life. It pervades all classes, and may make itself heard above the wiser theories of the Cabinet officers." In truth the storm that Palmerston and Russell had feared and done their best to guard both countries against had burst in all its fury. It is clear to-day that possibly there has never been a bigger ass in American history than Wilkes, but the problem at the time was, could the British government so guide the situation as not to be forced into declaring war, and could Seward get the American people to return to common sense and pursue any policy that Congress, as asinine as Wilkes himself, having committed itself so intemperately, would approve?

When we so pride ourselves on what we consider the self-evident value of modern inventions, we may be given pause when we realize that, had there been a submarine cable in 1861, it is almost certain that England and the North would have been

at war in that December.   As it was, the slowness of communication gave both sides time to think, and allowed Seward in
America and Palmerston and Russell in England, with Adams
as the connecting link, to guide the situation.

Gradually the insensate mob emotion spent itself.   America
began to question whether Wilkes, after all, had been legally
right, and England to realize that by going to war with the
North she would be establishing a great slave state in the South.
Adams wrote to his son Charles two days after Christmas, "I
have never before met with an instance of so striking a simplicity in a nation.   You do not even resort to the most ordinary habit of judging others by yourselves.   Here is all Europe
from end to end arrayed in opinion against you, and not a shade
of suspicion that you may not be right yet rests upon your
brows. . . .   A day or two will show whether the [English]
government will prove true to its ancient well-established principles, or whether under the paltry inducement of personal
pique it will strike out into a new path that will lead it neither
to glory nor success.   My own convictions are that it will
determine right.   Thus far it has not shown a false color as I
feared under the first popular impulse that it might.   Yet I
confess I dread the effect of the pressure to which it may be
subjected.   The result will soon be upon us."

Fortunately Russell and Palmerston stood firm against the
storm in their country, and Seward had by now wholly recovered from his earlier delusion of a European war as a panacea
for domestic troubles.   The American government, under the
wise control of Seward and Lincoln, finally, almost at the last
moment allowed by the ultimatum from England, handed the
prisoners over to that country and admitted that reparation
was due.   Adams noted at the end that "so the danger of war
is at present removed; and I am to remain in this purgatory
a while longer."

The matter, however, left rankling feelings on both sides, and
on other occasions, such as the Federal sinking of stone boats in
Charleston harbor, vocal British opinion showed a desire to
criticize that was hotly resented in the North.   Even such a

man as James Russell Lowell fanned the flames of resentment in his *Biglow Papers*.

> Of all the sarse thet I can call to mind,
> England *doos* make the most onpleasant kind;
> It's you're the sinner ollers, she's the saint,
> Wut's good's all English, all thet is n't ain't.

The North had expected that British sympathy would be out-spoken in its favor and was bitterly disappointed and resentful when that proved not to be the case. On the other hand, the South complained that England, so far from being neutral, was consistently favoring the North.

We are not discussing Anglo-American relations as history, however, but merely so far as they afford the background of an episode in the story of an American family, and must pass over much that would otherwise be essential for understanding. The earlier months of 1862 passed fairly peacefully for the American Minister. At the very beginning of the year Henry had had a severe blow which had thrown him into a panic and completely stopped his correspondence to the American papers and ended, as he thought, his usefulness. A letter which he had sent to his brother on the cotton famine in the Lancashire district had been printed in the Boston *Courier*, unfortunately with his name indicated. This reached the London *Times*, which immediately published a biting leading article casti-gating Henry with irony and sarcasm. The episode was unim-portant to anyone but Henry, but for him it was, for the moment, fatal to his literary aspirations. Charles was still stationed with his regiment in South Carolina, seeing little of war but much of the Negro problem at first hand. In August he was transferred to the Army of the Potomac, and as a captain began to see real fighting. The three, father and two sons, exchanged long letters in which we get interesting glimpses of the life of all.

In May, the Minister took a larger and more comfortable house at 5 Upper Portland Place, which was indicative of a more assured position. Through the spring, the success of the Union armies had helped him considerably. "The change

produced in the tone towards the United States is very striking," he wrote the end of March, although the governing classes
were still hostile. However, Henry wrote at the same time,
"no one treads on our coattails any longer, and I do not expect
ever to see again the old days of anxiety and humiliation";
and again, in May, "people are very polite [in spite of their
prejudice] and we seem to be in a good set and likely to get on
well." Seward was still in hopes of getting the European
nations to withdraw their recognition of belligerency, although
there was obviously no real possibility of it and, in truth, no
reason for it. Adams, however, had to obey orders and press
Russell at intervals. Of the American Minister and Foreign
Secretary, Henry wrote his brother in the letter just quoted that
"the contest between the two gentlemen is getting to be
flavored with as copious dashes of vinegar as you could wish to
see. About once a week the wary Chieftain sharpens a stick
down to a very fine point, and then digs it into the excellent
Russell's ribs. The first two or three times the joke was
borne with well-bred politeness and calm indifference; but the
truth is, the stick's becoming so sharp that now things are
being thrown around with considerable energy, and our friend
Russell is not entirely in a good humor. The prospect at this
moment is that the breeze will soon change into settled rough
weather and perhaps we shall soon have a regular storm."
The South was pressing hard for full recognition, which it hoped
to achieve through Napoleon's ambition and schemes, and
Adams was warily watching. Suddenly the American Minister
was given a jolt.

He had been for an afternoon walk on the eleventh of June,
when on his return he found a note from the British Prime
Minister. He read it and then in amazement threw it across
the table to Henry asking, "What does this mean? Does
Palmerston want a quarrel?"

The day before, the *Times* had published the famous order
issued by General Butler in New Orleans threatening to treat as
a "woman of the town" any woman who should insult a
soldier. The situation in that captured city had become

a very difficult one to handle. Taking advantage of their sex, Southern women had made a practice of insulting soldiers in the street, even spitting on them, and worse. Although the military order meant that such women should merely be locked up in jail with all the street riffraff, it was unjustifiable in expression although characteristic of Butler's coarse and vulgar mind. In England, however, the treatment would have been different, and the order signified to the English mind much more than to the American.

The extremely undiplomatic letter which Mr. Adams read began, "I cannot refrain from taking the liberty of saying to you that it is difficult if not impossible to express adequately the disgust which must be excited in the mind of every honorable man by the general order of General Butler given in the enclosed extract from yesterday's *Times*," and ended with "if the Federal Government chooses to be served by men capable of such revolting outrages, they must submit to abide by the deserved opinion which mankind will form of their conduct."

Adams was as anxious as he was angry, fearing that the tone of Palmerston's note might portend a change of attitude on the part of his government. No such change was contemplated in fact, and Palmerston had, apparently, called the American Minister to account merely because he wished to be in a position to reply to the questions which were going to be put in Parliament on the subject of Butler's order. Adams at first, in a note to the Prime Minister, felt his way cautiously, asking whether he was to regard the communication as addressed to him officially or "purely as a private expression of sentiment between gentlemen." Requesting an interview with Russell, he showed him the note from Palmerston, and was able to assure himself that it did not spring from a change in ministerial policy. Assured on that point, he could afford to play with the Prime Minister as an angler plays with a trout. The opportunity was superb. Palmerston had laid himself open to attack from several sides at once. He had exploded over a newspaper clipping without inquiring first as to its validity, though in fact it was valid enough. He had chosen to approach the representative of a foreign government directly, and in most undiplomatic language, instead of through the proper channel of Lord Russell as Foreign Minister. He had written officially, although marking his letter "confidential and private."

To Adams's letter he returned, after two days, a rather evasive answer. In reply Adams pressed his advantage. "I have read it with attention," he wrote suavely, "but I regret to perceive that it inadvertently omits to favor me with an answer to the question which I respectfully asked." He called attention to the fact that the second letter was also marked private, and that the Prime Minister had acted on merely a newspaper report. He remarked that his government was fully competent to care for its own reputation, and that it would certainly object to having its representatives abroad "receive under the seal of privacy any indignity which it might be the disposition of the servants of any sovereign however exalted to offer to it in that form," and he again pressed for an answer to his question. Palmerston was now squirming. He had seriously involved himself in a wholly unjustifiable quarrel with a foreign representative, and had not unlikely been told by Lord John Russell to attend to his own affairs and to leave *him* to attend to his.

The Prime Minister was in a delicious quandary. He could not insist upon the letters being private, as Adams justly pointed out. Neither could he afford to have them considered official and appear as such publicly. On the other hand, Adams was anxious to settle the matter without turning a private quarrel and a diplomatic mistake of the Prime Minister into a quarrel between their respective countries. He had Palmerston at his mercy and both men knew it. Palmerston in reply to Adams's last letter made a shuffling answer, which, however, was enough for Adams to seize upon to end the correspondence very satisfactorily to himself. Commenting that Palmerston had apparently withdrawn his imputations, Adams closed by noting that a copy of the correspondence would be transmitted to his government and that "the difficulties in the way of this anomalous form of proceeding seem to me to be so grave, and the disadvantage under which it places those persons who may be serving as diplomatic representatives of foreign countries at this Court so serious, as to make it my painful duty to say to your Lordship that I must hereafter so long as I remain here in a public capacity decline to entertain any similar correspondence." Both Palmerston and Russell were men who were quite capable of appreciating keenly the skill with which Adams had won a complete victory and even to chuckle over it as a beautiful example of diplomatic rapier play.

The general situation, however, was becoming serious enough. In the middle of July, 1862, although the French Foreign Minister Thouvenel was opposed to involving France in war with the United States, the Emperor was pressing hard for recognition of the South. While Thouvenel was in London, about the third week of that month, Napoleon telegraphed to him, "Demandez au gouvernement anglais s'il ne croit pas le moment venu de reconnaître le Sud," and the Southern party in Parliament was also becoming restive. The opinion was spreading that the North could not win even though it might drag the war out for a long time, and meanwhile both France and England were suffering severely for want of cotton. Owing to the fact that the cotton crop of 1860 had been the largest on record, and to the condition of the trade itself, the scarcity due to the war had not been greatly felt at first. The South, however, as is well known, had counted on the famine which was bound to occur later as its trump card which was bound at length to win it recognition if not intervention. Throughout 1862 the distress in the cotton districts of England had been growing almost steadily greater. Operatives out of work and receiving public or private relief mounted from about 72,000 in December 1861 to 550,000 in December 1862. There seemed to be no end to the war, and if no end to that, no end to the possible distress in Europe. Recognition and even intervention seemed to be daily drawing nearer.

The summer was a most unpleasant one for Adams, and as for Henry, he wrote forty years later that he himself could never think of it without a shudder. In May 1861, when England had proclaimed her neutrality, she had passed a law providing among other points that British subjects were forbidden to build, equip, or fit out any vessel which should be employed in the service of either belligerent, and that punishment of the offenders and seizure of the vessel would follow upon proof of the offense. This last clause took all the teeth out of the law, as was unfortunately to be discovered. On passing the law it had seemed plausible enough that a person or act should be considered innocent until proved guilty, but in this case proof could only follow after neutrality had been broken.

The Confederacy had no navy and the Confederate agents were busy trying to get one built in England. On August 1, one of these made a contract with the shipbuilding firm of the Lairds at Liverpool to build what was afterwards known as the *Alabama*, which was to be used as a commerce destroyer. The ship was launched on May 15, 1862, and lay in the Mersey. The law officers of the Crown, who have been the plague of Anglo-American relations since 1770, had ruled that there was nothing illegal in building an unarmed ship, in buying arms, and then in combining the two outside of the territorial waters of Great Britain. If, therefore, the Confederacy acted through third parties and if the above two modes of conduct were complied with, there seemed no reason why the English were not acting legally, and if the British government interfered it would do so with the certainty of being cast for heavy damages in court. The situation was farcical, but dangerous and disgraceful. A smaller vessel, the *Florida*, had already been allowed to escape by the law officers when Adams warned Russell, on June 23, that the *Alabama*, which was unquestionably being built for the Confederacy, was nearly ready for departure, and asked that she be detained unless the fact was proved that she was not to be used against the United States.

The letter was referred to the proper department and by that referred to the port authorities at Liverpool, notoriously Southern in sympathy. A report was returned that there was no evidence against the ship. Russell then asked Adams and the American Consul at Liverpool for evidence on which he might detain the ship. Adams presented evidence which later was considered absolutely convincing, but which the law officers did not consider sufficient. The work on the vessel went on. Adams secured the opinion of the well-known solicitor Sir Robert Collier, who wrote that a stronger case could not be made out, and, again later, Russell admitted that he should have accepted his opinion and stopped the vessel. Everyone was convinced that the *Alabama* was being built for the South, but it was claimed that there was not legal evidence. Finally, on July 23, a full set of the documents in the case were submitted to the law officers of the Crown. At least they were sent to the senior officer, Sir John Harding, the Queen's Advocate. Harding, though no one but his wife knew it, had just gone insane, and she left the papers unopened on his desk in his own house for five days. Finally, on July 28, the Attorney-General and the Solicitor-General got hold of them. Instantly their decision was conclusive, and they recommended to the government that the vessel be seized without a moment's loss of time. It was too late. The *Alabama*, warned also that not a moment was to be lost, had sailed, unfinished.

Russell was deeply chagrined, and at least three other members of the cabinet. The damage to American shipping done by the *Alabama* was later to cost England dear, but that was nothing compared to the damage done to Anglo-American good feeling, for it is a curious circumstance that we nurse every grudge against England while we forget readily every wrong done us by any other nation. Throughout the Civil War the British government was far more friendly than was the French. Had it not been for England, Europe would unquestionably have recognized the Confederacy, and as it was, France committed that overt act of armed hostility, the seizure of Mexico, but somehow has managed to remain in popular feeling the "traditional friend."

By midsummer of 1862, however, even the British Cabinet was beginning to waver. The *Alabama* matter had been clumsy and insane folly, complicated at the critical point by the genuine insanity of the man on whom, for the moment, everything depended. It had not sprung, however, from any change of policy toward the United States, and the French Emperor's desire to recognize the South had been coldly received. The trump card of the South, on the contrary, was beginning to have weight. We have already spoken of the steadily increasing destitution in the cotton districts of England. It has been estimated that during the fifteen months when the cotton famine was at its worst over $12,000,000 was contributed in England to tide the sufferers over, and that the latter lost $50,000,000 in wages, huge sums for seventy years ago. In France the situation was also extremely bad and 300,000 persons were destitute, receiving about $800,000 a month in relief. The news from America about the beginning of September was equally discouraging. There had been the great defeat before Richmond, the second battle of Bull Run, and Lee was invading Maryland. It looked as though the end, with defeat for the North, was only a matter of time.

Adams, who, with diplomatic wisdom, had sensed in July that a change of policy might be impending in the British ministry, had written to Seward for instructions in such a case. Seward had replied with great dignity and firmness, after consultation with Lincoln, instructing Adams that if the British government approached him for an opinion as to how an offer of mediation would be received in Washington, he was to say that he was not instructed but had no reason to believe that it would be entertained; that if the British government, singly or with other nations, should acknowledge the Confederacy, he should at once suspend his functions as Minister; and that if England declared war, he was at once to ask for his passport and return to America. Seward, a very different man now from the first months in office, added that, although they were now gravely facing the possibility of a war with England and possibly other states, "I trust that you will have perceived that the crisis has not appalled us."

What Adams had feared was in truth almost coming to pass. In September, Russell, although throughout the rest of the war friendly rather than otherwise to the North, for a moment lost faith in the possibility of its conquering the South, and, with the desire of ending the strife in America and the suffering in Europe, proposed mediation to the cabinet. For some weeks the question was debated critically, and when Gladstone made his famous and indiscreet speech Adams expected to be on his way home in another fortnight. In the end, however, the government decided to keep its hands off, and in November, when the French Foreign Secretary proposed to England and Russia a joint intervention, England declined, and the most dangerous diplomatic corner of the whole war had been passed. The English operatives in Lancashire, who were the greatest sufferers from the conflict, had shown throughout a remarkable courage and a sympathy for the cause of the North. While the decision of the government hung in the balance, English working-class opinion, in public meetings and in print, was gradually making itself powerfully felt. Lincoln's Emancipation Proclamation helped the cause materially among the lower though not the upper classes, which latter professed to believe that he was bringing on a servile war.

In fact, Lincoln was the *bête noire* of British society. *Punch* had a cartoon depicting him as a devil, and Henry Adams wrote that "London was altogether beside itself on one point, in especial; it created a nightmare of its own and gave it the shape of Abraham Lincoln." Running into Thackeray by accident one evening, the novelist burst into violent reproaches to Henry on the subject. Carlyle indulged in coarse jibes. As Henry wrote, "at that moment Thackeray, and all London society with him, needed the nervous relief of expressing emotion; for if Mr. Lincoln was not what they said he was — what were they?" Yet to-day a statue of Lincoln, in one of the thoroughfares of London, calmly faces the main portal of Westminster Abbey, although no statue of an English king, however great, could be erected in America. Perhaps one of the greatest mistakes in international relations is to believe that the British and the Americans are psychologically kin.

The very week that the *Alabama* had slipped out of the

Mersey on its disastrous career, work had been begun on two more vessels by the Lairds, one of the vessels to be completed by March and the other by May, 1863. They were to be the most powerful ships afloat, equipped with rams, and were counted upon to raise the Southern blockade and to put New York and Boston under tribute. It devolved on Adams to stop them if possible. Owing to delays, the first of the rams was not launched until July and the other in August. Meanwhile, Adams had been busy. The *Alabama* was in full course of her destruction of American ships, and steadily Adams listed her depredations, with the amounts of the damage demanded from England, in letters to Lord John Russell. Captain Semmes, who was in command of her, estimated the damage up to May 21 as $3,100,000.

So important did the United States government consider the rams that it sent two business men, with $10,000,000 in government bonds, to buy them, an ill-advised attempt which came to nothing and which fortunately was not confided to Adams. Russell, a high-minded man and much irritated over the escape of the *Alabama*, had no intention of being caught a second time in so disastrous a blunder, and the Confederates began to have a strong suspicion that they would never get their ships. At this point the matter was taken up by John Slidell, who after his capture on the *Trent* had been representing the Confederacy in France. Unlike the obtuse Mason, who was in London, he was a man of much shrewdness and ability, and the contest over the Laird rams now came down to a duel between him and Adams. It was, as the United States government admitted, a matter of "life and death" for the Union cause, and was equally vital for the Confederates. Slidell was an adept in intrigue and no mean opponent in the more dubious paths of diplomacy, but Adams finally won by cool judgment and above all by the force of character.

Slidell felt himself completely sure of the more than benevolent attitude of the French Emperor to the Southern cause. His first move, and it was an extremely important one, was therefore to transfer the nominal ownership of the rams to a

French firm, Messrs. Bravay & Cie., who were reputed to be acting for the Pasha of Egypt. The real fact was that they agreed to purchase the vessels and to resell them, once safely out of British jurisdiction, to the Confederacy at a very handsome profit. The legal papers covering the purchase, which could be shown to any official, were in perfect order and apparently unassailable in law. The Lairds were given £5000 to induce them to change the contract to the new owner, and appear to have been imposed upon themselves and to have been convinced that the French firm was the *bona fide* contractor acting for the Pasha. Slidell also floated a loan of £3,000,000 at 90, putting himself in possession of nearly $12,000,000 to carry on his campaign, which included a bold attempt to manipulate the British parliamentary situation in such a way as to force Lord John Russell out of office, an intrigue in which Louis Napoleon was involved with second-rate members of Parliament. The campaign also included recognition by that body of the Confederacy. It was estimated that two-thirds of the members were Southern sympathizers and there seemed to be a fair chance to work out the scheme in all its ramifications. Fortunately the men whom Slidell was forced to work with as tools in England were, as we have said, all second-raters, and when one of them, Roebuck, attacked the government and attempted to secure recognition for the South, he handled the matter so badly as to procure a complete defeat for himself although two-thirds of his fellow members were in theory on his side. On July 13 he withdrew his motion for recognition, and on the sixteenth, much to the angry mortification of London society, as Adams recorded, came the much-needed news of the Union victory at Gettysburg. Moreover, a very happily timed insurrection in Poland injected an unexpected complication into the international situation for all European foreign ministers.

The first Laird ram, however, had been launched on July 4. Seward in somewhat of a panic was bombarding Adams with instructions that if shown to the British government or acted upon would have knocked all the fat in the fire. Adams did neither. He put them in his pocket and courteously intimated to Seward that as he, Adams, was on the spot he believed that he knew best what course to pursue and would assume the entire responsibility of pursuing it. Meanwhile the rebel political attack on Russell continued. Efforts were made to show that he was too much under the influence of Adams, though, as Adams wrote in his diary with delicious sarcasm, "Russell is too old and skillful a politician not to understand the necessity, for his own security, of keeping the minds of his countrymen free from all suspicion of his being superfluously courteous to any foreign power. From my observation of his correspondence since I have been at this post, I should judge that he seldom erred in that particular."

Adams, as he watched the progress of the rams, regularly addressed notes on the subject to Russell, studiously suave and correct. He had, however, other channels of communication with the cabinet, and to Cobden and others he stressed the extreme gravity of the situation, knowing that these remarks to friends would find their way to the Foreign Secretary. Russell was becoming insufferably uncomfortable. The recollection of the *Alabama* fiasco, and the frequent notes presented to the government detailing the damage she was doing to Union shipping as a basis for ultimate claims, both made him exceedingly uneasy as Adams kept writing his polite notes about the rams. In addition, even Adams admitted that the Secretary was a high-minded man and sincerely wished to do the right thing. However, Slidell had done his work so well that not only did there seem to be no loophole in the legal ownership of the rams by the French, but even such sincere friends and upholders of the Union cause as the Duke of Argyll had become convinced that the transfer of ownership from the Confederacy to Egypt had been honest and complete. As the case stood, if the British government condemned the rams, it would lay itself open to having to pay heavy damages and become involved with both France and Egypt, with no legal case on which it could make any stand and with popular opinion against it.

On September 4, Adams received notice from the American

Consul in Liverpool that one ram was ready for sea. The Minister at once sent a note of solemn warning to Russell, though he feared it would do no good. It did not, for the same afternoon he received a reply stating that the government could find no evidence on which to stop the vessel. Adams was deeply affected. Others, even some of the Union's best friends, might be hoodwinked by the ruses of Slidell. Adams had not been, and he knew that if the ram got to sea it could result only in war between England and America. That evening he received a telegram announcing the Union destruction of Fort Sumter and the shelling of Charleston. Given time, the North would win, but the departure of the ram would ruin all. It was not merely the damage she herself would do, though that was very great, but the inevitable war which would follow with England, ending perhaps in a world conflagration. Adams spent an anxious night pondering the problem from every angle, and then in the morning, with deep depression and with a sense of the great responsibility he was assuming, he penned one last note to Lord John Russell.

He resolved on a desperate throw. He restated his case to Russell and reiterated his request that the ram be detained, and then added that in case it were not "it would be superfluous in me to point out to your lordship that this is war." Russell was in Scotland and Adams waited three anxious days. On the eighth he received a brief note informing him that the British government had given orders to prevent the sailing of the rams. Adams, self-repressed as always, had been in agony of spirit. The relief was almost overpowering, but with characteristic restraint he merely noted in his diary, "I know not that even in the Trent case did I feel a greater relief." The price of Confederate bonds fell to 65. The cause of the South was irretrievably lost.

The threatening phrase that Adams used as quoted above, which has become famous, may or may not have been the determining cause in the government's decisions. I am inclined to think it was not. A few hours after he had dispatched the note containing it, and before it was read by Russell, Adams received a note from the latter stating that his two preceding notes had been read and were receiving the earnest and anxious attention of the government. Russell was sincerely anxious to detain the rams. Adams, whether or not he had convinced the cabinet, had not been able to make out a legal case, and, indeed, so little had the legal aspect of the matter to do with the government's action that it did not try to defend itself in court and settled with the Lairds by paying £225,000 for the ships. The decision of the cabinet was not based on law but on policy, and the note received by Adams just after he sent his last one indicated even to him that there might be one last chance on that score. As a matter of fact, it later transpired that Russell had given orders to detain the rams on September 1, four days before Adams wrote his last note, but he had been anxious to obtain legal evidence to support that action if it were possible, which it proved not to be. Adams, ignorant of this at the moment, later wrote approvingly of the "firm stand" Russell had taken unknown to him. Had there been any wavering policy between the first and the sixth, Adams's note might have clinched the matter, but with all the documents now before us there is no indication that there was, and Adams's note may well have been superfluous, although this in no way detracts from the stand which he took.

In one aspect, however, the note may be considered to have been unfortunate, in that it gave the impression that the British government had yielded only to the threat of war. A serious attack on Russell in Parliament was later made on that very point, and it has become implanted in the popular mind on both sides of the water. The government's policy clearly appears to have been adopted before they received the threat, though they could not announce it, even to the American Minister, until they had secured all the legal evidence that they were trying to obtain secretly in order to justify that policy when announced. There is no indication — indeed, there is evidence to the contrary — that they had any intention of abandoning the policy even when they found they could not justify it on legal grounds. However, even though Adams's last note, embodying the only phrase of his that has become popular, was superfluous, it is unquestionable that to him is due the entire credit of having brought the British government around to adopting the policy of detention. It was, moreover, the last great diplomatic struggle that Adams had to wage in London, although he remained until 1868. On the diplomatic front the war had been completely won. Adams's position in London was now secure, and even Seward left him alone to do as he saw fit. Throughout 1864 and 1865 his reputation was enhanced by the brilliancy with which he carried on a correspondence with Russell over the *Alabama* claims, but they were merely being made the basis of the arbitration proceedings that we shall have occasion to discuss later, and had no effect on the diplomacy of the war itself. By March 1865, he wrote to his son that his position was at last getting easy and comfortable.

During all these years, young Brooks was at school, and Henry, after his career as newspaper correspondent had been nipped, devoted himself to the absorbing occupation of watching the diplomatic webs spun and unraveled, to study, and to society. "As the years went on," he wrote, "he began to find the advantages in having no position at all except that of young man." He was, however, far from idle. He read widely, often studying till the early hours of the morning in the silence of London nights, and the social life in which he took part was education in itself. His society, indeed, lacked one essential element in that it was almost wholly masculine. If London social life was far removed from the boy-and-girl or husband-and-wife affair that was typical of Boston's, Henry nevertheless had no intimates among the other sex of his own, or any, age. With most of the male celebrities of the day — the politicians like Palmerston and Russell, the literary men like Thackeray and Browning, science embodied in Lyell, and a host of others such as Lord Holland, John Bright, or Richard Cobden — he had a speaking acquaintance, and in several of the cases more intimate relations. As he later described it, he "met in England a thousand people, great and small; jostled against every one, from royal princes to gin-shop loafers; attended endless official functions and private parties; visited every part of the United Kingdom and was not quite a stranger at the Legations in Paris and Rome; he knew the societies of certain country houses, and acquired habits of Sunday-afternoon calls." His closest friend proved to be a young Yorkshireman, Charles Milnes Gaskell, whose father was member for Wenlock in Shropshire, and who in 1856 had bought the beautiful old ruined abbey at that place. The prior's house was in fair preservation and the family turned it into a charming country home, where Lady Gaskell, the widow of Henry's friend, yet lives. Set in the exquisite Shropshire country, within walking distance of Wenlock Edge and the Wrekin, it is to-day a perfect haunt of ancient peace, and was to remain a refuge for Henry all his life.

Toward the end of the war, in 1864, his English experience was interrupted by six months in Italy. The London climate had told on his sister, and Henry was appointed to escort some of the ladies of the Legation household to the south for the winter. He enjoyed it hugely. "Travelling," as he remarked, "in all possible luxury, at some one else's expense, with diplomatic privileges and position, was a form of travel hitherto untried." The Cornice, Naples, Sorrento, Rome at Easter, Perugia, Siena, all were passed in a panorama of loveliness and interest much more lively, apparently, than on his first trip. At Rome came the news of Lincoln's assassination. Back in London, Henry began to face the problem of a career. His father showed no signs of going home, and the government showed no signs of wishing to release him. The son, in spite of all the troubles of the war, had come to love London. All men are born Londoners or Parisians, as they are Platonists or Aristotelians, and Henry was a Londoner. The whole family, indeed, in all their character were English through and through, in nothing more than in their constant growling against the English. There is a quality about London that it is impossible to analyze. The city makes no effort to capture the stranger, but if he is a born Londoner in spirit he merely sinks softly into its vastness and wakes to find himself bound by a hundred filmy threads of affections, interests, habits, and sympathies that, when he considers leaving, he finds have become steel chains. Henry, when facing the problem of a career, made only the slightest of motions toward breaking them.

For three generations the family had had their hand on the lever of power, and Henry had ambition. Of the struggle over the rams, he notes that he "began to dream the sensation of wielding unmeasured power. The sense came like vertigo, for an instant, and passed, leaving the brain a little dazed, doubtful, shy." Some months before that episode, however, he had written to his brother that he had no confidence in himself, that his mind was too balanced to be successful in action, that he never saw good in anything unmixed with evil or evil unmixed with good, and that nothing seemed important enough to call forth full energy.

The weight of the family was beginning to be a heavy one. Three generations of the highest attainment in statesmanship would make any achievement, except the highest, spell failure. The front and back doors of the Adams House, through which they had so easily and regularly passed since the change of phase in John, had been the doors of law and diplomacy, but Henry rather oddly and characteristically considered both these to have been closed to him, and he says that his father agreed. He claimed that diplomacy had unfitted him for law, though he had merely been a youthful looker-on, from an extremely advantageous seat, and as yet was only twenty-six years old. His grandfather, at thirty-four, after he had himself been a minister for seven years, had gone back to Quincy to start to build a legal practice. As for diplomacy, young Henry considered that he had been too near the centre of things to take a post as secretary in some out-of-the-way legation, and in this he was probably wise, both as a matter of training and temperament and because diplomacy, in the American political system, was nonexistent as a career. It could never be anything but an episode. To a political career, Henry never gave a thought. Yet he wanted action and power. As he says, the press seemed the only resort, and for that Henry now decided to fit himself.   He knew that London was not the place to begin such a career, which, for him, was bound to be American, but he stayed on under the impression that he could not go home. His father had now become one of the great figures in English life.   Palmerston died in 1865;   Russell fell from office six months later; but Adams was "almost a historical monument." Mrs. Adams had achieved in her own sphere an even greater success, if possible, than her husband.   Adams was only fifty-eight, the boy Brooks was seventeen, the war was over, and life at the Legation had ceased to be difficult and had become merely easy and delightful.   It is hard to see why Henry could not leave, and why, having chosen to apprentice himself to the American press, he should not have gone home and set about it.

However, he remained and made his first essay, at the suggestion of the historian Palfrey, by, so to say, breaking one of the stained-glass windows in the old American hall of fame with a critical essay on Captain John Smith, which was an excellent bit of work and was published in the *North American Review*. His next article was of considerably more importance in the development of his thought.   Sir Charles Lyell, who was one of his father's friends, published his *Principles of Geology* in 1866 and dropped in at the Legation one day to inquire of Mr. Adams how best to get it noticed in America.   Henry undertook to review it, and thus began his first serious study of science.   This essay, like his other, duly appeared in the *North American*.   At this time, however, he had no intention of devoting himself to the field of either history or science.   What appealed to him as an Adams was statesmanship, and in America there was no bigger problem in that field at the moment than that of the currency.   Hoping to make his reputation among financiers and statesmen at home by showing how the major task of the moment, the resumption of specie payments, had been performed by England after the classical suspension of 1797–1821, he spent six months studying and wrote two long articles.   These were also accepted by Charles Eliot Norton, who was then editing the *North American*, and Henry was enrolled on the permanent staff.   "Precisely what this rank was worth," he wrote later, "no one could say; but, for fifty years the *North American Review* had been the stage coach which carried literary Bostonians to such distinction as they had achieved." The circulation of the journal was only about three hundred copies, but it served as a storehouse of ideas and material for newspaper editors all over the country. The influence of a writer in it was great. "It was an organ," Henry added, "worth playing on," and in his fancy "it led, in some indistinct future, to playing on a New York daily newspaper." While still in London, he had thus made a notable progress toward placing his hand, albeit from the study, on the lever of power.

At home, his brother Charles was similarly confronted by the problem of a career. Of his three and a half years in the army it is not necessary to speak in detail. He had made a courageous and competent officer. Beginning as a first lieutenant, he had risen solely on his merit to be colonel of the Fifth Massachusetts Cavalry, a Negro regiment, and had been mustered out, on account of a breakdown in his health, in May 1865 as a brigadier-general. His reputation had been well earned and General Humphreys had offered him the highest position on his staff, which he had declined from the mistaken sense of duty which he believed required him to remain in command of his regiment in the field. He had served in the great battles of Antietam and Gettysburg, as well as smaller skirmishes, and throughout the war had written extremely vivid descriptions of camp and war life in his long letters to his father. His health had broken down once before in the course of his service and he had made a visit of a few months on furlough to the family in London; but, of greater importance, he had also visited Newport and there become engaged to Mary Hone Ogden, the daughter of Edward Ogden of New York, whom he married on November 8, 1865, six months after he was discharged from the army and when still in wretched health. The next eleven months he passed in Europe, mainly in London, Paris, and Rome, getting back to America, restored in health, in October 1866 to face the problem of a career. He was now thirty-one, and although he had a small income which enabled him to live, both ambition and the need of means made the problem one to be faced without delay. The brigadier-general of war days had to start somewhere at the bottom again. "Nominally," he wrote in his old age, "I found I had to go back to a law office. I had no choice. I had to do something; but I did it with a sinking heart. I felt I had no aptitude that way. In my case people have always been over-ready to talk of 'family influence' and all that sort of thing in an owlish way, so accounting for about everything I ever accomplished. So far as I have been able to see, however, 'family influence' never was of any assistance to me; and in those ordeal days, never I am sure was put forth in the faintest in my behalf."

We have spoken a number of times of the divergence of the lines of force that directed on the one hand the development of the family and on the other the trend of social organization. In the case of Charles there was a deliberate and self-conscious effort to bring the two into the same path. Charles, instead of merely looking for a job, looked about him to determine what was likely to prove the major force of his time. "Surveying the whole field," he writes in his *Autobiography*, "instinctively recognizing my unfitness for the law — I fixed on the railroad system as the most developing force and largest field of the day, and determined to attach myself to it. I now stand amazed at my own inexperience and audacity; but, having made up my mind, within a fortnight of my dreary home-coming, and, in perfect good faith, evolving my facts from my inner consciousness, I proceeded to write an article on 'Railroads' for the *North American Review!* James Russell Lowell and Charles E. Norton were then editing that periodical — trying to infuse new life into its aged system; for it was being slowly but surely crowded out of existence by the newer and more superficial, but also more readable swarm of monthlies then coming into vogue. . . . I wrote the article — *currente calamo* — at Newport, while wondering what I was going to do for a winter shelter; and I hardly consulted a book, while, certainly, I knew nothing of the subject." The appearance of the article was to prove of great help to him, and it is interesting to note that both the brothers turned instinctively to their pen and the *North American* to start their careers. The pen, indeed, since it was first grasped by John, seems never to have fallen from the fingers of the family. "The dreary clientless months crept on," Charles continues, "but my pen was always busy; I wrote article on article, almost always on railroads, or railroad law, for the *North American* or the magazines, law and other, and in that way identified my name with railroads; but it was a discouraging process. I never seemed to get anywhere; the outlook did not brighten." The day, however, was suddenly to break, but not until after his father's return from England, and the further story belongs to the next generation.

At last, Adams resigned as Minister and left London the end of June, 1868. There was yet ahead of him one great act of public service, but no further continuing career, and we must turn to the younger generation, now pressing ahead. Henry sailed with him, and noted that, after seven years, "London had become his vice. He loved his haunts, his houses, his habits, and even his hansom cabs. He loved growling like an Englishman, and going into society where he knew not a face, and cared not a straw. He lived deep into the lives and loves and disappointments of his friends. When at last he found himself back again at Liverpool, his heart wrenched by the act of parting, he moved mechanically, unstrung." The family's third mission to a hostile England was over, and Henry loved her.

THE FOURTH GENERATION

JOHN QUINCY, CHARLES FRANCIS, HENRY, AND BROOKS ADAMS

JOHN QUINCY, CHARLES FRANCIS, HENRY, AND BROOKS ADAMS

"At ten o'clock of a July night, in heat that made the tropical rain-shower simmer, the Adams family and the Motley family clambered down the side of their Cunard steamer into the government tugboat, which set them ashore in black darkness at the end of some North River pier." Thus Henry chronicled their return. "Had they been Tyrian traders of the year B.C. 1000," he added, "landing from a galley fresh from Gibraltar, they could hardly have been stranger on the shore of a world, so changed from what it had been ten years before."

For an Adams, indeed, with his eighteenth-century tradition and fresh from eight years in London, engaged in eighteenth-century diplomacy, there was scarcely a recognizable landmark. In spite of the war, population had continued to increase and the nation now numbered about 38,000,000 people, most of whom, from the latest immigrant to descend the gangplank to the highest Senator in Congress, were bent with insane concentration solely upon the most rapid possible advancement of their personal fortunes. Mere increase of population had been witnessed by each succeeding Adams, but new elements were entering into the matter now. Even during the war, the remarkable phenomenon had been evident of a steady inflow of foreign immigrants, sometimes ten thousand in a week. Eight hundred thousand had arrived in the five war years alone, and with the end of the war the flood had swelled. At the same time, although in the decade from 1860 to 1870 the total population had increased only about 22 per cent, the urban population had increased 60 per cent. It was the era of vast increases in the cities and in the political corruption which has always characterized our municipalities.

The national government and politics were also, however, at their lowest ebb. Perhaps Congress has never offered such a disgraceful exhibition as in the administration of Andrew Johnson following the death of Lincoln. On May 26, scarce a month before the Adamses landed, a vote of acquittal had hardly been won for the President in the moronic farce of the impeachment proceedings. American public life smelt to Heaven. Government over a large part of the country was being carried on in complete defiance of the Constitution. In the South, the "carpetbag" governments were in full swing with their attendant orgy of theft on a colossal scale. In the West were limitless forests and boundless areas of land from which perjury and corruption could wrest wealth almost overnight unhampered by complacent government officials. Railroads and new inventions seemed to open vistas to hitherto undreamed-of riches. As the nation turned aside from whatever idealism there had been in the war it was to throw itself into an insane rush for power — money, land, mines, politics, railroads, any form of control that would lead to power for the individual. No one appeared to have any idea what he was going to do with wealth and power when he got it. There was merely a mad urge to get it. There was no time to think, or someone else would get it first. The opportunities were stupendous and life was short. To pass from the tranquil ordered life of England, with a sense of values, to the roaring tide of America, with no sense of values other than monetary, was like suddenly finding one's self jerked out of a quiet punt on the Cam to be sent over Niagara in a barrel.

No wonder that, after looking about a bit, Henry decided that "his world was dead," and that "not a Polish Jew fresh from Warsaw or Cracow — not a furtive Yacoob or Isaac still reeking of the Ghetto, snarling in a weird Yiddish to the officers of the customs — but had a keener instinct, an intenser energy, and a freer hand than he — American of the Americans, with Heaven knows how many Puritans and Patriots behind him." His father came home with a great reputation and no place to fill. One of the founders of the Republican Party, he could look only

with disdain and disgust upon the immoral filth and the unconstitutional courses in which that party was now wallowing,
whereas he also found much to criticize in both the record and
the political methods of the Democrats.

His son, John Quincy, who had served on Governor Andrews's
staff during the war, who had been a staunch supporter of
Lincoln, and had served in the State Legislature in 1866, had
found himself unable to stomach the Republican methods of
Reconstruction, and in 1867 had run for both the Legislature
and the governorship on the Democratic ticket. He ran again
unsuccessfully the following year, but in 1869 was elected to the
Legislature and became the leader of the Democratic Party in
the state, running for governor again in 1870 and 1871. His
father, however, merely retired to his house at Quincy and
busied himself over the family papers, the result of his labors
proving eventually, perhaps, of more lasting importance than
any office he might have held. In 1869 he was asked to accept
the Presidency of Harvard, but declined on the ground that he
did not consider that he possessed any special fitness and that
acceptance would interfere with the plans which he had made.

The boy Brooks had naturally entered Harvard, with
advanced standing, to graduate in the class of 1870 and continue his studies, according to family tradition, in the law
school. For Charles and Henry the problem was less simple.
Charles had, indeed, nearly worked his out. We have already
noted that he had been struggling with his pen to make a name
for himself in connection with the railroads that he believed
would prove one of the major forces of the new world then
arising. It was a force, however, which called for control.
There had been, for the time, too much mileage built and
altogether too much corruption in the building and subsequent
stock gambling. In 1869, largely owing to Charles's preparation of the public mind, Massachusetts took the lead of all the
states in establishing a State Railroad Commission, and
Charles was named one of three Commissioners. Although
the youngest, he was much the ablest and most active, and
three years later he was named Chairman, holding that post

until 1879, when he declined a renomination. We may merely note here that during those years he wrote a series of Reports that, apart from their own great value, were highly influential in securing the establishment of the railroad commissions of other states and developing the policies that such commissions have followed.

When his father returned from England, Charles and his wife had moved out of the family house in Boston and into one at Quincy on the Neponset turnpike, a change that was to have considerable influence upon his later interests. There, in his own home, his play for influence by means of the railroads having been successful in making him State Railroad Commissioner, in which position he could largely guide the policies of others as well as his own state, the young man began to find himself quickly. The same year that he was made Commissioner he was elected president of the Kansas City Stock Yards Company, then a small concern with $100,000 capital and earning about $20,000 a year. He was to remain president for forty years and to build up the company to a capital of $10,000,000 and earnings of $1,200,000, making it at that time the largest concern of the kind in the world. Visiting Kansas City when he first became interested in his company, he worked out logically the inevitable huge growth of that city and made large purchases of real estate, which were eventually to prove very valuable. At thirty-four he thus found himself a retired brigadier-general, started in civil life with a public post of importance and influence, and with the foundations skillfully laid of a great fortune. We shall see that disaster later nearly overtook the last, but the young man was well on his way. If his brother, John Quincy, had made something of a break with tradition in going over to the Democrats, he was in reality maintaining it, not merely in adhering to law and politics, but in his independence of mind. In the case of Charles, the break was distinctly more marked. He had not indeed gone over to State Street, for State Street did not look on commissions to control business with any too kind an eye, but in undertaking the management of large business enterprises Charles was clearly out of the family tradition. It was the nearest approach between the family line and the line of social forces that the new age was to be able to effect.

The three lines that would possibly lead to power in the new world might prove to be politics, money, and the press. John had combined his law with politics and become a brilliant leader in his state, whose influence was to extend beyond its boundaries, but for power he was in the wrong party. The Democrats did not reach the White House from 1861 until 1893, and in 1894 John was dead. Charles combined his law with big business, but the power that the latter brought him was slight compared with what came from his pen, and it cannot be said that the alliance was a fruitful one for an Adams. Henry, who also had his law, decided to strike straight for the press. The power that he was to gain, however, was outside the scope of his first endeavor and the family tradition. It was never to be political power.

He spent the first few months after his return in looking about him, discovering, as he said, "the worthlessness of a so-called social connection." "He was for sale," as he puts it, "in the open market. So were many of his friends. All the world knew it, and knew too that they were cheap; to be bought at the price of a mechanic. There was no concealment, no delicacy, no illusion about it." But nobody would buy. Henry, like his grandmother, had never fitted into Boston. "The mere thought of beginning life again in Mount Vernon Street lowered the pulsations of his heart." Besides, Boston "was full of his brothers." Moreover, a connection with the Boston press led nowhere, any more than did connection with Boston politics. Boston had come to be business. Henry decided on Washington, where possibly in some way he and Charles might play into each other's hands, each having, as he noted, "no one else to play with."

Washington in 1868, however, was outside the universe for a Bostonian. For a Bostonian to go there, except as a member of government, was to proclaim himself an adventurer, "a person of deplorably bad judgment." Henry did not have his eye on a government post. He had it on the New York press, and wished to use Washington merely as a stepping-stone. He intended to make his political articles a genuine weapon of power, and later wield that power as a New York editor — in other words, as a national figure. Beyond that all would be fate, with which one need not meddle too far in advance. Henry, however, was trying to plan his career with the same regard to the lines of force in his generation as did Charles. The weapon he chose, the political press, was to prove as useless for the purpose to an Adams as Charles's money, and to break much sooner. But he set out to fit it to his hand.

To win national power, he needed a national press, which — outside the *North American Review*, upon which he could count — meant the New York dailies. It was necessary to be in Washington to be a Washington correspondent, but it was equally necessary to have something to correspond with. The *Nation* he could get entry to, but that was not a daily. Raymond, the editor of the *Times* and Henry's friend, had just died. The *Tribune*, under Greeley, was politically out of the question. Henry felt he could do nothing with the *Sun*, for, "with the best intentions, he must always fail as a blackguard." The *Herald* was nothing but Bennett, so, "for the moment," as he wrote, "the New York daily press offered no field except the free-trade Holy Land of the *Evening Post* under William Cullen Bryant, while beside it lay only the elevated plateau of the New Jerusalem occupied by Godkin and the *Nation*." These offered only the same circle of readers as the *Review*, but such as the opportunities were, Henry took them.

So, in October 1868, he started for Washington in company with William M. Evarts, who was then Attorney-General and who kindly took him into his house for some months. After London society, the Washington world was simple enough. It would obviously take Henry but a short time to know every-one he cared to. He began with the President. "The inter-view was brief," Henry noted, "and consisted of the stock remark common to monarchs and valets, that the young man

looked even younger than he was. The younger man felt
even younger than he looked. He never saw the President
again, and never felt a wish to see him, for Andrew Johnson was
not the sort of man whom a young reformer of thirty, with
two or three foreign educations, was likely to see with enthusiasm." Yet as he looked back in later years he came to realize
Johnson's strength. Henry's social training in London was
worse than useless in political Washington and he amused
himself trying to learn how to talk with Western Congressmen
and hide his own antecedents. The lobby he found picturesque,
notably in the figure of "old Sam Ward, who knew more of life
than all the departments of the Government together, including
the Senate and the Smithsonian."

If Henry wished for political power from the press, he also
wished for literary fame, and he spent some months writing a
long article on finance, which he sent to the *Edinburgh Review*,
appearance in which, to his mind, would give a man at that
time as high standing as it was possible to attain in the literary
world. The article was accepted and published in April 1869.
At the same time, with his other aim in mind, he conceived the
idea of writing a periodic political article for the *North American*
on the lines of the so-called "Session" published by Lord Robert
Cecil in the *London Quarterly*. This he hoped in time to make
a political authority. "With his sources of information, and his
social intimacies," he wrote, "he could not help saying something that would command attention. He had the field to
himself, and he meant to give himself a free hand as he went
on. Whether the newspapers liked it or not, they would have
to reckon with him; for such a power, once established, was
more effective than all the speeches in Congress or reports to
the President that could be crammed into the Government
presses." Two of these "Sessions" appeared in the *North
American*, 1869 and 1870, as well as articles on Civil Service
Reform and the Legal Tender Act.

In 1869 the Republican régime was quite evidently rotten,
but the country, including all the Adamses except John Quincy,
had not been able to turn to the Democrats. John, who had

none of the crotchets and kinks of the family mind and manner, had, as we have seen, gone over to that party in complete disgust with the one in power, and was campaigning for the governorship in Massachusetts. He was not only "one of the best talkers in Boston society, and perhaps the most popular man in the state," but a clear thinker and a noted orator. In his speech of acceptance he turned heavy fire on the Republican extravagance, tax system, and tariff. Reconstruction had to be accepted, but he had already given his views clearly as to the policy to be employed toward the South. Some months earlier, in October 1868, he had accepted an invitation from Wade Hampton to speak in South Carolina, and it was a notable moment when the grandson of old John Quincy rose to address a Charleston audience on Union and fraternal relations after the war. He took the ground that Reconstruction questions were questions of a social, not of a political, order, and the various speeches he made in the South were among the ablest of his day, although, even when published, without effect on the vindictive policies of the dominant party supported by a majority of the people of the North.

In the campaign all the Adamses, except John, were for Grant, and Grant, whom Henry helped by a vote to put in the White House, ended Henry's political leader-writing career. Of all the family, John's judgment had been the clearest, but Henry could see clearly enough also after an interview with the new President and the announcement of his cabinet appointments. Henry had wanted to find an administration that he could support. Obviously he could not support Grant. America had reverted to the Stone Age. After an interview he contrasted him with Garibaldi, and decided that the Italian was the more intellectual of the two. In neither, however, did intellect count. Grant's closest friends "could never follow a mental process in his thought. They were not sure that he did think." Henry had spent the summer of 1869 at Quincy, and in September came Gould's attempt to corner the gold market. Whatever Grant's character might be, its effects had shown up, "startling — astounding — terrifying."

Henry and Charles decided to work up the whole problem of Gould, the Erie Railroad, and the conspiracy, Charles writing the railway part and Henry the gold corner. They worked for months with infinite pains and Charles's "Chapter of Erie" was published in the *North American Review*. Henry, although he had to wait for Congress to convene, finally finished his "New York Gold Conspiracy." "The worst scandals of the eighteenth century were relatively harmless by the side of this," he wrote in his *Education*, "which smirched executive, judiciary, banks, corporate systems, professions, and people, all the great active forces of society, in one dirty cesspool of vulgar corruption. Only six months before, this innocent young man, fresh from the cynicism of European diplomacy, had expected to enter an honorable career in the press as the champion and confidant of a new Washington, and already he saw a life of wasted energy, sweeping the stables of American society clean of the endless corruption which his second Washington was quite certain to breed." "Grant's administration outraged every rule of ordinary decency, but scores of promising men, whom the country could not well spare, were ruined in saying so. The world cared little for decency. What it wanted, it did not know; probably a system that would work, and men who could work it; but it found neither. Adams had tried his own little hands on it, and had failed. His friends had been driven out of Washington or had taken to fisticuffs. He himself sat down and stared helplessly at the future." The result of his meditation was the second "Session" article mentioned above. At that time, any article in a foreign review attracted far more attention than in an American publication, so Henry had sent his "Gold Conspiracy" to the *Edinburgh*, never dreaming that it would not be printed. In the spring of 1870 he sailed for England and in May found himself once more driving up St. James's Street. "He sniffed with voluptuous delight the coal smoke of Cheapside and revelled in the architecture of Oxford Street. Mayfair never shone so fair to Arthur Pendennis as it did to the returned American. . . . He loved it all — everything — had always loved it!"

Reeves, the editor of the *Edinburgh*, however, declined Henry's article on Gould for fear of libel. Henry was shocked at the lack of courage shown and dispatched the article to the *Westminster Review*.

Just at that moment he received word from his brother-in-law Charles Kuhn, at Bagni di Lucca in Tuscany, saying that his wife had been thrown from her carriage and that Henry had better go on at once. He arrived to find that his sister had cut her foot in the accident, that tetanus had set in, and that the brilliant woman of forty was doomed. The end came in ten days. In spite of his "education," Nature had thus far shown Henry only her smiling side. Now, suddenly, in the midst of the summer-clad Tuscan landscape, never so beautiful and caressing as in the dreaming days of June, she had revealed her other side, known before vaguely, but as yet unfelt. The mask of ease and charm had been dashed aside and the face of horror gazed like a Medusa into the terrified eyes of the young man who had so far gone gayly through the pleasant paths of his intellectual world. For the first time Nature appeared to him "as a phantasm, a nightmare, an insanity of force. For the first time, the stage-scenery of the senses collapsed; the human mind felt itself stripped naked, vibrating in a void of shapeless energies, with resistless mass, colliding, crushing, wasting, and destroying what these same energies had created and labored from eternity to perfect." Henry had made a vast step in education. He had needed something to scorch off the intellectual trappings and burn him to the centre of his being. John, by nature the most courageous of the brothers, had, by inheritance rather than training, been able to throw himself into the struggle of the world with all his strength from the start. Charles had needed the army, which had made, as he always claimed, a man of him. He had urged Henry to get out of London and expose himself to hardship in some way during the Legation days, recognizing his deep need for it. "All a man's life is not meant for books, or travel in Europe," he had warned. Henry was not a type that would choose adventurous hardships. He was essentially an intellectual and had to take life through

the channel of mind and emotion. He had not, as his brother
had urged, gone to the North Pole to face difficulties. The
North Pole, in the shape of a sudden and searing vision of a
frozen cosmos devoid of human compassion, had come to him.
He was overwhelmed.

Slowly he made his way back to England, the Franco-
Prussian War breaking out with startling suddenness while he
was on his way, and betook himself to the peace of Wenlock
Abbey and his friends the Gaskells. While staying at Wenlock
a letter came from President Eliot of Harvard offering him the
post of assistant professor of history, which he declined. He
considered, he later commented, though not to Eliot, that he
knew nothing of history, less about teaching, and too much
about Harvard. On September 1 he sailed for home with no
definite plans, and with no prospect of being able to attach
himself, in any work on the press, to any President or party.
The only career ahead seemed to be that of a free-lance writer
on politics, which probably would not have got him anywhere.
To be sure, his "Session" article had attracted wide attention,
though it had not then, as he states from a slip of memory in
his *Education*, been published as a campaign document and
circulated by the hundred thousand, as it was to be later.
Moreover, October brought him the *Westminster Review* with
his Gold Conspiracy article published at last. In spite of these
promising beginnings, however, his family recognized that his
position was a very insubstantial one. The editorship of the
North American Review was open at the moment and that
post was offered to him as combined with the post at Harvard.

Not only was any public career in prospect in 1870 unprom-
ising, but in actuality none proved fruitful or really successful
in the next two decades. As, in late life, Henry surveyed the
epoch, he could find in the executive, legislative, and judiciary,
and the public press, only failures or damaged reputations.
Alone of his family, John kept the field and the family banner
flying, much to Henry's admiration, but it was only to be
defeated again and again, and to-day to be so nearly forgotten

by the crowd as even not to have been given a place in the *Dictionary of American Biography*. Henry yielded to his family's arguments, even his father taking a rare position as a giver of advice, and settled at Cambridge to edit the *Review* and teach mediæval history, one of the wisest steps he ever took.

Meanwhile the father, while living quietly in Boston and Quincy, preparing the *Diary* of old John Quincy Adams for the press, was watching with great interest and anxiety the negotiations between England and the United States over the *Alabama* claims. All was proceeding well until Charles Sumner introduced into the discussion an utterly fantastic claim for *indirect* damages amounting to $110,000,000, with the suggestion that if the prolongation of the war were also taken into consideration they might run to two thousand million. Such a suggestion from a chairman of the Foreign Relations Committee in the Senate was not merely absurd, it was criminal, and followed by even worse. The negotiations, however, were continued, and on March 24, 1871, England and the United States signed the Treaty of Washington in which England manfully admitted her fault in allowing the ships to escape and accepted an arbitration of the dispute. The Commission of Arbitration was to be composed of five members, of whom one each was to be named by the two countries involved and three others by the King of Italy, the President of Switzerland, and the Emperor of Brazil respectively. At the time of Grant's inauguration, Adams had frequently been mentioned as a possibility for the post of Secretary of State, though it is now obvious that a Grant would never have thought of an Adams for any post whatever. It was clear, however, that no one but Adams could well be appointed as an Arbitration Commissioner, as it was he who had built up our whole case day by day at the Legation during and after the war. He received the appointment, and, taking his son Brooks, who had just completed a year at the law school, as his private secretary, he sailed in time to be present at the convening of the tribunal at Geneva on December 15, 1871. The British had appointed Sir Alexander Cockburn, and the three neutral appointments were excellent. Unfortunately Grant's appointment of J. C. Bancroft Davis as agent for the United States to present its case was incredibly poor.

Both sides, through their agents, presented their cases, and then the Tribunal adjourned, instructing that the counter cases be handed to the Secretary by April 15 and that another sitting be held June 15. At the very opening it appeared that Davis had wrecked the possibility of arbitration entirely. Rhodes, with certainly as much reserve as candor, writes that the case as presented by him was "not one for an American to be proud of," and Adams noted that the contentions "were advanced with an aggressiveness of tone and attorney-like smartness, more appropriate to the wranglings of a quarter sessions court than to pleadings before a grave international tribunal." In the opening section of his case, Davis made not only unnecessary but untrue allegations when he stated that the British Government had shown "a conscious unfriendly purpose toward the United States," but when he came to later sections he aroused a storm of passion in England by reviving in still more fantastic shape the demands of Sumner by claiming that England should be required to pay the entire cost of the whole Civil War from the date that the *Alabama* escaped, July 4, 1863.

The English had bitterly resented Sumner's speeches in the Senate, but they had never dreamed that the United States would seriously propose anything so preposterous at Geneva. In Parliament, Gladstone denounced the "indirect" claims as "claims which not even the last extremities of war and the lowest depths of misfortune would force a people with a spark of spirit . . . to submit to at the point of death." The feeling was so strong, even among some members of the cabinet, that it seemed impossible that the treaty could be saved and that there should be any arbitration at all. In London, Adams urged that the Government stand fast by the treaty, and as soon as he reached America he had conferences with Grant and the Secretary of State. The latter, Hamilton Fish, and other leaders were anxious to save the treaty also, and had no wish to uphold either the bad manners or the impossible demands of their pettifogging attorney. On the other hand, that great deflector of American uprightness, a presidential campaign, was approaching, and "public opinion," which was anti-British, had to be taken into consideration. In England, Gladstone was also striving to hold his Government together in the face of the storm that Davis had so unnecessarily aroused. In the House of Lords, Earl Russell had announced that he intended to blow the Treaty and the Government both high in the air. Fish intimated to the British Government, through the American Minister Motley, that the United States did not intend to press the indirect claims nor did it expect any damages on account of them, and an amendment to the treaty was passed by the Senate excluding them.

When Adams returned to Geneva for the session of June 15, however, nothing had been definitely settled and the English wished an adjournment of eight months. Adams saw at once that the whole question of indirect claims must somehow be got out of the way immediately or the arbitration would be wrecked. On June 17 an adjournment had been taken, but the five arbitrators remained for informal conference. Unfortunately, Sir Alexander Cockburn had been almost as unfortunate a choice for the English as Davis for the Americans. If Davis had nearly broken up the Tribunal, Cockburn at any time would have been glad to have had it so broken. Other members of the British delegation wrote home complaining of his conduct, which, as one wrote, was "very damaging." Another wrote that he seemed possessed to insult everyone. He was as far below the other four arbitrators in mind as he was in manner, and was that most unpleasant type of Englishman which is both overbearing and a bad loser. Fortunately the three neutral members, Count Sclopis, Jacques Staempfli, and Vicomte d'Itajubà, were all intelligent and just-minded men, admirably fitted for their office, and, equally fortunately, Adams's perfect command of French acquired in his boyhood at St. Petersburg enabled him to carry on the negotiations without that usual handicap of an American, the need of an interpreter.

In the informal conferences following adjournment, Adams, with his plan now clearly in his mind, led Cockburn to intimate that possibly an extra-judicial pronouncement by the Tribunal might be made that would satisfy both countries and end the deadlock. Adams, having committed Cockburn to agreeing, then said that he would make a proposition, in making which, he added, "I shall be assuming a heavy responsibility; but I shall do so not as an arbitrator representing my country but as representing all nations." That an Adams should have assumed the responsibility for decision was in line with the whole family precedent and tradition. We call to mind at once John in Paris in 1783, John Quincy at Ghent in 1814, and again in the House when his words "I will put the question myself" rang out over the confused mob. That the trait of courageous individualism should have persisted is noteworthy, but even more so is the steady broadening of the family outlook from the day when John, then an English colonial, stood for the rights of Massachusetts in Quincy Town Meeting to the day when his grandson considered himself not even as an American, but as the representative of all nations and of international law in an international Tribunal at Geneva. The result of Adams's suggestions was the drafting of a protocol which was adopted by the court and which declared that upon principles of the law of nations there could be no consideration given to the indirect claims. The way out of the difficulty was received with an outburst of cheers on the Whig side of the House in the Commons and given the prompt adhesion of the American government.

The way was now clear and the Tribunal at once reassembled formally. After the arguments of counsel had been heard, the voting began on August 21. The five arbitrators unanimously decided that England was in no way responsible in the cases of the *Sumter*, *Nashville*, *Georgia*, *Tallahassee*, and *Chickamauga*. In the case of the *Retribution*, Adams and Staempfli voted yes; the others, no. In the case of the

Alabama the five were unanimous against England. In that of the *Shenandoah*, Adams, Staempfli, and Sclopis voted in favor of English responsibility, but only after February 18, 1865. In the last case, that of the *Florida*, the Tribunal was unanimous against England with the sole exception of Cockburn. He alone again dissented when the judges awarded the United States the sum of $15,500,000 to be paid in gold by England for the damages which had resulted from her failure to take adequate steps to maintain her neutrality. England had already manfully expressed her regret. She now promptly paid the indemnity. Adams had done far more than find a formula and save a conference. He had inaugurated a new era in Anglo-American relations and in settlement of international disputes. The effects of failure to arbitrate the *Alabama* claims can be contemplated only with a shudder. A dangerous corner in the history of the world had been safely turned. Adams and his son Brooks returned to Boston, and there the older man, now definitely through with public life, set himself resolutely to complete the editing of his father's incomparable *Diary*, which was by all odds the most important in American history and was published in 1877 in twelve volumes. Brooks opened a law office, characteristically in a different building from that in which all the rest of the family had theirs.

While Adams was absent on his second trip to Geneva on the Arbitration Commission, political events had involved the family which might have had an odd sequel. Many of the recognized leaders in the Republican Party, men like Sumner, Schurz, Trumbull, and Greeley, were openly in insurrection against the rule of Grant. The Democratic Party was also demoralized, and Schurz conceived the idea of holding a Convention of the Liberal Republicans and nominating candidates who might be expected to draw into the new party the discontented from both the old ones. Just before he sailed for Geneva, Adams had been informed that he would probably be the candidate for President. Although indifferent and refusing to commit himself, his name was far in the lead when the Convention met and began balloting, and it was only on the seventh ballot that the choice fell upon Greeley.   Adams, as a matter of fact, was well out of it, and was himself pleased with the result.

At the Convention of the Democratic Party, the Greeley candidacy was accepted and endorsed, but a large portion of the party were dissatisfied with what they considered a cowardly surrender of their principles, and as a result held another Convention at which Charles O'Connor was nominated for President and John Quincy Adams for Vice-President.   John accepted merely to stand up for his principles, although the result was never in doubt.   Grant, in spite of all the scandals of his administration, was reëlected by a larger popular majority than he had received the first time.   Had Charles Francis Adams made any effort to secure the Republican-Democratic nomination, he could probably have done so, and it would have been a curious political incident to have a father running for President on one ticket and his son for Vice-President on another.   It may be noted that in both cases the two generations were willing to lend their name and influence to movements toward independence from party policies and domination.   Both cared more for principle than for party and neither ever held high elective office, and the following year John was defeated for that of lieutenant-governor of Massachusetts on the Democratic ticket, although he was to serve again in the Legislature.

Meanwhile, Charles and Henry were pursuing their quieter courses.   In 1872 the former became the chairman of the State Railroad Commission, and Henry was complaining of the dullness of editorial and professorial life but continuing the grind, much to the benefit of both mind and character. On June 27, 1872, he had married Marian Hooper, a daughter of Robert William and Ellen Sturgis Hooper of Boston, and after a year in Europe, on leave of absence, had again settled to his work, living at 91 Marlborough Street in the Back Bay. It may be said here that all the brothers either through marriage, professional practice, fortunate investments, or a combination of the three, accumulated fortunes, moderate or large.   Brooks always appeared in later life to have ample means.   John was reputed in the newspapers at the time of his death to have been a millionaire. Charles accumulated a large fortune at one time, though it was seriously diminished by losses, as he himself tells us in his *Autobiography*. Henry, though never wealthy in the modern sense, appears always to have had means for easy and delightful living, independent of any occupation, from about the time of his marriage onward. That marriage was a happy one and must have been of beneficent influence on the social but singularly shy and sensitive man he was.

It was characteristic of him that in his work at Harvard he struck straight away from the theretofore normal method of teaching in American universities. He saw no use in lecturing to a room full of a couple of hundred boys. A teacher, he wisely believed, was at his best with a half-dozen students only. At that time, there was practically nothing which could be considered postgraduate teaching in America, and the English system of tutors and the German one of seminars were unknown in our colleges. The latter was introduced into the educational system by Henry, although, again characteristically, he gave it no high-sounding pedagogical name. It is difficult, and wholly out of character, to think of him as even being called "professor," if he ever was. His best work was done when he gathered a few students around his dining table or in front of the open fire in his study in Marlborough Street. He felt no call to bother with the second-rate and commonplace mind and frankly devoted himself to the mind above the average, which proved in his experience to be "barely one in ten." He had at least the happiness, which is not common, to teach some first-class men, his students including Henry Osborn Taylor, A. Lawrence Lowell, Henry Cabot Lodge, and others.

His theory was that a teacher who knew nothing of his subject should not assume to know but should join the boys in finding it out, and since in his subject "no textbooks existed, the professor refused to profess," he wrote long later, "and the students read what they pleased, and compared their results. As pedagogy, nothing could be more triumphant. The boys worked like rabbits, and dug holes all over the field of archaic

society; no difficulty stopped them; unknown languages
yielded before their attack, and customary law became familiar as the police court; undoubtedly they learned, after a
fashion, to chase an idea, like a hare, through as dense a thicket
of obscure facts as they were likely to meet at the bar." The
boys found him immensely stimulating. Mere facts bored him.
Adams-like, he was unhappy unless he could get at laws, principles. In 1876 a volume made up of the essays of some of his
students, with one of his own, was published as *Essays in Anglo-
Saxon Law*, but Henry had had about enough. Of all his own
education from life, he thought that derived from teaching was
the thinnest, and if teaching came to seem futile, faculty meetings and duties were even worse. As administrators he ranked
even Congressmen higher than professors, and no comparison
could be more damning. The same failure marked the university social life. The title of professor was strangling. James
Russell Lowell, Francis Child, John Fiske, Louis Agassiz,
William James, a dozen other brilliant men, were famished for
want of society, but could not make it so long as they were
dubbed professor. It was the mark of the beast. Had they all
lived in Cambridge without being professors, the society would
have been brilliant and charming. As it was, the social life of
Cambridge "would have starved a polar bear." In the summer
of 1871 he had had a very different experience. He had gone
on a hunting trip to the Rockies, and the West then was still
West. He did not do much shooting, but enjoyed immensely
the long days in the open, and there he ran across Clarence
King. The two men became fast friends at once. King knew,
so Adams said, more than he himself did of art and poetry; he
knew professors; he knew Congressmen; he knew science;
he knew women, even the New York woman; he had wit and
humor and was bubbling over with energy; he had charm of
manner and a limitless capacity for giving himself in friendship.
If he had no faith in the American woman, he had infinite
enthusiasm for everything of interest. At the end of the summer, bound in the closest friendship he was ever to know, Henry
returned to Harvard and the professors. By the end of seven

years he had had, as we have said, enough. He had maintained the *North American* on a high level, though the day of quarterlies was passing, if not past. He had got all Harvard could give him. Both his character and his position had solidified. To the teaching of mediæval history he had added American, and had made the plan of his great work to be written on the latter. He saw no reason for tarrying longer, and, never at home in Boston, he and his wife went back to Washington.

The same year, 1877, his brother Charles, as chairman of the State Railroad Commission, was confronted with the strike on the Boston & Maine. There had been an epidemic of strikes and the situation was becoming serious. Hearings were held before the Commission and then Charles set to work on his report, which was written in an evening at Quincy and adopted next day by the other members of the Commission without change of a word, and immediately published. As General Cogswell, a member of the Legislature, said, "it cleared the air like a thunderclap," and there was not another railroad strike in Massachusetts for a generation or more. Charles believed in such cases that the best appeal was that to an enlightened public opinion — "investigation and publicity as opposed to compulsory arbitration," as he named a pamphlet written on the subject long after in 1902. In labor troubles elsewhere, he repeatedly called attention to the way in which the Boston & Maine strike had been settled and stayed settled, but, as he said, his was a voice crying in the wilderness. It was, he suggested, perhaps too philosophical for the man in the street, the "practical man" who wants to settle specific things in a hurry. As contrasted with Adams's method, the world was to try constant tinkering of legislation, new legislative edicts all the time, a process that he believed in as little as he did in the "Dear Peepul." But, as he commented, "the lot of the man who talks of Reasons, Publicity and Patience now differs not greatly from the lot of him who three centuries ago questioned Divine Right, or gave open expression to a doubt as to the infallibility of the British Solomon. And so it goes! The potter's wheel has turned; the clay and the potter remain the same."

The world was going well with him. His fortune had increased and in 1871 he had built a house at Quincy on land given him by his father on "President's Hill," and there he lived until 1893, four of his five children being born there. He had had, it is true, some very anxious years. His extensive operations had involved him heavily in the panic of 1873, and in 1878 he estimated that his liabilities exceeded his assets by $15,000; but if his liabilities were large, so had become the assets, and at the turn of the tide, with the resumption of the gold standard in 1879, his affairs rapidly improved. These financially troublesome years had otherwise been very happy and had brought him two interesting experiences. In 1873 he had been appointed chairman of a commission appointed by Massachusetts to attend the Exposition at Vienna and make a report on it. He remained there from April to September and formed a lifelong friendship with the secretary of the Commission, Frank D. Millet. In 1878 his appointment as chairman of the Board of Government Directors of the Union Pacific Railroad entailed another trip, in a reverse direction and of great though quite different interest, to the Pacific coast. This period in his life was also notable as marking the beginning of his serious study of American history. Hitherto his writings had been almost wholly on railroad and other public topics of current importance, and he and Henry had united in publishing in book form a number of their articles under the general title of *Chapters of Erie and Other Essays* in 1871. Called upon to deliver the address upon the commemoration of the two hundred and fiftieth anniversary of the settlement of the Town of Weymouth, his mind had to turn to the past, and in the studies made for that purpose he found what was to prove the chief interest of his life thereafter outside of his public duties. The address, delivered in 1874, revealed a genuine historical mind, and the following year he was elected a member of the Massachusetts Historical Society.

Henry and Brooks had also turned to history as their main occupations. The former and his wife had taken the old yellow Corcoran house in Lafayette Square in Washington, and there and in his summer home at Beverly, Massachusetts, Henry kept steadily at work, his wife spurring him on. In 1877 there appeared, as we have already noted, the twelve volumes of John Quincy Adams's *Diary* edited by Henry's father. It was the last public service rendered by the elder generation, and in finishing the work on the final volume Charles Francis had remarked, "I am now perfectly willing to go myself. My mission is ended, and I may rest." He had written the life and edited the papers of his grandfather, John Adams, the life and letters of Abigail Adams, and with the completion of the vast task of editing his father's diary his work was indeed completed. He lived on quietly in Boston and Quincy until his death on November 21, 1886, his wife surviving until the sixth of June three years later.

While his father had been working on the John Quincy papers, Henry had been digging deep into the period of Jefferson and Madison, going through vast masses of papers available in America and ransacking the foreign archives, journeying to Europe with his wife for the latter purpose. Among his own family papers was the collection of documents that had been made by his grandfather, John Quincy, when writing his reply to the Massachusetts Federalists in 1828, which he had decided not to publish. These Henry prepared for the press and published under the title of *Documents Relating to New England Federalism, 1800–1815*, in the same year the *Diary* appeared. Among the papers of others which had been placed at his disposal were those of Gallatin, loaned to him by Gallatin's son, and in 1879 Henry published *The Life of Albert Gallatin* in one volume and edited the *Papers* in three supplementary ones. The four volumes mark an important turning point in the history of American historical scholarship. After fifty years the *Life*, in spite of all subsequent research by scholars, yet remains the authoritative and definitive biography of the statesman, but the influence of the work has been felt more from its method than from its mere facts. It appeared in the era when Bancroft's influence was the supreme one upon historians and the public, used to lavish praise of men and institutions.

In contrast, Henry's work exhibited a very marked restraint. In editing the *Papers* he added no footnote comment and allowed Gallatin to speak absolutely for himself without the intrusion of editorial commendation or disagreement, and there was equal restraint shown in the *Life*, which, without loss of color, was as deliberately cool, dispassionate, and unbiased as the author could make it. Just as in his teaching Henry had struck out and adopted a new method, so he did in his writing, and in both cases left a lasting impression.

Meanwhile Henry was looking at the world about him as well as the past, and these were for him the happy years. Although shy and sensitive, he was fond of society if it came to him easily, and both his mind and his training had made him demand only the choicest of social fare. Mere celebrity or the meretricious fame due to money or office was no passport to the house in Lafayette Square. No more was mere intellectuality or knowledge, unaccompanied by social grace and charm. Nowhere else in America has the line ever been so closely and inviolably drawn, and with Mrs. Adams as the gracious and discriminating hostess the house became the most noted *salon* this country has evolved. Clarence King on his Washington visits and John Hay and his wife were the closest friends of the household, and so inseparable as to be dubbed with Adams and his wife "the five of hearts." The Cabot Lodges and Don Cameron, with his brilliant and beautiful wife, were also of the inner circle, which with, later, the Roosevelts and a few others constituted in the eyes of Europe as well as America the one really worth-while social group on this side of the water, beside which the gilded splendors of New York and Newport were merely *bête* and insufferably dull.

From his window in the Square, Adams watched the passing show of Washington social and political life — the vulgarity of the new rich, the pomposity and venality of Senators, the secret strings by which the puppets of public life were made to dance, the whole human show of the national capital in the 1880's, which had to be taken lightly and ironically if it were not to be utterly dull and sickening. From the study of Jefferson's day, Adams turned aside for a few months to paint an incomparable picture of the contemporary scene in his novel *Democracy*, which was published anonymously in 1880. It was biting satire in which living figures who took themselves with intense seriousness were shown to the public under pseudonyms and with but scant disguise. The book at once became the rage in London, where Adams and his wife were passing the spring, and, having acquired that British approval which in spite of anti-British feeling was still essential for a work of literature, it was then seized upon by the American public. Its authorship, known to not more than three or four persons, was attributed to Hay and almost everyone else, including Mrs. Adams, who might be suspected of being in a position to know the inner workings of Washington. One of the best novels ever written in America, Adams himself laid but little stress upon it, and it was many years before the authorship became authoritatively known. He had enjoyed writing it, however, and in 1884 published a second and last novel, *Esther*, under the pseudonym of Frances Snow Compton. In this the scene was laid in New York, a scene rather notably unfamiliar to Henry, whose knowledge of Washington, Boston, London, and Paris was far greater than that of New York, which city apparently he rarely even visited, and the book was less successful than the first and is to-day scarcely known even by name.

The *Gallatin*, important as it was in itself, had been merely a preliminary study in the progress of Adams's great work on the Jefferson and Madison administrations, and in these years he wrote two more, which, however, added nothing to his reputation. John T. Morse, Jr., who was then editing the excellent *American Statesmen* series, conceived the idea of getting Henry to write the life of his grandfather John Quincy's bitter enemy John Randolph, of Roanoke. He counted, as he has told me, on Henry's sense of humor, a sense in which the Adamses have always been largely lacking; and the choice was an unfortunate one. Henry should never have been asked to write the book, and, if asked, should have declined. It was not merely that

Randolph was, so to say, an hereditary enemy, but his character and entire career were deeply antipathetic to Adams, any Adams; and although Henry wrote of him in a manner that would make the book more welcome to an undiscriminating public than the *Gallatin*, he was not sufficiently interested himself, or perhaps unbiased, to do for Randolph what he had done for Gallatin. At this time also, the *Randolph* appearing in 1882, he wrote a life of Aaron Burr for the same series, but apparently without consulting Morse. On October 8 of that year he wrote to John Hay that "Houghton declines to print Aaron Burr because Aaron was not a statesman," which certainly could also have been truly said of Randolph. Whatever became of the manuscript of the Burr is unknown, although tradition avers that Henry promptly put it in the fire with the remark that no one was to tell an Adams who was or was not a statesman. However that may be, the gesture would have been sufficiently characteristic and the manuscript has disappeared.

Adams, however, had now settled down to a life of steady literary production. He and Hay had bought remarkably cheaply the large plot of ground on the corner of H and 16th Streets on the north side of Lafayette Square, Hay retaining the larger part of the property, that on the corner, and Adams taking the smaller part on the back, facing on H Street. In the summer of 1885, with H. H. Richardson as architect, they built two adjoining houses, with a door between, and Adams was happily looking forward to moving into the new home before Christmas. On December 6 his wife suddenly died under peculiarly tragic circumstances. She had been in poor health all summer. There was an overdose of a drug, and, without warning, Adams's life was shattered. He moved into the new house alone, but found it intolerably lonely, and in the spring he went to Japan with John La Farge, whose son had married a niece of Mrs. Adams.

He remained only a few months, becoming interested, however, in Japanese art and more particularly in the brooding calm of Oriental philosophy and religion. Returning to the house at 1603 H Street, he picked up life as best he could and began again on the history. His nieces stayed with him from time to time and at other times he had men living with him in the lonely house. Cecil Spring-Rice, later Ambassador from England but then a young Secretary of Legation, wrote a few months after Adams's homecoming that "the Adams family are as odd as can be. . . . I like the one here, who since his wife died has no friends and no absorbing interest and takes an amused view of life, tempered by an attachment to Japanese art. He lives in a beautiful house and works at a history of ten years, 1800–1810. He has a friend who lives with him, the librarian of the State Department, who corresponds with Aubrey de Vere."

Rice wrote this in the summer, when everyone was away, soon after he had been admitted to the H Street house, and the casual remark about Adams having no friends had to be revised. He did not, indeed, go into society. Society had to come to him, but, as the editor of Rice's letters notes, the ultimate test of admission to the best coterie in the capital "was at the threshold of 1603 H Street, the house of Henry Adams," a man "who called on no one, and never left a card — not even on ambassadors. They, like the rest, had to be introduced by those permitted to stand sponsors, and such introductions were eagerly sought after." By December the young Secretary could write that Henry Adams "is a great friend of mine. He is queer to the last degree; cynical, vindictive, but with a constant interest in people, faithful to his friends, and passionately fond of his mother and of all little children ever born; even puppies." "He lives in a Japanese house," Rice added, "full of strange trophies from Japan and a precious idol given him by the Japanese Minister." Another has described it as "an odd home for so fastidious a man as Mr. Adams. The leather chairs which abounded were all so low that they seemed made for the host's own use. Things which he had brought home from Europe and the East were everywhere, and though they were beautiful their total effect was not beauty but miscellaneousness. To the eye it was a very Bostonian house, though Mr. Adams did not care to have you think so." Hay used frequently to come through the connecting door, the Lodges and Camerons were there, and gradually life was resumed with friends constantly in and out, especially at the famous breakfasts which became a Washington institution.   Adams turned back to his work, and in 1889 the first two volumes of his *History of the United States* was published.   A considerable part of them had already been printed privately and shown to a few, including Adams's brother Charles, for criticism.   The remaining seven volumes followed in rapid succession, until in 1891 the series was complete.   The work was monumental and will forever remain one of the great productions of American historical scholarship.   Although dealing with friends and enemies of his family, the author returned to the detached point of view of his *Gallatin*, though clothed in a far more brilliant style, and the judgments as far as could be were unbiased.   Characteristically he had not waited to see the last volumes issued, but, careless of their reception, had again started for the Far East with La Farge.

Before leaving, he had commissioned Saint Gaudens to execute a bronze figure as a memorial to be placed over the grave of Mrs. Adams in Rock Creek Cemetery.   The Orient had made a profound impression on Adams, and for those who are inclined to think of him as a dilettante we may quote a Japanese statesman, who after spending an evening with him in his home declared that he had found him one of the only four Occidentals who had a thorough comprehension of the East and its problems.   Even more than to the politics of the East, Adams had been drawn to its mysticism, and in his instructions to the sculptor he laid great stress on his putting a deep philosophic calm into his figure, which should embody the spirit but not copy the form of any definite Oriental one.   He turned him over to La Farge, who understood his mood and thought, and suggested in addition that he keep by him not only a Buddha but copies of the Michael Angelo frescoes from the Sistine Chapel.   Knowing that Adams was off on a long trip, Saint Gaudens tried to get a model of the figure ready for him to see before he left, but Adams declined to look at it, saying that if he were not exactly suited it would spoil the pleasure which otherwise he could anticipate on his return.   With that, and caring not a jot about his *History*, he set out for the South Pacific.

Meantime, while Henry had been busy with his work in Washington, his brothers had been equally so in Boston and Quincy. Brooks had entered the lists in 1887 with his first book, *The Emancipation of Massachusetts*, a work which attracted much attention and which ran counter to the accepted view of New England history as derived from Palfrey and the whole school of filio-pietistic clerical historians. An attack upon the smug tradition when made by an Adams had telling force and the author naturally encountered much resentment. The book was not important as history, but was extremely so for its point of view, and the old Puritan self-complacency had received a killing blow. New England history could never be written in the old style again. If, however, Brooks chose to explode false views and beliefs, he had a deep regard for whatever in his opinion was genuine in early New England life, and it was with as much sincerity as courage that this Adams rose in the Stone Church at Quincy to make public profession of his faith according to the old manner which had long ceased to be customary.

It must have taken much courage, for Brooks had in an excessive, almost an abnormal, degree that shyness characteristic of the Adamses, as of many Englishmen, which in both cases so often results in a self-defensive brusqueness of manner that is misunderstood. Visiting England in 1888, the summer after his book appeared, he was taken down to Oxford for a visit by Spring-Rice, who was then in the Foreign Office. On his return to London, Adams wrote a warm note of thanks, followed a few days later by another in which he said, "My dear fellow, I 'm a crank; very few human beings can endure to have me near them, but I like to be with you, and I suppose I like to be with those who are sympathetic, the more since they are so few." He had given up his law practice in 1881, and without regular occupation or the steadying effect of public office and duties, there was a tendency, in the restlessness of the day, to

CHARLES FRANCIS ADAMS II AND BROOKS ADAMS AS UNDERGRADUATES

(By permission of Miss E. O. Adams)

disperse the energies of the youngest and most erratic member of the family.   In the autumn of 1889, however, his marriage on September 12 to Evelyn Davis, daughter of Admiral Charles H. Davis, and a sister of Mrs. Henry Cabot Lodge, helped to give him a central interest in life.

The most active of the brothers, Charles, had been doing an overwhelming amount of work in his several fields.   He had, first, his own extensive business operations, and appears to have looked after the affairs of some of his brothers.   In 1878, as we have noted, he had become chairman of the Board of Government Directors of the Union Pacific, his report on the affairs of that road meeting with the anticipated result when placed before Senators with whose interests it conflicted.   In the same year he published his *Railroads: Their Origin and Problems* and *Notes on Railroad Accidents*.   In 1884 the position of president of the Union Pacific was practically forced upon him, although he was ousted six years later by Gould, as an echo of the *Chapters of Erie*.   He himself felt, as he looked back, that he should have gotten out at the end of the first four years, at which time he had done a very good piece of work in rescuing the road from bankruptcy.   The last years he considered as his "least creditable experience."   "During the last eighteen months of my connection with the Union Pacific," he wrote with candor in his *Autobiography*, "I was — there is no use denying it, or attempting to explain it away — wholly demoralized.   I hated my position and its duties, and yearned to be free of it and of them.   My office had become a prison-house.   Loathing it, I was anxious, involved, hopeless.   I had accordingly become a plunger; rapidly getting beyond my depth, I have nothing to say in extenuation.   I displayed indecision and weakness — almost as much as Napoleon showed in his Russian campaign.   Comparing little things with big, and a small man with a great one, the one situation had become as impossible for me as the other for him.   I simply rode for a fall; nor did I really care when or how I got it."   Certainly few men occupying a great position in the public eye can ever have written more frankly of themselves.   His plunging was to have serious consequences when the panic of 1893 swept the country.

His real interest during these years had been his historical research and his public service. In 1883 he had written his *Three Episodes of Massachusetts History*, which, first printed privately, was published in enlarged form in 1892. In the earlier year, 1883, he also published his scholarly edition of Morton's *New English Canaan*, and in the next year his *Antinomianism in the Colony of Massachusetts Bay*. There were also scattered articles, and in 1890 came his two-volume biography of Richard Henry Dana.

As we have seen, after the return of his father from Europe, Charles had gone to live at Quincy. His brother John, although he had a summer place at Cohasset, also had a five-hundred-acre model farm at Quincy, where he spent much of his time, and the two brothers were deeply interested in the affairs of the town, both serving as moderators in town meeting for twenty years. The people of Quincy practically handed the town administration over to the brothers, who considered themselves "bone of their bone, flesh of their flesh." The town meetings were reduced "from a mob to a model." Charles wrote of this service, in which he took great satisfaction and delight, "I worked with and through my brother, J. Q. Adams. I never was sympathetic or popular; he, somehow, was. He was in close touch with the people of Quincy; me, they were disposed to look at a bit askance. But he and I, in town matters, always acted together. I was much the more active-minded; he was inclined to indolence. But, when set in motion, provided he did not encounter too much opposition, he had a really remarkable faculty of accomplishing results." Charles was, in reality, the active directing intelligence of the combination, which worked together perfectly. Finding the school system thoroughly antiquated and functioning as badly as rural schools could, they gradually developed a wholly new system which attracted much attention throughout America and became known as the "Quincy System," Charles's book on the subject, *The New Departure in the Common Schools of Quincy*, quickly passing through six editions. Both a public library and building were secured for the town, as was also Mount Wollaston Park. When the Adamses took charge of town affairs, the town had a debt of $122,000, which they extinguished in eight years, and when they ended their work the tax rate was one per cent. When, later, they had given up their work, the character of the place had changed with increasing population, and a city government had been instituted, the debt rapidly rising to $2,000,000 and the tax rate to two and a half per cent. The work of Charles for his town had given him a wide reputation and in 1892 he was appointed on the State Commission to plan a system of parks and reservations for Boston and its vicinity, and he was mainly instrumental in saving the Blue Hills and the Middlesex Fells from commercialization. It is impossible to record all his activities of this period, but we may note as an additional one that he was made chairman of the state commission to study the relations between municipalities and street railways, and was sent abroad for the purpose, making a report which influenced legislation in many American cities.

That America was coming more and more to be really governed by business men, the great capitalists, was evident then as it has become plain since, and it is of interest to note this Adams's comment on them. "As I approach the end," he wrote, "I am more than a little puzzled to account for the instances I have seen of business success — money-getting. It comes from a rather low instinct. Certainly, as far as my observation goes, it is rarely met in combination with the finer or more interesting traits of character. I have known, and known tolerably well, a good many 'successful' men — 'big' financially — men famous during the last half-century; and a less interesting crowd I do not care to encounter. Not one that I have ever known would I care to meet again, either in this world or the next; nor is one of them associated in my mind with the idea of humor, thought or refinement. A set of mere money-getters and traders, they were essentially unattractive and uninteresting. The fact is that money-getting, like everything else, calls for a special aptitude and great concentration; and for it, I did not have the first in any marked degree, while to it I never gave the last. So, in now summing up, I may account myself fortunate in having got out of my ventures as well as I did. Running at times great risks, I emerged, not ruined."

Meanwhile, Henry and La Farge were roaming from island to island in the South Seas. Reaching Hawaii on August 30, 1890, they spent a month there, living in a house lent them by an old college acquaintance of Henry's. From there they drifted on leisurely — a couple of months in Samoa, Papeete in February, then Tahiti, and Fiji by June, reveling in color and the native life. Henry himself left no account of the year, — his *Education* jumps across a gulf of twenty unrecorded years from 1871 to 1892, — but one may follow him in La Farge's *Reminiscences of the South Seas*. He was essentially an intellectual, and even as a youth his æsthetic sense seems to have been stirred but slightly by what Europe had to give. In music, painting, and poetry he developed slowly, but living month after month with La Farge amid the indescribable and unpaintable color of the Pacific, trying with his own sketching to catch a faint impression of it, a new sense awoke, and he found a new approach to reality. The wide stretches of the Pacific, the surf on island beaches, the dazzling silver nights, the dancing of lithe and naked young bodies, Greek in perfection of form, the sensuousness of a primitive life that knew nothing of the burdens of civilization, opened a new world with which that of the legation experiences in London or the research of a scholar or the cynical contemplation of the Washington scene had nothing whatever to do. By September the travelers were at Kandy, and, after a visit to the sacred Bo Tree, Henry, while passing up the Red Sea, wrote one of the only two poems that have been left to us by him — the "Buddha and Brahma." He sailed directly from Colombo to Marseilles, stopped in Paris to see the Camerons, made a flying visit to old friends in Scotland, and by the end of 1891 was again in Washington.

There he at once went to Rock Creek to see the memorial

Saint Gaudens had erected in his absence, as he did, time and again, to dream and remember to the end of his days. He found the sculptor's masterpiece, the master work of all American sculpture, austere and beautiful, expressing, in the words of John Hay, "infinite wisdom, a past without beginning, and a future without end, a repose after limitless experience, a peace to which nothing matters." Saint Gaudens himself described it as "the mystery of the hereafter," "beyond pain and beyond joy." The American people, because they have not suffered, have not understood, but the day may come.

The *History*, which had occupied so many years of his life, was completed. It had met with immediate recognition on the part of scholars, which caused his election as a vice-president of the American Historical Association, an office which in due course, according to the custom of that body, would lead by annual stages to the presidency. Hay had also got his monumental *Lincoln* off his hands, and the two friends sat down to watch life from Lafayette Square. Adams amused himself by putting into shape some of the legends he had picked up in Hawaii, and published them privately in a quarto under the title of *The Memoirs of Marau Taaroa, Last Queen of Tahiti*, and was sufficiently interested to expand and print them again in Paris in 1901. But it was a fallow time for his mind and he was awaiting a new lead. Wandering over to Europe, he was in Lucerne when he received a cable from his brother Charles announcing the panic of 1893 and the possible financial ruin of them all. Henry at once went to Boston, where he found himself "suspended, for several months, over the edge of bankruptcy." Charles, who, as he himself records, had become somewhat reckless from a long course of prosperity, ran into the storm with altogether too much sail spread on his own account and with additional burdens which he had incautiously assumed on account of the Union Pacific.

Henry's investments weathered the blow and by September he was back at 1603 H Street, fairly secure, but for Charles, although he too had weathered the gale, "its results were felt continuously through five long precious years," as he wrote.

"They were for me years of simple Hell — years when I had to throw everything aside, and devote myself to rehabilitating a wreck. It made no sort of difference that the wreck was the result of my own improvidence; there it was right under me, and the question of again reaching port was the only one to consider. The dislocation this event caused — coming just when it did — shattered my whole scheme of life. I was sixty-three years old, and a tired man, when at last the effects of the 1893 convulsion wore themselves out, and my mind was once more at ease so that I could return to my calling." He sold his house in Quincy, a move he had long seen to be inevitable, owing to changed conditions, and took one at Lincoln. The break with old ties and the place where he "had lived vicariously or in person since 1640" was a cruel one. The worst of the financial strain was over by 1897, but he spent that year with his family living in Florence, Italy, to recuperate, working over the papers of his father and a report on the study of English at Harvard, which he had been asked to draw up as head of a committee of the Overseers, to which body he had been elected in 1882.

The unrest of the times had resulted in return to power of the Democratic Party, for the first time in over thirty years. Cleveland offered John Quincy the post of Secretary of the Navy, but about this time his health began to fail and he declined the offer. He spent the summer of 1893 in Europe, and on August 14 of the following year died suddenly after having suffered two strokes of apoplexy. The only member of his generation who had fought the political fight in the open arena, he had deliberately and consistently chosen to do so on the side of the party whose principles most nearly coincided with his own, but which offered no path to office. When at last such a possibility opened, he was himself at the end of his career. Of the three children who survived him — two sons had died — we shall have occasion to mention one later.

Meanwhile Brooks, with the true Adams insistence upon law and generalization, had been trying to find for himself some

leading thread through the tangled skein of history. He became convinced that conscious thought had played a negligible
part in the historic process, and sought to link the latter up to
the physical universe. His fundamental assumption was that
history was governed by law, and that the movements of intellect seemed to follow the laws governing the material universe.
As the human movement accelerated, he found that centralization increased and that energy took the form of capital. He
illustrated his thesis by the rise and fall of trade routes, and his
whole theory was deterministic and pessimistic. The book,
although it reached a second edition, failed of gaining as much
attention as it otherwise might have done on account of the
financial theory and preoccupation of the moment when it appeared. Brooks was in frequent communication with Henry,
and in view of what we shall have to say about the theories of
history that came to be propounded by the latter, it is an interesting speculation as to which influenced the other, a problem
that cannot be settled until the correspondence of both appears.
Brooks received scant attention in America, although his
Law of Civilization and Decay, which he published in 1895 to
embody the above thesis, was translated into French and German, and a later volume into Russian as well; but Henry, of
course, was familiar with his thought.

Henry, called back so brusquely from Switzerland to face
bankruptcy, had, after looking into the Gorgon's face for the
month of August at Quincy, gone to Chicago to see the Exposition, which proved a multifold revelation to him. It was not
merely that out of the muck and materialism of the Chicago of
the stockyards had arisen this unpredictable vision of beauty.
That was one problem to be solved. But Henry appears also
to have been brought face to face with the new forces that were
being harnessed by man. Between the control over environment shown in Samoa and the possibilities of control shown in
Machinery Hall there was a gulf that required spanning by some
process of thought. If the physical forces of the universe could
be harnessed by discovering "laws," how about social forces?
Were there any laws of social change? Was there a law in his-

tory? Apparently Henry and Brooks began to approach the same problem at the same time.

For the moment Henry merely pondered. He and his family had survived the panic, but Clarence King had gone down. In the winter of 1894 Henry took him to the West Indies to recuperate. The summer was spent with Hay in the Yellowstone, the autumn running over the new lines of railway in the Northwest, and then a sudden dash down to Mexico, the Gulf, and the Caribbean. In six months he had covered about twenty thousand miles. Being in Mexico in December, he was unable to attend the annual meeting of the American Historical Association, of which he had attained the presidency, and in place of a presidential address he forwarded a letter which was published under the title of "The Tendency of History," and which Brooks said Henry had originally intended to use as a preface to Brooks's *Law of Civilization and Decay*. Its main thesis was a plea to historians to try to place history on a footing comparable to that of the exact sciences. Henry's mind was now definitely on a new track, which it was to follow to the end. He had never cared for mere unrelated facts. "I have never loved or taught facts, if I could help it, having that antipathy to facts which only idiots and philosophers attain," he was to write to Henry Osborn Taylor in 1915. But he had sifted them and documented them, as carefully and painstakingly and meticulously as any "scientific" historian of the present day, as his *History* alone amply indicates. He was no dilettante, no seeker after mere impressions, no writer striving only for effects. From now on, however, what he was to seek was a general law, some order in the chaos of historical facts. After his return from Mexico he turned from historical manuscripts to the study of statistics, indicating his changed point of view. The next few years, however, were to be devoted to travel and reflection rather than to any definite formulating of his theories, and we may pass over them somewhat briefly.

In 1895 he was again in Europe, as he was to be constantly from this time on until the close of his life. He spent the summer in England with the Henry Cabot Lodges and in the autumn crossed with them for a long motor tour in Normandy which marks an era in his outlook. In all his European experience hitherto he seems never to have been very sensitive to æsthetic emotion or interested in the spiritual aspects and currents of its past. Chartres had stirred him as little as had the Sistine Madonna. When he hung over Wenlock Edge gazing over a score of miles of the exquisite Shropshire landscape to the blue hills of Wales in the hazy distance, it was not to yield himself to the influence of beauty but to ponder over the *Pteraspis* and the *Terebratula*. Suddenly, however, in Normandy in that autumn of 1895, he began to see the world with fresh eyes. It was as though a new sense had been given him. The change was probably not as sudden as he himself considered it, but had been preparing within him through the lonely years following his wife's death, through his wanderings in the South Seas with La Farge, through the slow maturing of his nature. Europe, however, did cease to present to him only a charming social scene and friendships, a diplomatic puzzle and a political drama. He became aware of a new world. He attributed much of his initiation to the guidance of Mrs. Lodge, as he was always wont to attribute much influence over him to women. Whatever the channel may have been through which it came, a new conception of the forces which might dominate man's development did come to him as he leisurely visited Amiens, Caen, Coutances, Mont Saint Michel, Chartres, and other towns where he was vouchsafed a vision of Gothic and the spiritual atmosphere of the Middle Ages. It was an approach utterly different and far more moving than that through Berlin and the civil law. In October he "drifted back to Washington with a new sense of history."

He still wandered restlessly. The next year he was again in Mexico, with the Camerons, in the spring; in Europe, including Italy, with Hay in the summer, and back in America by autumn to vote for McKinley. There he wrote what may be considered his only state document, a long and able report on intervention in Cuba, which was presented, without the authorship being acknowledged, to the Senate by Senator Cameron. In

December, Hay was appointed Ambassador to England, and Henry went over with him, passing on to Paris, where he was picked up by the Hays in January 1898 and carried on by them to Egypt, where a new civilization of the past was revealed to him. Alone he passed on to Smyrna and Damascus, and with Rockhill, then Minister to Greece, he visited Constantinople and Athens. The winter was spent in Washington, and the spring found him in Sicily and Rome with the Lodges, followed by a solitary summer in France, where he was joined in November by La Farge, who helped to initiate him into Chartres and mediæval glass. In January he sailed for Washington to "look after" Hay, who had gone home to be Secretary of State. There he posed for himself a new problem, very different from his mere untangling of the threads of the ten years of the administrations of Jefferson and Madison. If history were a science, how, he pondered, could the Washington of McKinley and Hay be brought into mathematical relation with the twelfth-century Chartres and the world which had brought that into being? If no relation other than that of mere casual, not causal, sequence could be predicated, obviously history was a chaos and not a science.

In 1900 Brooks published his volume on *America's Economic Supremacy* and two years later his *New Empire*, which, however, added nothing essentially new to his earliest volume. The development of historical theory was now in the hands of Henry. In 1896 both brothers had been seeking to correlate history to science, based on the assumption, in Brooks's words, that "the law of force and energy is of universal application in nature." Brooks had developed a theory largely based on trade routes and the shifting centres of trade balances and foreign exchanges. He had tried to establish a hypothesis that the centralization of society was proportionate to its velocity, and that velocity was proportionate to energy and mass, a suggestion that he did little but repeat and amplify in his later works.

For Henry the problem assumed a different shape. In 1900 he passed the summer in Paris, as usual, and spent long days at the Exposition, where the dynamos in Machinery Hall made a profound impression on him. In the soft purring of this triumphant achievement of man he recognized a new and illimitable force to transform society. But since 1895 he had had also to recognize the force of the Virgin, for that, too, had been almost illimitable in its power to transform man and society. "All the steam in the world," he recognized, could not have built the Cathedral of Chartres, which was merely a symbol of a whole world of spiritual forces. It was probably in this summer, in his rooms near the Trocadéro, that Henry wrote that strange "Prayer to the Virgin of Chartres," embodying in its middle passage the "Prayer to the Dynamo," that was found in his wallet at his death eighteen years later. But if history were a science relating facts otherwise than poetically, some formula had to be found to embrace at once two such apparently unrelated facts as the force of the dynamo and that of the Virgin, for both had unquestionably to be regarded as driving forces in the historical process. Henry set to work.

The following year, partly with the Lodges, he made a long trip through Austria, Germany, Russia, and Sweden, but we need be little concerned from now on with his travels, which for the most part came to be merely annual crossings between Washington and his established haunts in Great Britain and France.

From the days when he had had his first glimpse of modern science through Lyell, he had followed its development — as an amateur, of course, but with a trained and powerful mind. By 1900 that development had led to giving the supreme place to physics. The whole trend of opinion was that eventually all the sciences would be fundamentally resolved under the laws governing physics, and with the strong bent of the Adams mind away from facts and phenomena toward primary laws and principles, it was natural, indeed, inevitable, that Henry in seeking a law for history should attempt to apply to historical phenomena the concepts and relationships used in the basic science of physics. I need not in this history of a family enter upon a critical analysis of his doctrine, with which I have dealt elsewhere. Briefly, the mere distinguishing of a force was not sufficient for his purpose. What he had to do was to establish velocity and direction, and to do this it was necessary to establish points of reference.

For the first point he decided to take the period of Chartres Cathedral, the period in which "man had held the highest idea of himself as a unit in a unified universe," and for the second the twentieth century, in which unity had given place to multiplicity. As a means to this establishment he started to make an analysis of each period. If the attempt did little or nothing for his theory, shifting, indeed, under his hands even in the making, it resulted in two of the most remarkable books in American literature, the *Mont Saint Michel and Chartres*, first published privately in 1904, and the *Education of Henry Adams*, also published privately in 1907. The first of these is not so much a study of its period as a re-creation of it, of the soul of the Abbey of Mont Saint Michel, of the stones and the glass and spirit of Chartres, of the heroes of Roland, of Nicolette and Marion, of Abelard and Saint Thomas, of the Queens of France and the Queen of Heaven. The intervening centuries pass away and we live again in the thirteenth and share in its thought and action, its earthly loves and its heavenly hopes. Much against Adams's will, he finally consented, after another private printing, to have it published under the auspices and at the request of the American Institute of Architects in 1912, that body having proclaimed it unique and invaluable to every artist whatever his form of expression.

In the *Education*, which was not published until after his death in 1918, and then in a form that Adams would probably have not considered as final, he gave us the most thought-provoking autobiography, though it was not so intended, that America has produced. The book, like the *Chartres*, is unique, and no other American could have written it. It has its faults and we may admit that the irony is a bit overdone, but even without revision by the author it has already taken its place among the very few American classics.

In neither volume, however, had Adams succeeded in his primary effort to establish points from which the lines of force in

history might be measured.   He continued, however, to ponder
the problem.   Life was closing in on him.   Hay died in 1904
and King a few years later.   Nieces stayed with him and he
maintained his annual migrations from Washington to Paris
and back to Washington.   Running across Willard Gibbs's
book on phase, his thought took a new direction, and he postu-
lated phases of human life and psychical activity more or less
corresponding to the physical phases of solid, liquid, gaseous,
ethereal, electrical, and so on, and finally worked out a mathematical formula based mainly on the well-known law of squares.
He calculated roughly the length of the phases of instinct and
religion in the past and predicted a change of phase about 1917,
and the breakdown of human thought about four years later.
Fantastic as all this seemed when read in his *Letter to American
Teachers of History*, published in 1910, and his essay on
"Phase," written in 1909 but only published by Brooks in
The Degradation of the Democratic Dogma after Henry's death,
his last prediction has had a most curious and unpredictable confirmation in the sudden development of the new physics after
1917.   In 1909 to have predicted that we should reach the end
of human reason seemed too absurd to be taken as anything but
the vagary of an ironical and erratic old gentleman, but it has,
in an utterly unforeseen way, come about, and the physicists
themselves have been most unwillingly forced to admit that we
have reached a point beyond which our reason is now powerless
to proceed in our investigation of the structure of the universe,
a blank wall which marks the end of knowledge and on the
other side of which the categories of human reason no longer
hold sway.

This strange corroboration by no means proves the correctness of Henry's theory or formulæ, and in view of the rapid
change in our views, the development of the theory of relativity,
and the realization that concepts applicable to one field of reality cannot be applied to another, most of Henry's doctrine of
"phase," "force," "acceleration," and so on, falls to the ground.
On the other hand, he must, I think, be considered as the first
pioneer in scientific history.   The essence of science is not in

mere impartial, painstaking accumulation of facts and examination of evidence. That is simply intellectual integrity, in the exercise of which a historian may differ less from an artist than the modern type likes to believe. I see no use, and, indeed, much disadvantage, in calling anything a science which has not so succeeded in arranging the facts under observation as to have disclosed "laws" — that is, uniform modes of behavior which show regular recurrence and thus possess predictability. This, I think, is the main value of Henry's theory. He was not content, as so many historians are, to masquerade as a "scientific historian" in the eyes of a science-worshiping public, if history were not really a science, and in his opinion it was clearly and emphatically not a science unless its phenomena could be made to fall into patterns that would permit of establishing mathematical formulæ that would allow of a fairly definite predictableness. It was precisely the sort of thought that the family had been following since the change of its own phase in the person of the first John: the reduction of an unintelligible chaos of mere uncorrelated facts into an ordered cosmos subject to law, — that is, recurrent and predictable modes of behavior, — and a refusal to be put off from the search by any popular acceptance of easy but unmeaning misuse of terms.

These essays were Adams's last contribution to the problem, a contribution whose value has not seldom been overlooked because of the somewhat fantastic shape it assumed. It was a contribution, however, of the utmost value in this age of loose thinking, which so prides itself on being "scientific"; and I believe Henry's insistence upon the fact that history is a chaos, and not a science, unless its phenomena are capable of being arranged under laws, or modes of behavior, that permit of predicting both the direction and velocity of change in society, is unassailable.

In 1911 he published a brief *Life of George Cabot Lodge*, a memoir of the young poet who was one of his intimate circle, and in the following year he suffered that stroke of paralysis which put an end to his active literary career. Evening, indeed, was beginning to fall upon the fourth generation. John had been gone for nearly twenty years, and his children, George Caspar, Charles Francis III, and Abigail, were now well advanced in careers of their own. The second of the four remarkable brothers of the fourth generation, Charles Francis II, after having recovered from the effects of the panic of 1893 had devoted himself mainly to his writing. In 1900 he had published a brilliant short life of his father, the Minister, in the *American Statesmen* series, which had been followed by a rich harvest of other volumes and short studies, many of the latter published in the *Proceedings* of the Massachusetts Historical Society, of which he had become president and of which both Brooks and Henry had also been elected members. In 1911 he published his volume of *Studies: Military and Diplomatic*, and two years later was invited to deliver a series of three lectures at Oxford which were published under the title of *Trans-Atlantic Solidarity*, a fitting colophon, after nearly a century and half, to John Adams's Declaration of Independence. In 1905 he bought a house in Washington which thereafter became his winter home, and in the closing years he devoted himself to accumulating material for an extended life of his father, for which purpose he went to England several times to search both public and private archives which were thrown open to him. He had originally planned a diplomatic history of the Civil War, but he was not to be permitted to finish even the less extensive enterprise of narrating his father's part in it, and died with the work only partially finished, on March 20, 1915. His own *Autobiography* was published the year following his death by the Massachusetts Historical Society, to which he had left the manuscript.

The doctors had pronounced Henry's recovery from his stroke in 1912 as hopeless, but after a few months spent at South Lincoln he recovered somewhat, although never enough to do more writing. He resumed, however, his life in Washington and France, with even occasional trips elsewhere, as to Ireland in 1915. His nieces were constantly with him, and it was in a château in the French country that the news came to him of the outbreak of the war and the collapse of the civilization he had known. In these last years he had taken great delight in collecting old twelfth- and thirteenth-century songs and having them sung to him in the evening, looking on at the changing world meanwhile with as keen an interest as ever, but with a greater detachment. Always liable to brusqueries of manner, which made him a terror to those who did not know him well, he had, as had his brothers and forbears, a great tenderness and depth of affection. Not only, like old John Quincy, was he always gentle and devoted to children, but no man was ever more loyal and tender to his friends. *Porcupinus Angelicus* he was dubbed by Hay, who also wrote, —

> Oh! Adams, in our hours of ease
> Rather inclined to growl and tease,
> When pain and anguish wring the brow
> A ministering angel thou.

Of his thoughts in the last years perhaps we can get as clear a glimpse as anywhere in an unpublished letter which he wrote to his old pupil, Henry Osborn Taylor, in 1915, thanking him for a copy of his then newly published *Classical Heritage of the Middle Ages*. "My dear Scholar and Master," he begins, and then, after a passage that we have already quoted, he passes on to his own thoughts about the book. "Perhaps I ought to say first, that once, at the most trying crisis of my life, and of his, — our old teacher in wisdom, Gurney, said to me that of all moral supports in trial only one was nearly sufficient. That was the Stoic. I cannot say that I have found it so, except in theory. Putting myself in that position, I read your book. You see at once what must follow, — what did in fact follow. Of course all that goes before is futile except as failure; all that follows after is escape — flying the ring — by assuming an unprovable other world. Logically, the religious solution is inadmissible, — pure hypothesis. It discards reason. I do not object to it on that account; as a working energy I prefer instinct to reason; but as you put it, the Augustinian adjustment seems to be only the Stoic, with a supernatural or hypothetical supplement nailed to it by violence. The religionists preached it and called it Faith. Therefore to me the effect is of ending there. The moral adjustment, as a story, ended with Marcus Aurelius. There you lead us with kind and sympathetic hands; but there, over the door to the religious labyrinth, you, like Lord Kelvin, write the word Failure. Faith, not Reason, goes beyond. What you intend, either as reason or faith, is another matter. I am giving the effect on one mind. At the present moment, perhaps, the moral is somewhat pointed, — to me decidedly peaked. If you are writing Failure over one door and Lord Kelvin over another, and the Germans over the third and last — that of energy without direction — I think I had better quit. I said so ten years ago, but I put it down to my personal equation then, and I cannot believe that you mean it now. Are we, then, to go back to Faith? If so, is it to be early Christian or Stoic? The early Christian I take to have been abandoned long ago by the failure of Christ to reappear and judge the world. Whatever faith is to save us, it cannot be that. Is it, then, the Stoic? . . . Marcus Aurelius would have been my type of highest human attainment. Even as it is, I would give a new cent to have a really good book on the Stoics. If there is one, lend it to me. I need badly to find one man in history to admire. I am in near peril of turning Christian, and rolling in the mud in an agony of human mortification. All these other fellows did it, — why not I?"

Years before in that strange twin poem, the "Prayers to the Virgin and the Dynamo," he had ended with the appeal to the former : —

> Help me to see! not with my mimic sight —
> With yours! which carried radiance, like the sun,
> Giving the rays you saw with — light in light —
> Tying all suns and stars and worlds in one.
>
> Help me to know! not with my mocking art —
> With you, who knew yourself unbound by laws;
> Gave God your strength, your life, your sight, your heart,
> And took from him the Thought that Is — the Cause.
>
> Help me to feel! not with my insect sense, —
> With yours that felt all life alive in you;
> Infinite heart beating at your expense;
> Infinite passions breathing the breath you drew!

Faith, reason, a science of an unreasoning chaos of colliding atoms and blind force — in a century and a half the four generations had lived through them all, and the unquestioning affirmation of the first had ended in a passionate and unanswered question for the last.   On the twenty-seventh of March, 1918, the question was ended or answered, and after quietly passing away in his sleep Henry Adams was found in the morning with an expression of peaceful wonderment upon his dead face.   He was laid to rest beneath Saint Gaudens's symbol of brooding thought and infinite calm.

Brooks alone was left.   Except for a brief period of teaching in the Harvard Law School he had continued to devote himself to his writing, mostly trying to discover the laws governing human society, ending, as he had begun, in a pessimistic doctrine of scientific determinism undeflected by human reason. His *Theory of Social Revolutions*, published in 1913, presented the thesis that civilization was based upon centralization, but that centralization was dependent upon administrative capacity, and that the capitalists of a complex industrial state were incapable of coping with the problem.   On the other hand, in his opinion democracy had failed.   In his address on "The Revolt of Modern Democracy against Standards of Duty," delivered before the American Academy of Arts and Letters, he pointed out how far democracy in America had become rebellious against self-sacrifice on the part of the individual and "incapable of continuous collective thought except at long intervals under the severest tension."   His criticism, although it roused a storm of abuse, was never answered save by slushy laudation of democratic ideals and statistics of material progress.   In 1920, in a long introduction to his printing of some of Henry's essays under the title of *The Degradation of the Democratic Dogma*, he pointed to the doctrine already enunciated by Henry that degradation of energy applied to the intellectual as to the material world, and that democratic society as a form of collective energy must lose in intensity in direct ratio to its expansion.   He contended that in his opinion, supported both by his theory and by a mass of observational facts, all the fears of John Quincy Adams, nearly a century before, for a democracy that placed material above spiritual and intellectual values had proved all too well founded. In an introduction to a new edition of his *Emancipation of Massachusetts*, he analyzed the story of Moses and made him out as a magician and a suicide.

Much more unstable than any of his brothers, of whom he was always rather jealous, Brooks had neither the political courage of John, the practical ability and desire of public service of Charles, nor the intellectual capacity of Henry, but he had a brilliant if unregulated mind. He was the last of the line to live in the "Old House" at Quincy which had sheltered so many generations of this American family, and after his death, February 13, 1927, only two months after that of his wife, the house was given to the public to serve as a permanent memorial of the family. The flood of modern American democracy and industrial life had so overwhelmed the Quincy of old John Adams that it could no longer serve as a place of residence and shelter his descendants. The fate of the "Old House" was symbolic.

EPILOGUE

ON September 20, 1824, John Quincy Adams wandered among the tombstones of the family burial plot at Quincy musing on the past and future of his line. "Four generations, of whom very little more is known," he wrote in his *Diary*, "than is recorded upon these stones. There are three succeeding generations of us now living. Pass another century, and we shall all be mouldering in the same dust, or resolved into the same elements. Who then of our posterity shall visit this yard? And what shall he read engraved upon the stones? This is known only to the Creator of all. The record may be longer. May it be of blameless lives!"

The century has passed. We have seen the generations, and to-day a third Charles Francis, a son of John Quincy's grandson John Quincy, is head of the family. A Harvard graduate, like all his family since John; for thirty years treasurer of the University; a lawyer, like all his family; a famous yachtsman who defended the American Cup against the British; a man true to the family tradition and honored in his community, he sits in the Cabinet at Washington as Secretary of that Navy which was founded by John.

John Quincy's wistful hope has been fulfilled: "The record may be longer."

INDEX

INDEX